Futures of Education for Exceptional Students:
Emerging Structures

Maynard C. Reynolds, Editor

A publication of the National Support Systems Project under a grant from the Division of Personnel Preparation, Bureau of Education for the Handicapped, U.S. Office of Education, Department of Health, Education, and Welfare.

This project was performed pursuant to Grant No. 600-75-9013 from the Division of Personnel Preparation, Bureau of Education for the Handicapped, U.S. Office of Education, Department of Health, Education, and Welfare. The points of view expressed herein are the authors' and do not necessarily reflect the position or policy of the U.S. Office of Education, and no official endorsement by the U.S. Office of Education should be inferred.

Minneapolis, Minnesota
1978

Copies may be ordered from The Council for Exceptional Children, 1920 Association Drive, Reston, Virginia 22091. Contact CEC Publications Sales Unit for current single copy price and for quantity order discount rates.

Preface

The conference reported in this book was concerned with where special education is going and how — what the future will bring and how we can improve what it is that we are involved in. It was a pleasure to be a participant in such a conference and to know that the Bureau of Education for the Handicapped had a part in planting the seed that got it started. The conference met a need for people in the field of special education to get together with people in other fields and to think through some issues together.

As I was thinking about the conference and our purpose for meeting, I recollected the process we went through in developing P.L. 94-142. It started about eight or nine years ago when, in preparing to meet with the new Presidential Task Force on the Physically Handicapped, I consulted with Fred Weintraub at the Council for Exceptional Children and others about how we would approach that Committee. We decided that we were looking for a "commitment" to children. We felt that this commitment should replace the charity orientation that seemed to be the basis for government policy. Charity implies giving. We wanted more. We wanted a federal policy based on an analysis of the full task and a policy that would meet all the needs identified. To obtain our goals, we first enlisted the support of then U.S. Office of Education Commissioner, Sidney P. Marland; he agreed that an education for all handicapped children would be an appropriate goal to accomplish by 1980. Then we convinced the Educational Commission of the States to adopt our goal as a policy statement. The Educational Commission of the States, an organization of governors, legislators, and educators was the logical place to start as parents had been more successful in dealing with legislators than with the schools, which were often reluctant to change. The Council for Exceptional Children decided to study state legislation in an effort to assist those states that were interested in developing statutes and to put all the available state legislation on the computer. They did an analytic study of the legislation and reported the findings to the states. They also helped by developing a model state statute, which they distributed to the states for use in designing their own statutes.

At the same time, it was our good fortune that the civil rights lawyers, extending their interest from the civil rights of black persons, began pursuing the rights of handicapped persons. Once the first breakthrough in the federal courts was made in Pennsylvania, it greatly increased the possibility that we would have a federal law. P.L. 94-142 was finally passed four years after it was first introduced in Congress to assist the states financially and to insure that the job would be done.

The process was based on a theoretical formulation of the forces that could coalesce to bring about a desired public policy. We need to repeat this process as we implement the law. We need, if we can, to identify what the major public policy issues are in relation to the children we are interested in, and once again to find the forces that could help us to achieve our goals.

The meeting reported in this book is a beginning step in such a process. We met as an interdisciplinary group to examine the issues that will be the basis of our future policy decision. But it seems to me that even before we can examine the issues we need to examine some assumptions underlying the issues. One major assumption that needs to be examined is that our behavior toward disabled people is accidental. It is not. It just is not accidental that disabled people have not been able to get into school, that they still do not get on to buses or elevators or into buildings. There is a whole underlying structure of assumptions that is a part of the fabric of society which has resulted in the exclusion of disabled people from most of our public places. These assumptions need to be identified and consciously faced. Educators can not do it alone; we need the sociologists, anthropologists, and others to work together. We need to find a way to extend the broad social revolution that is already underway and is beginning to change these assumptions.

We also need to examine the assumptions that have led us to think of regular education and special education as dichotomous constructs. This kind of thinking has led to the treatment of common problems by separate groups who use different language constructs, publish in different journals, and, in general, cannot communicate. It has also affected the way our personnel are trained. If handicapped children are going to receive the best possible education, we need to find a way to share our knowledge and to work together, rather than to continue to divide our tasks in such a way that regular and special education personnel have difficulty in communicating with each other.

In addition, we need to examine our use of constructs, such as "mentally retarded." Because we have a construct and we use it, we think we know something about the people who are called "mentally retarded" and the programs that are called "programs for the mentally retarded." We tend, because of this construct, to assume that we can train children who are labeled mentally retarded as if they were essentially identical. However, this approach has not succeeded because children labeled mentally retarded are not as homogeneous as it may seem. But neither are so-called "normal" children.

Other problems are based on the way the label has been applied. For example, if, in a given community, 85% of the children in programs for the mentally retarded are black and, in the same community, 95% of the children in programs for the learning disabled are white, what does that tell us about the use of that particular construct — "mental retardation" — and the meaning of it, or about the construct "learning disabled?" We also need to look at the construct "mainstreaming." We do not think of it in the same way we think of mental retardation because it represents a process rather than a generic label that is applied to people. But by its very existence, the construct can limit our thinking. As an example, I think most people would say that a deaf child would achieve more in an environment where there are hearing persons; that the child would be stimulated by the normal environment. However, some of the data on achievement show that deaf children in schools for the deaf achieve higher on standard achievement measures than children in schools not for the deaf.

Another example is that of learning disabled children. If, for instance, in the third grade these children are reading at the third-grade level and over the next few years they learn to read to the fourth-grade level, we have evidence that they have been instructed and have gained an achievement. Suppose, however, when a measure is taken of the children's self-concepts it turns out that as they have grown older, their self-concepts have suffered. So, despite the fact that they have been in a mainstream setting, despite the fact that they have actually learned, the farther along they have gone in that setting the lower their self-concepts have become. A theory or assumption that is not necessarily accurate but that is extrapolated from these data is that as children grow older, they become more and more aware of the differences between themselves and their peers, who have grown at a faster rate. The point I am making is that most of us support mainstreaming because we have seen segregated schools for black children, because we have seen institutions for the retarded, because we have seen Indian reservations, and because we are struck dumb by what has happened in segregated settings. But we do not have any real data to help us understand whether that which we generically call "mainstreaming" brings about positive results. Our support for mainstreaming, it seems to me, is based on our assumptions and values rather than on any research that indicates that mainstreaming is the best solution for all children.

As we examine public policy issues, we have an obligation to be aware of the notions that are based on values rather than on knowledge and to examine those notions in our research. I do not think the issue is to decide "yes" or "no" on mainstreaming. The real issue is to examine our constructs so that we are aware of how they affect our thinking and influence our solutions to problems.

There is no magic limit on the numbers of issues that face us in the future of special education, but these are some that interest me, not only because they reflect practical problems, but because they are problems that will be influenced by how we think, by how we conceptualize.

Edwin Martin
Deputy Commissioner of Education
Bureau of Education for the Handicapped
U.S. Office of Education

Contents

Edwin Martin . . . . . *Preface* iii

Introduction

Maynard C. Reynolds . . . . . *Introduction* xi

Presenters

Seymour Sarason . . . . . *Mainstreaming: Dilemmas, Opposition, Opportunities* 3

R. P. McDermott & Jeffrey Aron . . . . . *Pirandello in the Classroom: On the Possibility of Equal Educational Opportunity in American Culture* 41

Reginald L. Jones . . . . . *Special Education and the Future: Some Questions to be Answered and Answers to be Questioned* 65

Arthur W. Chickering & Joanne N. Chickering . . . . . *Life-Long Learning by Handicapped Persons* 89

James J. Gallagher . . . . . *Organizational Needs for Quality Special Education* 133

Henry M. Levin . . . . . *Some Economic Considerations in Educating Handicapped Children* 151

R. L. Schiefelbusch & Robert K. Hoyt, Jr . . . . . *Three Years Past 1984* 175

Critics

Nicholas Hobbs . . . . . *A Critical Perspective of the Papers on "The Futures of Education"* 197

Michael Timpane . . . . . *Theories and Their Applications* 209

Geraldine Joncich Clifford . . . . . *Issues Relating to the Future of Special Education* 217

Dan C. Lortie . . . . . *Some Reflections on Renegotiation* 235

Dean Corrigan . . . . . *The Present State of Teacher Education and Needed Reforms* 245

Discussants

S. Phyllis Stearner . . . . . *Who (What) is the Handicapped Child? Conceptions and Misconceptions* 263

Hadi Madjid . . . . . *Some New Ways of Thinking About Handicapped Children* 269

John W. Melcher . . . . . *Reactions from a New Believer* 275

George P. Young . . . . . *Reactions* 277

Closing Comments

Nicholas Hobbs . . . . . *Closing Comments* 283

Conference Participants   289

Publications List   291

Introduction

Introduction

Change is not made without inconvenience, even from worse to better.
(Quoted by Samuel Johnson in the Preface to *English Dictionary*)

We are in the midst of a most remarkable period in the history of providing educational services for handicapped persons. The courts, state legislatures, and the Congress have mandated schools to seek out and assume the responsibility for providing appropriate educational services for all children, including those with the most profound handicaps, to maintain in the mainstream of education as many children as possible, to individualize the education of children considered to be handicapped, and to observe due process in all decisions affecting such children. Essentially, a major renegotiation of the relation between special education and regular education is under way, and the renegotiation carries implications that may change all of education for children.

The judicial and legislative mandates are based on the right of all children to equal educational opportunity. The courts have set forth the purpose of education as the enhancement of the individual's life. These principles shift the focus of concern from children's handicaps to their learning needs, and the educational setting from segregated classrooms and institutions to the "least restrictive environment." Thus, the barriers between so-called "regular" and "special" education programs have been breached and strong pressures have been created for unification.

The rights of handicapped children have been extended to include due process. Handicapped children and their parents or guardians now have the right to participate in the processes of determining placements and programs. We can anticipate that this right will be extended in the near future to include individual programing for all children.

A great deal of new activity is underway in the schools at this moment in response to these mandates and principles. There is growing recognition that the changes are fundamental and that as procedures are extended to all children—as in negotiating placements and programs individually with parents—the potential of the impact is very great indeed. The practices of schooling have undergone radical changes of several kinds in the United States, over the past century, and perhaps we are at a watershed once again.

The Upward Climb to Equality

The present provisions for handicapped children bring together two strands of education which developed independently of each other. Historically, children who were born deaf, blind, crippled, or mentally retarded were considered to have been spawned by the devil or cursed by God. Until the Age of Enlightenment, they were more feared than pitied and grossly abused or neglected. With the rise of humanitarianism, a handful of pioneers, mostly in Europe, proved that handicapped children were capable of learning, and special education made its appearance in residential institutions for the blind, the deaf, and the mentally retarded. Special education practices and the idea of the residential school were carried to the United States from Europe in the 19th century.

Early concepts of special education for the handicapped involved many doubtful assumptions. For example, one of the motives for establishing institutions for mentally retarded persons was the belief that sensory training could cure their handicaps. When this belief proved false, another came along to justify separating retarded persons from society, that is, that their handicaps were allied with criminal or deviant tendencies. In many segments of our population, the latter belief is still the basis for isolating handicapped persons from their nonhandicapped peers.

Regular education in the United States was conceptualized initially as the means of instructing the populace to become citizens of a democracy — no small feat in a world in which democracy was still a revolutionary idea. However, free public education was not adopted as a national policy until after the Civil War. Industrialization required a large influx of immigrants to build the railroads and man the factories and mills, and public schools were given the task of Americanizing the newcomers. As industry came to depend more on technology and a hierarchy of skills than willingness and strong backs, schooling was conceived of as preparing youngsters for future employment. Indeed, the enthusiasm with which academic and psychological testing was adopted by the schools has been attributed to the role imposed on the schools of sifting young people for differential participation in the nation's economy. The handicapped were left aside; if they showed little promise as future employees and as independent self-supporting persons, then they could be shunted off to the byways of schooling as well.

Although education has been compulsory by law for decades in most states, until recently the focus has been more on children's attendance than on the suitability of programs for them, and the laws rarely have been enforced with vigor. The schools were never required to be all inclusive. In fact, they were free to exclude or to provide only minimal services to those segments of the school-aged population that were considered unlikely to contribute to society. For example, when the prime role of women was as wife, mother, and homemaker, educating women was considered a waste of time and resources beyond the acquisition of basic skills; indeed, the long struggle of women to gain equal educational opportunities is not yet over. A disproportionately meager share of educational resources was also expended on the education of minority groups, especially blacks, Chicanos, native Americans, and poor whites, who were expected to remain on the agricultural or unskilled fringes of society. And handicapped children, who were regarded as a burden to the state, were either refused entry to the schools or were served on a privileged basis in separate and isolated facilities.

The picture changed only very slowly until after World War II. The war aims listed in the Atlantic Charter by President Franklin D. Roosevelt and Prime Minister Winston Churchill included in the sixth clause a phrase that gave hope to the dispossessed, not only in the small beleaguered nations of the world but in the United States as well. It was, "... [to] afford assurance that all the men in all the lands may live out their lives in freedom from fear and want." In the United States, "freedom from fear and want" became a political rallying cry for the poor, the disenfranchised, and the handicapped; what had been expressed as an ideal was translated into an immediate goal. It gave impetus to a broad civil rights movement and led, through the courts, to a broader interpretation of the Fourteenth Amendment of the Constitution. In Brown v. Board of Education, in 1954, equal educational opportunity was established as the right of all black children in the United States, and in the landmark PARC case in Pennsylvania, in 1971, and the many related cases which followed, the right was extended to all handicapped children.

The development of special education services in local public schools since World War II has been largely the result of the strivings of parents of handicapped children. The marginal basis on which such services were provided for many years, mainly in the form of special classes and special schools, established the pattern of one system of education — regular or general education — for "normal" children and another quite separate system for the "others." Yet parents continued to work for increasing opportunities for their children, at first in separate, and then in more inclusive arrangements.

Given the public sympathy for handicaps that followed World War II, middle class, white, politically oriented parents formed strong national organizations that lobbied successfully for appropriations to increase special services in the schools. As appropriations increased, school systems expanded the definition of handicap and classified more and more children as requiring special services. Categories of handicap were stretched to include children who were difficult to teach or who did not respond well to the usual instructional approaches, and to those who differed culturally. By the late 1960s, consequently, special education classes were made up of disproportionately large numbers of children who were not handicapped in the traditional definition but who displayed some difficulty in learning, and the story began to have many complications. Some parents began to interpret the assignments to special education classes as discrimination. To them, special classes and classification systems stigmatized their children and deprived them of future opportunities for advancement. Since these parents tended to be poor, black, or Spanish speaking, they had very limited funds to lobby state legislatures or Congress. There were available to them, however, civil rights organizations that had learned to use the courts to gain their ends. Through a series of court cases brought in the names of individual children (see Weintraub, Abeson, Ballard, & LeVor, 1975),[1] the whole system of testing and categorizing children for special education purposes was placed in question. Thus, while middle-class parents were petitioning the courts for the expansion of special education services for handicapped children, poor and ethnic parents were petitioning the courts to keep their children out of special classes.

It is important to note that growing numbers of special educators also were distressed by the naive expansion of special classes in the 1960s. Despite the massive support and appropriations earmarked for special education, it was recognized that more did not mean necessarily enough or better. The special classes sometimes were used as a dumping ground for the children who were rejected by regular classroom teachers. More important, perhaps, there were never enough teachers or rooms for all the children who were classified and referred for special education. Thus, a sizable proportion of children who needed special services were retained in regular classrooms.

The 1960s were a decade of social upheaval in this country and the schools were caught up in the middle. It was fashionable, at the time, to see in the schools a reflection only of society's ills. It is true, of course, that in northern cities the concentration of blacks and other minority group children in some school buildings reflected the concentration of ethnic groups in certain sections of the city. And it is also true that most school personnel were white with a middle-class orientation. But the critics tend to forget that a great deal of experimentation was also going on in the schools during that period. For example, there were developed during that decade the ungraded classroom, the open school, alternative programs, contracts between students and teachers, criterion-and domain-ref-

---

[1]F. J. Weintraub, A. Abeson, J. Ballard, & M. L. LaVor (Eds.). *Public Policy and the Education of Exceptional Children.* Reston, VA: Council for Exceptional Children, 1976.

erenced testing, individualized instructional programs, and the application of behavior modification principles to education.

In addition, some new structures for the delivery of special education services, such as the resource room and consultative model, which stressed bringing services to the mainstream of education for students with special needs rather than removing the students to special settings, began to appear. In a parallel development, some colleges of education began training special educators as resource teachers, consulting teachers, and diagnostic-prescriptive teachers—the three most popular terms— whose main function is to help regular education teachers to maintain children with learning problems in regular classes. An extensive literature on mainstreaming began to accumulate.[2] During the 1960s the schools were beginning the long climb that might have brought most handicapped persons into integrated arrangements in the schools. Time ran out on the schools, however, with the consent decree in the PARC case, in 1971, and, subsequently, the enactment of P.L. 94-142.

It is important to note that education is only one area in which a "civil rights revolution" for the handicapped is taking place.

> Among the others are the right of institutionalized handicapped persons to be free from unusual and cruel treatment; the right of institutionalized handicapped persons to be freed from employment without reimbursement and without rehabilitative purpose; the right to avoid involuntary institutionalization on the part of persons who represent neither a danger to society nor to themselves; the right of the handicapped to exercise the power to vote; the right of the handicapped both to marry and to procreate; the right of the handicapped to travel on the nation's public conveyances; and the right of the handicapped to access to America's buildings by means of removal of environmental barriers. (Weintraub et al., 1975, p. 5)

With the enactment in 1975 of Public Law 94-142, the Education for All Handicapped Children Act, the Congress established an educational Magna Charta for all those children who have been kept out of the mainstream of education for whatever reason. The provisions are not directed against special education but against the prevailing practices of delivering special education and related services. Most school systems in the country, therefore, are in the process of reorganizing their practices to comply with the provisions of P.L. 94-142. The task is especially difficult for those school systems in which special education personnel were scarce and services were minimal.

---

[2]See the publications of the Leadership Training Institute/National Support Systems Project listed at the end of this book. One of the projects undertaken by the LTI was a bibliography on mainstreaming. In the third edition (1977), close to 1000 publications are listed.

The Conference

It was against this background that the conference, "The Future of Special Education and Its Implications for Personnel Preparation," was called in April 1977. The conference was proposed (a) to provide an avenue for productive reflection upon the issues and problems of education from a range of perspectives, (b) to bring into focus the new or emerging features of school systems in a changing society, and (c) to envision school systems in the near future—the mid-1980s, say—given the present judicial, legislative, social, and theoretical influences on education.

The conference was organized about primary papers which seven participants were asked to write from their individual perspectives. The latter were Anthropology (McDermott), Psychology (Sarason), Economics (Levin), Educational Research (Schiefelbusch), Special Education (Gallagher), Minority Group Education (Jones), and Adult Learning (Arthur and Joanne Chickering). The papers were discussed by a number of critics, with papers written by five who also represented different disciplines: History of Education (Clifford), Teacher Training (Corrigan), Psychology and Public Policy (Hobbs), Federal Policy Analysis (Timpane), and Sociology of Education (Lortie). In addition, two handicapped persons, S. Phyllis Stearner, who is cerebral palsied, and Hadi Madjid, who is blind, participated in the conference and contributed their written observations to this volume.

Other conferees had been invited to participate in the discussion and, subsequently, to contribute their written reactions. This report, therefore includes brief papers by a large city superintendent of schools (Young), and an administrator of state special education services (Melcher).

The order of the seven major papers is somewhat arbitrary. Sarason's presentation provides an historical perspective for the analysis of the impact of P.L 94-142 on schools and school personnel. McDermott and Aron report their observations of the sorting function of the classroom which is at odds with the intent of P.L. 94-142. Jones reviews the literature on (a) teacher attitudes toward innovation and change, (b) assessment and modification of attitudes toward the handicapped, (c) individualization of instruction, and (d) the delivery of inservice education, four areas that are critical to the understanding of probable future directions in special education. The Chickerings report enthusiastically on new modes of education for adults that provide opportunities for higher education for handicapped persons and offer models for teachers' inservice training. In order to insure continuous quality in special education, Gallagher advocates (a) the generation of comprehensive and widespread support systems, and (b) the creation of organizational entities to move innovative and proven ideas and skills through those systems to the consumer. Levin analyzes four theories of public funding that are applicable to special education in general and mainstreaming in particular. In the final major paper, Schiefelbusch and Hoyt extrapolate from the implications of recent research and development to an idealized conceptualization of education by 1987.

In the papers by the five critics and four discussants, issues raised in the major papers and the conference discussions are the starting points for individual observations on the future of special education and the preparation of teachers for mainstreaming.

If, on the whole, the papers seem to be more concerned with the present than the future, it is because we must understand current events before we can try to predict where they will lead us. At the present time, the mandates of P.L. 94-142 are stimulating a great deal of complex, many-faceted changes in the schools in the ways that handicapped students are served, in the relations between special and regular education, and in the training and retraining of special and regular education personnel. It is not surprising, therefore, that much of the conference discussions centered on change, not so much theories of change as the factors within education that foster or impede change. Opinions varied on how fundamental and far reaching the current changes in the schools may prove to be.

There is a popular belief that schools, in general, are the instruments of conservatism, that is, that they function mainly to transmit the culture, preserve the political status quo, maintain social classes, sort children for vocational and social roles, and provide upward mobility to only a selected few youngsters. All of this fits a theme that the powerful few use the schools to maintain their privileges. At the same time, there is an equally popular belief that schools are the spearhead of progressivism, that is, that they are the gateway to upward mobility, socially, politically, and economically, and that they are forces for social change. In the conservative view, schools resist changes that are not evolutionary in nature; in the progressive view, schools are capable of planned change if they are given the resources and support to do the job. In 1949, Clyde Kluckhohn, an eminent anthropologist of the period, took the progressive view of the role of the schools in our society when he wrote, "... we have come to believe in education as an instrument for creating something new, not merely for perpetuating the traditional" (Kluckhohn, 1949, p. 169).[3]

During the conference, the discussions reflected the polarity of conservative-progressive views. A sampling of some of the observations follows:

... in any organization, structural resistance to change can "domesticate" change.

... there is a powerful tradition of cost-saving in the history of education and mainstreaming will be expensive.

[3]C. Kluckhohn. *Mirror for Man.* New York: McGraw Hill, 1949.

...there is cost saving in maintaining the traditional curriculum.

...there is the inevitable gap between the extravagance of our claims for schooling and the paucity of resources to do the job.

...when we expect people to act differently, we have to confront the limits and constraints imposed by their roles.

...large organizations without a profit motive are governed by the need for tranquility rather than excellence.

...the first law of any social organization is to preserve itself.

...resources and support must be increased if organizations are to be permitted to explore with freedom.

...teachers do not like the perception of themselves as at the end of a chain of insight.

...the dilemma of social action is that we know we have been wrong but we are not altogether sure about where to go and in what way, yet we realize that we have to move.

...there is a lot more standardization on commercial television than in our schools today.

...schools are far more equal now than any other institution in American life; we are always asking the schools to do something the rest of society is not able or willing to do.

...as a society, we have a tremendous drive toward change, innovation, and technology; but as individuals we are terribly rigid and unwilling to see change.

...as a society, we are trying to cope with a greater amount of diversity and degree of change than anyone ever has; over the longer pull, we have probably accommodated far more than anyone ever has.

It well may be that P.L. 94-142 has become effective at a time when schools and educational personnel are quite receptive to change. The criticisms leveled against public education during the 1960s led to considerable examination of practices by educators and to conscious attempts to make education more useful for children with more diverse backgrounds. New leaders are emerging rapidly whose concerns encompass both regular and special education and who conceptualize schooling as preparation for an unknown future rather than as the single transmittal of skills that were valued in the past. Scholars and leaders in many fields, including law, philosophy, public administration and finance, sociology and others, are giving close attention to changes occurring in education of the handicapped and to the broad implications of such changes. A new and comprehensive literature on handicapped persons is emerging.

Teachers' associations and unions are moving topics concerned with handicapped students to the top of the agenda for negotiation with school boards because they sense that fundamentals, such as class size, supports for regular teachers, provisions of wide-ranging instructional materials, and like matters, are at stake. Political leaders are paying more attention to this busy scene as more dollars, more people, and more concerns are involved.

The old procedures of testing and classifying children by simple standards are passing from the scene. Although, in the past, lip service was paid to the concept of individual differences, we are seeing today the recognition that "individual differences" means far more than deviations from an arbitrary norm. This recognition is an essential basis for the determination of individual educational plans for all handicapped children.

In sum, the schools of today are in a period of tough but promising renegotiation of relations between special education and regular education. The results are by no means certain. Perhaps what looks promising will be indeed "domesticated" and opportunities for the handicapped will be but little improved. On the other hand, the concepts at issue appear to be rooted in societal aspirations and goals that support the confluence of the many forces for constructive change and even the provision of some essential resources for the change. Agreement is fairly general that, at base, the problem is moral and education is headed in the right direction. It is this realization that is generating so much soul searching among educators even as we confront the difficulties of deep change.

The concern with the future, therefore, is not so much whether we will provide education for the handicapped but how the provision can be carried out within the goal of providing all children with quality education.

Acknowledgements

The conference on "Issues Relating to the Future of Special Education" and the preparation of this publication reflected the dedicated efforts of a number of colleagues and associates. I am indebted to all of them and especially to the following persons:

From the Bureau of Education for the Handicapped, Dr. Edwin Martin, Director, for his continued interest and support and for his participation in the conference as a critic; and Dr. Thomas Behrens of the Division of Personnel Preparation, who, with Dr. Dean Corrigan of the University of Maryland, helped to design the conference.

From the University of Minnesota, Dr. Clyde Parker, for chairing the sessions with unflagging good humor, Dr. Bruce Balow, for serving as a critic, and Dr. Mary Corcoran, for acting as a discussant.

From Chicago and Boston, respectively, Dr. Phyllis Stearner and Dr. Hadi Madjid for taking the time from their busy professional lives to share their personal experiences as handicapped persons.

From the National Support Systems Project, Karen Lundholm, Sue Bye, and Reece Peterson for carrying the burdens of preparing for and managing the conference; Kathryn Bass, for her typing skills, and Sylvia W. Rosen for editing the papers and managing the production of this book.

All the contributors to this volume have my special thanks for their participation in this venture.

Maynard C. Reynolds, *Chairman*
Department of Psychoeducational Studies
University of Minnesota
and
Director, National Support Systems Project

Presenters

Mainstreaming: Dilemmas, Opposition, Opportunities[1]

Seymour Sarason[2]

Yale University

and

John Doris[3]

Cornell University

The speed with which mainstreaming has emerged as a concept, value, and public policy in our society is little short of amazing. Indeed, its emergence has come about so fast and with such apparent general approbation that the question of what people understand about mainstreaming and its implications for schools must be examined. The issues that are relevant to the question are very complicated. We cannot assume that institutions will accommodate appropriately to mainstreaming because we think it is desirable. Let us start, then, by trying to gain some historical perspective on these issues.

Mainstreaming Before 1950

Imagine that it is any time before 1950 and you are attending a convention of people who work in the field of mental retardation. Suppose, at the general meeting, that someone makes the following statement from the floor:

> This is the first time I have attended these kinds of meetings and I am no end impressed and encouraged by what I have heard. Thank God there are people like you who are fighting for justice for mentally retarded people. For too long society has ignored the needs of these people so that our state institutions are, as many of you have said, overcrowded and understaffed: We call them training

---

[1]This paper is adapted from *Educational Handicaps, Public Policy, and Social History: A Broadened Perspective on Mental Retardation,* a forthcoming book by the authors.
[2]Professor of Psychology
[3]Professor of Psychology, School of Human Ecology.

schools but, for the most part, they are custodial institutions, and pretty bad even at that. What really gave me a lift was to hear so many of you call for many more community facilities to reduce the need for institutionalization. For example, you are on record as favoring more special classes in our schools, attracting more and better people into special education, and, in general, upgrading training programs in colleges and universities. But one thought has been nagging at me: Why do we have to segregate mentally retarded individuals in our schools? Why are we so ready to separate them from the mainstream? Why can't they be accommodated in the regular classroom? Are you in favor of separate but equal facilities in exactly the same way we treat blacks? Does not this type of segregation affect the retarded person adversely, and does it not rob the normal student of a kind of knowledge and experience that will make the student a better moral person? I would like for this convention to go on record as in principle opposed to the segregation of mentally retarded children in our schools. Indeed, I move that we go on record as opposed to segregation any place.

The speaker would have been regarded, at best, as a misguided idealist of the bleeding heart variety and, at worst, as dangerously mentally disordered and quite out of touch with both social reality and the nature and needs of mentally retarded people. After a stony silence, the meeting would have moved on to more "realistic" considerations. It would be an egregious injustice to judge that response to be a symptom of callousness, immorality, or narrow self-interest serving the status quo. The fact is that those would have been dedicated people sincerely trying to make society more responsive to what the most advanced knowledge, research, and experience suggested about the nature and needs of mentally retarded people. In fact, those conference participants well understood societal prejudice because they were devoted to the welfare of mentally retarded people! Why else would anyone "choose" to work with "them"?

Let us do some more imagining. One participant, who regrets that no one responded to our speaker, feels obliged to seek him out and to explain why his recommendation was so misguided, however lofty his motivation.

> You are an idealist and there is a part of me that accepts what you said about segregation, although in the case of mentally retarded people you are simplifying the complexity of the issues. But let's assume that everyone at this meeting agreed with you. How do you think the "outside world" would react? I'll tell you: either with the same stony silence you received at this meeting or with anger because you are telling them that their communities have been immoral, callous, and irresponsible. And how do you think school people would respond? They don't even want the special classes they now have, so how do you think they would cotton to the idea of putting mentally retarded people in regular classrooms? Put them into the mainstream? It would be unfair to say that they would like

them to drown, but it is not unfair to say that they want them on isolated islands surrounded by an awful lot of water. Mainstream them? If we came out and said *that*, it would be used as evidence that *we* were mentally retarded.

Today, some 25 years after our imagined meeting, mainstreaming is public policy. In the interim, did opposition melt away? Was there an unprecedented attitudinal and moral change in our society? Were welcome signs (welcome-wagon style) erected by schools and communities? Or is present public policy a variation of the 1954 Supreme Court desegregation decision? Racial segregation in schools has been declared unconstitutional, but changing school practices to accord with that decision turned out to be beset by a host of obstacles, deliberate and otherwise. Some naive people greeted that decision with a sigh of relief: Thank God the moral cancer was spotted and could now be excised, maybe not tomorrow or next year but certainly in a decade or so. We have learned otherwise. Deeply rooted attitudes, reinforced by traditions, institutions, and practices, are not changed except over long periods of time (Sarason, 1973). And mainstreaming is no exception, as is shown in a later section.

Let us examine more clearly the contributions to the present policy. The first set of facts represents a convergence of events and forces (e.g., the quick growth and power of a national parents' group; the Kennedy family's personal and political interest in mental retardation powered by the financial resources of the Kennedy Foundation; and exposés of degrading conditions in state institutions) that made mental retardation a topic of public interest, in itself a remarkable social change. But this change is not comprehensible unless one sees it in the context of an even more drastic social change which was accelerated by the Great Depression: the widespread acceptance of the idea of governmental responsibility for citizens rendered dependent or handicapped for reasons beyond their control (Sarason, 1976). Before the 1930s (and even during much of them) the federal government was not expected to intervene in matters of education and health. For a few handicapping conditions (e.g., blindness) there were modest programs, but they were the exceptions and not considered to be forerunners of an increased federal role. The philosophy that "that government is best that governs least" made it extremely difficult to mobilize or sustain national attention to issues in education and health. At best, they received attention in the states, but even the states were guided by the prevailing philosophy. It took a national economic calamity to start the process of philosophical change; thus today, our prepotent response to a social problem is in terms of federal policy and programs.

At the same time that mental retardation started to receive national attention and the pressures for a federal role in meeting the needs of mentally retarded persons began to mount, other social forces came to the fore. At first, they were unrelated to the political issues of mental retardation but, later, they had the most influence on how these issues were resolved. They were the forces of the civil rights movement. The major impetus for this movement came from the desire to eradicate racial discrimination but, soon, spread far beyond race to women, arrested and institutionalized persons, gays, older people, members of the armed services, children, and people in general. What were their constitutional rights? What constituted their equality before the law? How did tradition and practice come to rob them of their basic constitutional rights as citizens? On what constitutional grounds can mental patients be confined to state hospitals? What are the legal restrictions to the use of psychological tests as a basis for job promotion? What constitutional or legal procedures must be observed before a child can be suspended or expelled from school? What guarantees must be observed to preserve the privacy of self-information given by an individual or obtained by others about him/her?

Scores and scores of similar questions, some old, most new, but all testifying to an upsurge of attention to and concern for individual liberties, rights, and equality, can be asked. They have led to the law's and, therefore, the courts' becoming agents of social change. The most pervasive changes have been through judicial decisions that essentially reinterpreted or enlarged the scope of laws and existing constitutional language. Many of these decisions have not been greeted with anything like unanimous approval because they call for radical changes in institutional thinking and practice. And that is our point here. Although these court decisions were initiated by plaintiffs who are seeking change, they were opposed by defendants who are by no means few in number or lacking in strength. To interpret a decision in favor of a plaintiff as a victory is understandable, but one should never underestimate how long it can take for the spirit of the victory to be accepted and manifested appropriately in practice.

When mental retardation first became, so to speak, a topic of public discussion, moral-humane rather than legal-constitutional considerations were in the forefront. Mentally retarded people "deserved" as much attention and programmatic support as groups with other disabling conditions. In fact, advocates for mentally retarded persons wanted no more and, certainly, no less than "separate but equal facilities." No one was calling for the elimination of state training schools or special classes. However, it was not long before the rationale behind the historic 1954 Supreme Court desegregation decision began to influence the thinking of the advocates for the mentally retarded. Central to that rationale is the argument that segregation has pernicious effects on both the person who is segregated and the person who does the segregating. The 1954 decision was the first time that the Supreme Court ruled that segregation had adverse effects on white and black children. Generalizing from that rationale, it is not surprising that its judicial and logical relevance to mentally retarded people began to be examined. As a consequence, the status of mentally retarded people in our society, generally, and in schools, in particular, became a focus of interest for legal scholars, regardless of whether they had interest in or knowledge of mental retardation. As lawyers, they did not have to be sophisticated about mental retardation per se to study and write about the legal-constitutional issues of mental retardation which had been long ignored by everyone. And once the supporters of the movement for more and better facilities started to go down the legal-constitutional road, their goals became more encompassing and radical — radical in that they found themselves at a familiar principle: segregating mentally retarded people in schools or elsewhere was demeaning to all involved. Blatt and Kaplan's (1966) *Christmas in Purgatory* is a pictorial essay of what happens to segregated persons in institutions. The picture of the scandalous conditions was given a big play in the mass media and was placed in the hands of every United States senator and congressman. In his subsequent books (Blatt 1970, 1975, 1976), Blatt rounded out the picture of telling us what happens to the segregators.

Opposition

The reason for this very brief historical overview is to make a point that is too easily overlooked: The change in societal attitudes and social policy was spearheaded by a dedicated minority relying on political pressure and the courts; but at every step of the way, this minority encountered opposition, especially from personnel in schools, institutions, and state agencies who saw how drastic the proposed changes would be for them. Their opposition, of course, is quite understandable. After all, few (if any) people look with relish at the necessity of redefining their roles, activities, and values. Opponents to the proposed changes were not evil or unintelligent people; far from it. They were people engaged in public service, carrying out their tasks in ways that their professional training as well as long-standing custom had supported as right and effective. To be told, then, that their values were wrong, that they had been contributing to the evil, and that they would have to accommodate to new procedures and practices — it is no wonder that far from dissolving opposition the adjudications may have had an opposite effect.

Consider the structural-administrative relation of the fields of mental retardation and education, first in colleges and universities. In our schools of education, mental retardation has always been "special" or "exceptional," that is, whatever it was, it was off pretty much by itself, away from the mainstream of "real" education. Faculty and students in mental retardation were rarely viewed with a sense of pride or as indispensable members of a department or school of education. It is not fortuitous that in departments of education in our private colleges and universities mental retardation was hardly represented, and most of the time it was completely unrepresented. When it was represented, it was less because it was viewed as indispensable and more because it was a reaction to pressure or legislation to prepare teachers to take positions in state institutions. And even then the department of mental retardation or special education tended to be small and politically weak.

If these departments were more tolerated than warmly embraced, it bespoke of snobbishness reinforced by and reflecting societal attitudes. Mental retardation was seen, if not as a dead end, as an unrewarding field in which to work. It had a "hopeless" quality. If people entered it, it was because they could not make it in the mainstream of education, were misguided, or were nobly self-sacrificing individuals.

A more fundamental assumption undergirded all these perceptions, however, and it was one that everyone accepted. To understand and educate mentally retarded students required theories and techniques that were different from those required for "normal" human beings. That is like saying that you need one theory to explain the helium atom and a different one to explain the hydrogen atom. Obviously, it is one thing to say that helium and hydrogen are different, and quite another to say that they require different theories because each is "made" differently. There is or should be one human psychology based on principles applicable to all people. Women are different from men, Republicans from Democrats, and Catholics from Protestants, but to conclude that these differences arise out of psychological-developmental-social principles and processes that are unique to each group is gratuitous and a massive denial or misinterpretation of what we have learned about human behavior. Because people develop differently does not mean that the development is governed by different processes. Diversity in behavior among people does not require resorting to a theory of diversity in underlying principles.

In any event, the separation between special and "regular" education, a separation accepted by both, was based on the assumption that retarded individuals required special theories, that they were different kinds of human beings. Therefore, people trained to understand and work with retarded children could not (should not) work with normal children, and vice versa. For all practical purposes, they could not talk with each other! The groups segregated themselves, and the thought that perhaps they should be together in the mainstream was considered ludicrous. The opposition to mainstreaming children was long contained in the political-administrative-social structure of departments and schools of education in our colleges and universities.

We would have seen much the same set of relationships in public schools except that special class teachers *and* their students were isolated from the mainstream. Only in recent years has the special classroom been as physically well-appointed and situated as the regular one. Since not all schools had special classes, some children were bussed to schools that had them. To the rest of the school faculty the special class teacher was a second-class citizen, someone who was expected to be a good custodian rather than an effective educator. Students were placed in the special class "for life"; there was no expectation that they would or could be returned to the regular class. And it was by no means infrequent for children to be placed in the special class because of behavior rather than academic inadequacy. Because special classes were not numerous enough to accommodate all retarded children, it is not surprising that these classes were used selectively for purposes of behavioral control. Aside from the special teacher, no one was concerned about what or at what rate the children learned because they were not expected to learn very much, and even that would take years. The school principal, either by tradition or administrative regulations, came from "regular" education and considered himself incompetent to advise or guide the special class teacher; not infrequently, the principal saw the special class as either an unasked-for burden or a blemish on the school's image. In urban settings, a supervisor of special education visited the classroom occasionally. If the special class teachers felt alone and unwanted, the feelings were warranted by reality. It would be a gross mistake to see this situation in personal terms or, better yet, to react to it in personal ways. *It was a situation that was pretty much viewed as "natural" by almost everyone, including the special class teacher; if she felt otherwise, she was careful not to articulate it.* At best, the special class teacher would have been delighted to achieve separate but equal status. We should not overlook the fact that this situation had the sanction of the community.

The pressures for mainstreaming did not come from within educational institutions. That fact alone allows one to predict that these pressures will be resisted. It is not a case of "good guys vs. bad guys" or "virtue vs. sin." Personalizing the polarities in such ways overlooks how both sides reflect tradition, history, *and* a fast-changing society. Institutional custom and practice are effective bulwarks to forces for change, a fact we too easily forget which has both good and bad features. On the one hand, we do not want our institutions to change in response to every new fad or idea; on the other hand, we do not want them blindly to preserve the status quo. In regard to mainstreaming, of course, how one views the oppositional stance of our schools and university training centers depends on how one feels about mainstreaming. If one is for mainstreaming, then one tends to view opposition as another instance of stone-age attitudes. If one is against mainstreaming, one tends to view it as another misguided effort that will further dilute the quality of education for everyone. The important point is that opposition to mainstreaming was and is predictable. To proceed as if it were not is to deny the obvious, especially when institutional custom and practice always have been congruent with and a reflection of societal values and attitudes.

But what happens when societal attitudes begin to change, at least among those segments of the population that are effectively organized to bring about change, and the change, like mainstreaming, is generally seen as related to many other matters involving basic constitutional issues? As we indicated earlier, the legal and human issues emerging from segregation practices in regard to mentally retarded persons can be understood only in the context of the upswell of protest against the discrimination practiced toward many other groups (e.g., blacks, Chicanos, women, the physically handicapped, aged people). What frequently happens is that public sentiments are translated into public policies through legislation and given the force of law. From that point on, institutions must conform to the law's intent and requirements or suffer sanctions. Of course, this requirement does not mean that by virtue of the law or some magical process long-standing attitudes and practices will be dissolved and reconstituted to accept willingly the new direction. There is conformity and conformity, and one must expect that ways will be sought to circumvent the new intent or to carry it out minimally, as in the case of discrimination against any minority group. Passing laws is far easier than getting them implemented in ways that are consistent with both the spirit and letter. This fact says less about the human capacity to be socially perverse than about the strength of institutionalized custom and practice. Opposition is based not on personality but on institutional custom, organization, and values.

Let us be concrete. There follows part of the summary of P.L. 94-142 which was prepared by the Children's Defense Fund (1976), an agency that, as its name implies, seeks to protect and enlarge the rights and opportunities of children.

> On November 29, 1975, the Education for All Handicapped Children Act (Public Law 94-142) was signed into law. This law builds upon, expands, and will eventually replace the Education of the Handicapped Act, including Part B, which provides assistance to states, as amended by the Education Amendments of 1974 (Public Law 93-380). P.L. 94-142 [became] fully effective on October 1, 1977 (Fiscal Year 1978).
>
> Both laws are extremely important for children who are handicapped, or misclassified as handicapped by their school districts, and for parents of these children because the laws (1) require states

to provide special education and related services to children with special needs, (2) provide financial assistance to states and local school districts to develop appropriate programs and services and (3) establish and protect substantive and procedural rights for children and their parents.

State Plan

To be eligible for money under EHA-B [Part B of P.L. 94-142], a state must develop policies and procedures in a "state plan" to insure that the requirements of the law are carried out in every school district in the state (whether or not that school district actually receives EHA-B money). State plans must be available to the public for comment and then submitted for approval to the federal Bureau of Education for the Handicapped (BEH) in the U. S. Office of Education. The state plan must demonstrate that the state has established and will enforce the following:

1) *Full Services Goal* — a goal of providing all handicapped children with "full educational opportunities"; at least 50% of the EHA-B funds must be given to children who are receiving no education at all (i.e., are not in school) and children who are severely handicapped. The plan must provide a timetable showing how services, personnel, equipment and other resources will be developed and assigned in order to reach "full services."

2) *Due Process Safeguards* — policies and procedures describing due process safeguards which parents/children can use to challenge decisions of state and local officials about how a child has been identified, evaluated or placed in a special education program.

   These safeguards must include:
   a. prior notice before a child is evaluated or placed in a special program;
   b. access to relevant school records;
   c. an opportunity to obtain an independent evaluation of the child's special needs;
   d. an impartial due process hearing to challenge any of the decisions described above; and
   e. the designation of a "surrogate parent" to use these safeguards for each child who is a ward of the state or whose parent or guardian is unknown or unavailable.

3) *Least Restrictive Alternative* — *local and state procedures to assure that handicapped children are educated with non-handicapped children to the extent possible. Separate schools, special classes or other removal of any handicapped child from the regular program are only allowed if and when the school district can show that the use of a regular educational environment accompanied by supplementary aids and services is not adequate to give the child what he/she needs.* (Italics added)

4) *Non-Discriminatory Testing and Evaluation* — procedures showing that tests and other materials or methods used to evaluate a child's special needs are neither racially nor culturally discrimi-

natory. The procedures should also assure that whatever materials or methods are used, they are not administered to a child in a discriminatory manner.

5) *Confidentiality of Information about Handicapped Children* — procedures to guarantee that information gathered about a child in the process of identifying and evaluating children who may have special educational needs, is kept confidential. State procedures must conform to regulations, issued in the February 27, 1976 *Federal Register* by the Commissioner of Education, which include requirements that parents must be given the opportunity to see relevant school records before any hearing is held on a matter of identification, evaluation or placement of a special needs child. These regulations also apply to the requirements for confidentiality of information under the Education for All Handicapped Children Act.

1) *Full Service Goal* — "free appropriate public education" must be available to all handicapped children ages 3-18 by September 1, 1978 and to all handicapped children 3-21 by September 1, 1980 unless, with regard to 3-5 year olds, and 18-21 year olds, "inconsistent" with state law. States must place a priority in the use of their funds under this Act on two groups of children: 1) handicapped children who are *not* receiving an education, and 2) handicapped children with the most severe handicaps, within each disability, who are receiving an inadequate education.

2) *Due Process Safeguards* — As of October 1, 1977 the policies and procedures describing due process safeguards available to parents and children in any matter concerning a child's identification, evaluation or placement in an educational program must include:

   a. prior notice to parents of any change in their child's program and written explanation in their primary language, of the procedures to be followed in effecting that change;
   b. access to relevant school records;
   c. an opportunity to obtain an independent evaluation of the child's special needs;
   d. opportunity for an impartial due process hearing which must be conducted by the SEA [state education agency] or local or intermediate school district, but in no case by an employee "involved in the education or care of the child." In any hearing, parents have the right to be accompanied by a lawyer or any individual with special knowledge of the problems of special needs children, the right to present evidence, to confront, compel and crossexamine witnesses, and to obtain a transcript of the hearing and a written decision by the hearing officer. Parents have the right to appeal the hearing decision to the SEA and, if they are still dissatisfied, the SEA ruling in federal or state court;
   e. the right of a child to remain in his/her current placement (or, if trying to gain initial admission to school, in the regular school program) until the due process proceedings are com-

pleted; and
f. the designation of a "surrogate parent" to use the procedures outlined above on behalf of children who are wards of the state or whose parents or guardians are unknown or unavailable.

3) *Least Restrictive Alternatives* — handicapped children including children in public and private institutions, must be educated as much as possible with children who are not handicapped.

4) *Non-discriminatory Testing and Evaluation* — the tests and procedures used to evaluate a child's special needs [a] must be racially and culturally non-discriminatory in both the way they are selected and the way they are administered, [b] must be in the primary language or mode of communication of the child and [c] no one test or procedure can be used as the sole determinant of a child's educational program.

5) *Individualized Educational Plans* — written individualized educational plans for each child evaluated as handicapped must be developed and annually reviewed by a child's parents, teacher, and a designee of the school district. The plan must include statements of the child's present levels of educational performance, short and long-term goals for the child's performance, and the specific criteria to measure the child's progress. Each school district must maintain records of the individualized education plan for each child.

6) *Personnel Development* — comprehensive system to develop and train both general and special education teachers and administrative personnel to carry out requirements of this law must be developed by the state, and each local school district must show how it will use and put into effect the system of personnel development.

7) *Participation of Children in Private Schools* — free special education and related services must be provided for handicapped children in private elementary and secondary schools if the children are placed or referred to private schools by the SEA or local school districts to fulfill the requirements of this law. The SEA must assure that private schools which provide programs for handicapped children meet the standards which apply to state and local public schools, and that handicapped children served by private schools are accorded all the same rights they would have if served in public schools. (Children's Defense Fund, 1976)

We should warn the reader that this federal law is very complex. It contains many provisions on, for example, priorities, time schedules, funding levels, diagnostic and testing practices, advocacy for children, and parental role. This law, related to and superseding a previous federal law, went into effect October 1, 1977 (some months following the writing of this paper). In late 1976, the *federal* regulations, spelling out in detail the criteria for the administration of the law, were published; these regulations determine the substance of required *state* plans and regulations which, in turn, determine the plans and regulations required of *local* districts. When the Congress passes a law, the executive branch interprets and administers it, and so on down the line.[4] At every step of the way one is dealing with interpretations of interpretations. At this time it is impossible, obviously, to evaluate the law's consequences. Some states (e.g., Connecticut, California, Massachusetts) already have legislation consistent with P.L. 94-142, but most do not.

In the following discussion, we examine some of the possible implications of a few of the law's provisions in relation to (a) the historical background (sketched above) and (b) discussions with numerous teachers and administrators in local school districts and the staffs of several state departments of education. From these discussions, we could come to only three firm conclusions: (a) There is unanimity that the law will have massive consequences for public education, although no unanimity on what these consequences will be. (b) Implementation of the law will require a tremendous outlay of time and energy and increase in paperwork for everyone. (c) Despite the provisions for federal funding in the law, the long-range effect will be to require local school districts to increase their school budgets. Less firm than these three conclusions, because it was clearly stated by some discussants and not others, was the view that a healthy skepticism about the relation between what school people say they will do and what they actually do (or will do) should be nurtured. In at least one instance, independent observations noted a glaring discrepancy between what we were told and what we observed; more correctly, the discrepancy between this person's definition of mainstreaming and what we consider to be the intent of the law was obvious.

So, what follows must be regarded not as an effort at prediction or evaluation but as a kind of analysis seeking to determine how past historical trends interacting with emerging attitudes and practices in today's realities can give us a glimpse of the future. Acceptance of mainstreaming as a concept and value is a kind of socially moral triumph, but just as we had no good reasons to accept the Supreme Court's 1954 desegregation decision as "solving" a problem, we have no reason to view P.L. 94-142 as a solution to other forms of educational segregation. Social pendulums swing from one pole to the other, in part because of our tendency to underestimate how deeply ingrained are the practices and habits of thinking that characterize us as individuals and as members of institutions; these habits of thought subvert our better intentions. If our discussion

---

[4]For readers unfamiliar with how Congress passes a law, we recommend Bailey (1950), *Congress Passes A Law*. Although the book is concerned with the Employment Act of 1946, it conveys well how legislation emerges from a welter of forces, past and present, leading inevitably to compromise and ambiguity. Those of us not saddled with responsibility for legislation underestimate the role of compromise, conflict, and competing values in shaping legislation.

cannot be characterized as sunshine and light, it is not because we are pessimists or cynics but because we cannot let our hopes blind us to obstacles to their fulfillment.

Legislation is often a strange mixture of ambiguities and precise statements about intent, consequences, time tables, payments, and punishments. P.L. 94-142 is no exception. Far from criticising this law, our characterization is intended to suggest that sometimes there is wisdom in ambiguities. For example, consider the item on *Personnel Development*: Why is personnel development necessary? If the aim of the law is to mainstream handicapped children, why is personnel development necessary for special and regular education teachers? If mainstreaming is an effort to eradicate discriminatory segregation, should not the law be explicit about phasing out special class teachers and classrooms? And why does the law require so many procedures and controls to insure that its intent will be implemented? Have the schools been so lawless about the rights of handicapped children, so cavalierly discriminating, or so unresponsive that all of these new procedures and controls are necessary? One might come away from a reading of the law with the conclusion that schools have been against rather than for handicapped children.

The fact is that the contents of the law make sense only if one assumes that they reflect the opposition of school personnel to the intent of the law and the need to "help" school personnel to adjust to conditions that are not of their making or desires. Indeed, without the federal money as an incentive and the few years as a kind of grace period, the implication seems to be that mainstreaming will be impossible to institutionalize.

Where the law is most clear, the rationale is most implicit. This is another way of saying that the people who wrote the law knew well that a radical transformation of the schools was being called for, that the transformation would encounter opposition for some time to come, and that the opposition could not be easily and quickly overcome, only, perhaps, blunted and somewhat controlled. Mainstreaming, like racial school desegregation, should take place with "deliberate speed," a phrase from the 1954 Supreme Court desegregation decision which was purposely ambiguous, although none of the Supreme Court justices expected that racial school desegregation would still be encountering mammoth obstacles a quarter of a century after the decision. A reading of P.L. 94-142 suggests that although its writers may have been aware of the nature of the opposition, their time perspective was remarkably far more optimistic than that of the Supreme Court justices in 1954.

What we have just said, however, assumes that the intent of the law (like that of the 1954 Supreme Court decision) is to end segregation practices. That this is an unwarranted assumption is clearly suggested by the item, *Least Restrictive Alternative*. The essence of this item is that when a school district can show that the use of a regular educational environment accompanied by supplementary aids and services is not adequate to give the child what he or she needs, educational segregation is permissible. Given the law's implicit recognition of the opposition to mainstreaming, one need not be a cynic to predict that school districts will find ways to justify the continuation of special classes, just as so many school districts found (and still find) ways to circumvent the 1954 decision. It would be a disconfirmation of every theory of individual and institutional behavior if school districts did not seek ways to continue practices which they regard as right and proper, not because they are less moral than other people or wish to discriminate pejoratively against handicapped people, but because both the law and the schools agree that there will be many children for whom mainstreaming is impossible. The law and the schools are not in opposition about principles. What the law intends is that the number of segregated individuals should be reduced somewhat. We should then amend our prediction as follows: The schools will seek to mainstream more handicapped people but the majority of them will continue to be segregated. Public Law 94-142 intends a modest quantitative change and, in that respect, it is miles apart from the 1954 decision which ruled segregation unconstitutional, no ifs or buts.

To someone unfamiliar with schools, P.L. 94-142 may appear to be a step to initiate mainstreaming. The fact is that most handicapped pupils always have been mainstreamed in the public schools. However schools may have defined a handicapped child there were never enough special classes to accommodate all the children so defined. Special classes for the mentally retarded go back a long way in our society, but never more than a very small fraction of these children has been placed in such classes because school personnel were unwilling to bear the costs. In recent decades, as the result of state and federal subsidies, special classes have been developed for children with other types of handicaps (e.g., perceptually impaired, learning disabled, emotionally disturbed), but the number of children assigned to the classes always has been a very small percentage of those considered to have the handicap. Why, then, this new push for mainstreaming? Several factors have been at work.

1. It is obvious that when a handicapped child is placed in a special class it is not because of the diagnosis; if it were, how did the schools decide to place one handicapped child in the special class and not many others with the same diagnosis? The most frequent answer has been that the children placed in the special class were those who disturbed the children and teacher in the regular

class. The statement says as much about teachers as it does about handicapped children. In short, special classes have been a kind of dumping ground for children with "behavior problems," and the dumping is not always deserved.

2. The dramatic increase in special classes of all sorts in the past two decades was a direct consequence of state and federal subsidies that made it "profitable" for school systems to set up these classes. As one teacher said, "Now we have a lot of places to dump children."

3. Particularly in our urban areas, special classes tend to have a disproportionate number of children from ethnic or racial minorities, a tendency that does not go unnoticed by the more militant members of these groups.

4. If the trend for increased numbers of special classes were to continue, both the state and federal budgets would have to expand considerably. In a sense, the process came full circle: Local school districts would not increase the number of special classes unless a good part of the costs came from the state or federal government, and now these governments are concerned that they may not be able to stand the increasing costs. Not surprisingly, economics has been and continues to be a potent factor. Economics, dumping, and overrepresentation of minority groups, together with a heightened sensitivity of the citizenry to civil rights, account for the recent push for more mainstreaming.

One other factor deserves mention, and it is no less potent for its lack of clear and direct explication: The polarization between school and community has become deeper and stormier. The reasons are many and need not detain us here. The fact is that school personnel have more and more become the objects of community hostility, derogation, and rejection. Never before have school programs and practices been so scrutinized and criticized. It is only somewhat of an exaggeration to say that school personnel are perceived as guilty until they can prove their innocence. And if that is an exaggeration of how the community views the school, it is not an exaggeration to say that that is how school personnel feel. It should occasion no surprise, therefore, that in the course of criticizing schools (e.g., types of tests used, confidentiality of files, criteria for suspensions and expulsion, racial discrimination, accountability), the questions of how handicapped children are diagnosed, managed, and educated should at some point come to center stage and the drama that is played out should reveal deep and opposing currents of feeling. Mainstreaming, in the near and distant past as well today, is not an educational issue or problem. It is a reflection of the nature of and changes in the larger society, if only because the definitions of deviancy, atypicality, or handicap arise out of societal norms.

Our analysis indicates that opposition to mainstreaming characterizes the history and structure of our educational institutions. One may ask, therefore, What has been the reception accorded Public Law 94-142? Before trying to answer the question, however, let us look at possible implications of the very title of the law: Education for *All* Handicapped Children's Act.

All Handicapped Children

P.L. 94-142 is not only for those children who are diagnosed as mentally retarded. They are only one of many groups to whom the law is applicable. To anyone familiar with the recent history of advocate groups for the mentally retarded, what is remarkable is not the law itself but the lack of strong opposition to the law by these advocate groups. Ever since the early 1950s, when the advocate groups became formidable, they have stressed the need of retarded people for more equitable and humane public support. That is, they were opposed to administrative arrangements that included responsibilities for all handicapped people because, in practice, that meant that the mentally retarded would be, so to speak, low man on the totem pole. For example, it was long the practice of the state department of mental health (or mental hygiene) to carry the responsibility for state programs (residential or otherwise) for mentally retarded people. That is, they were responsible for both the mentally ill and the mentally retarded, which meant that the latter received far less attention and support than the former, if for no other reason than that the heads of these state agencies were psychiatrists who had far greater interest in mental illness than mental retardation. In *Exodus from Pandemonium*, Blatt (1970) described and discussed the "politics" of a state department of mental hygiene, and there is every reason to believe that his story is not atypical.[5] It is small wonder that advocate groups began to fight for the administrative independence of programs for mentally retarded people.

Two examples follow:

1. Up until the late 1950s, Connecticut did not have a central state department of mental health. Each institution for mentally ill or mentally retarded people was administered by a board of trustees appointed by and responsible to the governor. Pressure for a centralized agency began to mount for three reasons: (a) growing public awareness of the extent of the mental health problem, (b) the inadequacies of existing mental hospitals, and (c) the combination of rising costs and the desire for efficiency. In the plans for the proposed state agency, both the mentally ill and the mentally retarded would be its charges. However, a number of advocate

---

[5]In order for Blatt to be appointed to the Massachusetts Department of Mental Hygiene as Deputy Director for Mental Retardation, a special act of the legislature was required because he was not a physician.

groups were aware of the consequences of this administrative arrangment in other states, therefore, they mounted a campaign that resulted in the placement of mental retardation in the Department of Health rather than in the new Department of Mental Health. It is not fortuitous that between 1935 and 1960, Connecticut pioneered nationally in new programs for mentally retarded people (Sarason, Grossman, & Zitnay, 1972). During this period Connecticut may well have been the only state in which mental retardation was "independent." Since then, the administrative separation of mental retardation from mental health has become more frequent.

2. In the 1960s, an act of the U. S. House of Representatives brought about the separation of mental retardation from other special education programs in the U. S. Office of Education. The reasons for the separation were less ideological than political, however. Testifying before a subcommittee of the House of Representatives in favor of a proposed bill that contained funding provisions for special education (i.e., mental retardation), the U.S.O.E. bureau head, Dr. Donald N. Bigelow, made an eloquent plea to bring special education, especially in regard to the training of teachers, into the mainstream of American education. This plea did not sit well with the subcommittee chairman who had fought for greater and separate recognition of the field of mental retardation. He interpreted, wrongly in this instance, Dr. Bigelow's plea as a kind of power grab that would have the familiar effect of robbing the field of the increased support it needed. The hearing was on a Friday; by the end of the following Monday, mental retardation programs had been separated from the bureau.

On the surface, P.L. 94-142 appears to be unobjectionable. Indeed, it is a tremendous stride forward. But, from the standpoint of partisans for mentally retarded children, especially those partisans who have a sense of history and know the culture of schools, there are grounds for unease: the fact that in the past 15 years there has been an exponential growth in special classes for emotionally disturbed, learning disabled, perceptual handicapped, and hyperactive children. The push for those classes came from within and without the schools; among the outside leaders were mental health practitioners who, theretofore, never exercised such leadership on behalf of the mentally retarded. This statement is not made in criticism but simply as a matter of fact. The various special classes that were spawned were, for the most part, for pupils who were not regarded as retarded; however, their handicaps in some way either disrupted normal class routine or put undue burdens on teachers who felt inadequate to deal with the children. These special classes and programs were also costly because the variety of educational and mental health specialists they required was much greater in extent than was ever deemed necessary for special classes for the mentally retarded.

The unease in this account stems from the fact that concern for mentally retarded children was not displayed by the proponents of P.L. 94-142; their concerns were for the bewildering assortment of children whom the schools considered "handicapped" and in need of segregated programs. We put quotes around handicapped because the basis for such a label or diagnosis is often ambiguous, prejudicial, and invalid. For example, few topics can engender more heated controversy than getting agreement on the criteria of emotional disturbance or the nature of learning disabilities. The unease now can be put in the form of a concrete question: Is it not likely that in implementing the mainstreaming intent of P.L. 94-142, less attention and effort will be given to mentally retarded children than to the others encompassed by the act? This question must be raised, not to suggest a conspiracy against mentally retarded children but to suggest that public laws are reactions to current perceptions of social problems, and, in the case of P.L. 94-142, the problems in our schools that seemed to need correction did not primarily center on mental retardation. Of course, this does not mean that the law is not genuinely concerned with mentally retarded children but, rather, that the law is so written that *it permits schools to give greater attention to other kinds of handicapped children*. P.L. 94-142 will be implemented in schools where traditions, structure, and perceived priorities will determine the law's effects. Individuals and institutions are rather adept at transforming a law's intent to their own purposes. If that were not the case, legislative bodies would spend far less time than they do amending laws and writing remedial legislation.

Consequences of P. L. 94-142

Passed in 1975, P.L. 94-142 builds on and expands a law passed in 1974. It requires each state to put "in effect a policy that assumes all handicapped children the right to a free appropriate public education" by October 1977, when funding begins. At the time of this writing, that deadline is several months in the future. Even if one were writing several years after October 1977 it would be difficult to judge the law's consequences, for reasons that are taken up later. At this point, it is possible to present observations of how some school districts have reacted to and prepared for the October 1977 deadline. Our observations are not based on any kind of representative sampling, but we have observed and talked to numerous school teachers, administrators, and policy makers — a sufficient number of them to give us some sense of the diversity of reaction and program.

Before turning to our observations and interviews, let us look at an article by D. Milofsky which was published in *The New York Times Magazine* on Sunday, January 2, 1977. The article is headed as follows:

Schooling for Kids No One Wants

A new Federal law requires 'mainstreaming' of handicapped children into regular classes. It could prove as controversial as busing.

The heading reflects the feelings of many people. Milofsky's article is based on observations of mainstreaming in Massachusetts consequent to the passage of the 1972 state law containing Chapter 766, on which P.L. 94-142 was later based. Mainstreaming has been in effect for five years in Massachusetts. Milofsky described it as follows:

> It requires local school districts to take responsibility for the education of all children who suffer from handicaps "arising from intellectual, sensory, emotional or physical factors, cerebral dysfunctions, perceptual factors, or other specific learning disabilities or any combination thereof." Chapter 766 discourages the labeling of handicapped children as much because of the "stigmatizing effect" this can have and instead emphasizes the individual needs of each child, determined through a "core evaluation" by a team consisting of a psychologist or social worker, doctor or nurse, the child's present or most recent teacher, and a parent. The law mandates the involvement of parents and lay groups in "overseeing, evaluating, and operating special education programs" through regional and state advisory committees, a majority of whose members are parents of handicapped children.
>
> The Massachusetts law has enabled the mainstreaming of the "vast majority" of handicapped children into public schools, says Dr. Robert Audette, Associate Commissioner for Special Education in Massachusetts. Most of these children divide their time between regular and special classrooms, with only the most severely afflicted children in segregated classes. (pp. 24-25)

Before giving some of Milofsky's observations, his examples of mainstreamed pupils should be noted; they are cerebral palsied, learning disabled, emotionally disturbed, and perceptually handicapped children. Mental retardation is never mentioned in the entire article. This omission may be an oversight but that is our point: The mentally retarded may well be overlooked. One could argue that it is a real step forward for our society to recognize that there are many handicapped children with different types of conditions, and that no more attention should be given to one group (e.g., the mentally retarded) than to others. We agree. However, ours is a society that places such a high value on "intelligence" that children who are considered to have less or little of "it" are devalued more than those who have "it" but who also have other characteristics that interfere with school learning. As soon as a child is diagnosed, formally or informally, as mentally retarded, the social-educational-productive worth of that child tends to be seen as lower than if the label given the child were "emotionally disturbed" or "learning disabled," the latter labels implying a more hopeful prognosis. Every teacher has been told, "You teach children, not subject matter." If that admonition is so often honored in the breach, it is for the same reasons that we so often react not to children but to labeled children, even if the label is not based on a formal diagnosis. So, if we seem to be partisans of mentally retarded pupils, it is not because we feel that they are owed more than other children (which is as silly as saying that we should devote more attention to "gifted" than to "run-of-the-mill" children), but because in our society they are likely to get less than other children.

Let us turn to Milofsky's observations:

1. Mainstreaming means being in the mainstream part of the time. "Most of these children divide their time between regular and special classrooms, with only the most severely afflicted children in segregated classes" (p. 25). In other words, some children are more segregated than others.

2. Many teachers feel unprepared for their responsibilities under the Massachusetts law; the school personnel who might be of help to teachers are too busy meeting their new responsibilities under the law. Some teachers, in the minority, report being able to cope with their new responsibilities.

3. Emotionally disturbed children are the most disturbing. School personnel feel that they are being required to deal with these children with very inadequate resources and with no expectation that the resources will ever be available. In the City of Springfield, "Most of these children are boys and many of them are blacks or Spanish-speaking . . . . [and] there is little hope of returning them to regular classes" (p. 28).

4. It is difficult for parents to assert their rights, in part, because they do not know the law and, in part, because "they are intimidated by the whole thing" (p. 33).

5. For some towns and cities, the law, despite its funding provisions, has created financial hardships.

The consequences of P.L. 94-142 will vary in terms of urban, suburban, and rural settings, that is, the consequences will vary not only according to the size of the school district but, also, according to the factors that are highly correlated with size: racial and ethnic composition, average achievement levels, serious problems of management and discipline, class size, frequency of moving of families within a school district, teacher morale, and level of conflict between school personnel and the community. Only if we were living in another world could one avoid predicting that the consequences in our urban settings will very likely be different from those in suburban and rural settings.

Someone once said that our urban school systems are really two systems, regular and special, and the regular exceeds the special in size by a surprisingly small amount. In 1968, the President's Committee on Mental Retardation found that children from poverty and ghetto areas are 15 times more likely to be diagnosed as mentally retarded than children from higher income families, and that, nationally, most of the retarded are found in our urban slums (and some rural ones as well). Reynolds (n.d.) noted that *"Awareness of the spreading presence of 'special classes' in ghetto schools has aroused resentment and resistance. As a result, administrators of school systems in our largest cities are under a virtual mandate to reverse the expansion of special education programs"* (p. 11; italics added). From the standpoint of urban school personnel, the existing special classes contain only a fraction of the pupils who would be in them if more funds were available. More than one urban school teacher has said, "I am a *regular* classroom teacher but don't kid yourself, I have a *special* class." This feeling increases in frequency and depth as one moves from elementary to middle to senior school levels.

If anything, these feelings have deepened in the past few years as cutbacks in funds have made for larger classes. But even before these cutbacks, teacher unions in our urban settings sought, often successfully, to insure that regular classroom teachers would not have to cope with children who, in one or another way, disrupted classroom routine and academic goals. From the standpoint of urban school personnel, the provision in P.L. 94-142 that restricts funding to the small percentage of pupils who may be diagnosed as handicapped by a school system is a gross misperception of the size of the problem. Furthermore, and again from the standpoint of urban school personnel, the provisions of the law safeguarding the rights of children and parents (or other advocates) will be not only costly in time but may well heighten the level of existing conflict between schools and the community. The fact that the law provides inservice training of school personnel to enable them to cope with the consequences of increased mainstreaming is explicit recognition that what is at issue is changing the attitudes of school personnel.

Our observations and discussions lead, unfortunately, to the conclusion that urban school systems are hardly prepared to implement P.L. 94-142. Several months before the deadline of October 1977, some school systems have no plan at all. As one administrator in a large urban school system said, "It's not that we don't want to be prepared but simply that we have not had the time and, frankly, the energy to think through what we should do and how we should do it. And to be completely truthful, I have not read the law and no one I know has either. We thank God when we get through a day or a week with our hearts and bodies intact, so when you ask what we are doing about the law, I get a sinking sensation. But then again, that's exactly the way we feel: sinking."

This administrator's reactions are paraphrased, not for the purpose of criticising, evaluating, or excusing, but to underline the beleaguerment that urban educators project. Several urban school systems reported that they had already instituted mainstreaming. Although the reports differed in a number of respects, they tended to have several features in common. (a) Centers (variously labeled) had been established to which handicapped children were sent for academic subjects and in which they spend a significant portion of the day. (b) These pupils were "mainstreamed" with the other children in the gymnasium, at lunch, for music, and during other comparable periods. (In some instances, children were bussed daily to the center and the mainstreaming took place there; in other instances, the center was in the school that the child normally attended by virtue of place of residence; in one instance, the center was in a mobile unit parked next to the school.) (c) In almost every instance, the descriptions indicated that primary attention was being given to children who were labeled emotionally disturbed or learning disabled. In other words, school personnel seemed to be defining mainstreaming, to see its intent, as less related to mentally retarded pupils and more to pupils whose labels did not suggest an intellectual deficit.

Mainstreaming: Begging the Question

24   Mainstreaming is a concept powered by a value: Every effort should be made to allow a handicapped child to be an integral member of his peer-age group, and only when such membership is not possible should one employ the least restrictive alternative. The question arises, however, by what criteria should one resort to a least restrictive alternative? The answer to this question, of course, will determine in practice what mainstreaming is. It is relatively easy to get agreement on a verbally stated value, but it is far more difficult to keep that agreement once that value is acted upon. Between intent and performance is a wide area containing obstacles that often obscure or defeat intent. Because you want to do "good" does not mean that you will, or if you do good by your lights that others will agree that your actions have been consistent with your values. In practice, on what basis is the least restrictive alternative being decided and how consistent is it with the underlying value?

The very fact that P.L. 94-142 was enacted, as well as the fact that it calls for inservice training, is testimony to the widespread belief that too frequently schools defined least restrictive alternative in ways that were congenial to their accustomed perception of their mission rather than to what was in the best interests of certain children. This attitude is not peculiar to schools; it is characteristic of how most organizations deal with troublesome individuals. P.L. 94-142 does not tell school systems how to decide the question; it puts the burden of proof on schools to justify the resort to a least restrictive alternative. How do some schools seem to be justifying the resort to the alternative? Keeping in mind that "modern" mainstreaming is, so to speak, in its infancy, and that our observations and discussion cannot be assured to be representative (although they may so turn out), the answer to the question is — relatively sincere tokenism. And by that confusing and self-contradictory answer we mean that there is a sincere desire to comply with the law at the same time that a tremendous amount of time and energy go into the development and maintenance of the new type of segregated setting. The very existence of these settings requires justification and use, which often play into the tendency to avoid asking to what extent the child is removed from the regular classroom because of the inadequacies of the classroom. This is not to say that the child labeled as handicapped is no problem in the classroom but, rather, that classroom problems are always a consequence of the interaction among characteristics of the child, teacher, and other children.

Problem behavior always has a situational component. Problem behavior is not "inside" a child, or a characteristic of the child, but a feature of a complex situation. For example, the most dramatic and sustained change in behavior we have ever seen has been when we could change a child's classroom placement, no mean diplomatic feat (Sarason, Levine, Goldenberg, Cherlin, & Bennet, 1965). The following case description is given in detail, not only because of the tactics that were employed and the outcomes achieved but, no less important, because it was written more than a decade before mainstreaming became public policy.

Tommy was a 7-year-old boy enrolled in the second grade. He was a well-developed, good-looking child of above-average intelligence who had entered the elementary school one year before when his family had moved into the area. Both academically and socially his performance and adjustment at the time were more than adequate and consistent with his abilities and talents. Although initially noted to be somewhat shy, he quickly made friends and was highly regarded by his first-grade teacher.

Tommy had had several of the usual childhood diseases (chicken pox and measles) and his last complete physical examination had been essentially negative. His teeth required attention, his vision was 20-20, and his hearing was normal. Thus, until the summer of 1964, Tommy was a relatively healthy, attractive and bright 7-year-old whose developmental and medical history was essentially unremarkable. Although he experienced some minor difficulty when he entered the new school situation, his adjustment, both academically and socially, was completely satisfactory.

During the summer vacation, Tommy, while delivering newspapers, was viciously attacked and bitten by a dog. As he went up to one of the houses on his paper route, the dog leaped on him, ripped his clothing, and bit him on the back and wrist. Tommy's screams eventually brought the dog's owner, who had to beat the dog repeatedly with a club in order to make him let go of the child.

Tommy was taken immediately to the office of a local doctor. His mother was notified and met Tommy there. His wounds were cauterized and injections administered for possible infection, and he was given sedatives. Soon after this experience Tommy became very quiet and extremely withdrawn, not talking or playing with other children, and refusing to leave his home. About three weeks later, he developed a cold and what was described as an "asthma attack" in which he was short of breath and had difficulty breathing. According to Tommy's mother, it was during this time immediately following the incident with the dog that Tommy "woke up nights screaming and crying and at times running out of the house. He complained of a pounding in his head and imagined seeing things."

With the passage of time and the approach of the new school year, Tommy's posttraumatic symptomatology appeared to become more involved and frightening. He began actively hallucinating and talking about "the ugly little man who's coming and putting bad feelings in my head." He became extremely frightened by loud sounds and constantly sought his mother's attention, reassurance, and protection. The only way in which she could calm him down was to hold him and speak to him in a soft quiet manner. After numerous consultations with the family doctor, it was decided to put Tommy under the care of Dr. S., a "nerve specialist in town." Dr. S. placed Tommy on a regimen of medication (phenobarbital) to be taken three times a day after meals. It was his feeling that Tommy's condition was "an emotional reaction related to the strain stemming from his traumatic episode with a brutal dog." Tommy was told that the "pill he took to school would help him get rid of the spells."

It will be recalled that when Tommy initially entered the first grade he had experienced some minor difficulties in adjusting to his new living and school settings. It was during this period that he first came into contact with the school nurse. According to her, he "often would come to me during the first few weeks of school complaining of a cold or stomach upset, but would be satisfied to just talk with me, have his temperature taken and return to class." Following his successful adjustment in school he contented himself with visiting the nurse whenever the holidays were drawing near, at which time he would wish her a happy holiday, and would often give her a card that he had made for her.

On returning to school this year Tommy was assigned to a second-grade class. At this time he was extremely nervous and upset, often running away from the loud noises in the schoolyard, and frequently hallucinating. His single anchor of security in school appeared to be the faith he placed in "the pill that would help my spells."

Tommy's second-grade teacher was an essentially unresponsive and reserved person. Her approach to teaching and to the children was all business. Her previous teaching experience had been confined to the parochial school setting and it was difficult for her to tolerate any interference with the academic standard and expectations she set for her students. Our observations in her classroom always revealed an academically competent teacher who was a stern and controlling disciplinarian and who used methods of shaming and rejecting to ensure the maintainance of an orderly efficient classroom. Although she was never harsh or uncontrolled in her interpersonal dealings with the children, neither would she allow herself or them to minimize their personal distance in a physical or psychological manner. In short, however competent her preparation and however well-intentioned her philosophy of teaching, she was a teacher who was essentially unable or unwilling to deal with the particular and idiosyncratic needs of her children. She tended to perceive these needs as unwelcomed and unrelated interruptions in the processes and aims of second-grade education.

In terms of the teacher's relationship with Tommy, although upset and somewhat frightened by his behavior, she perceived his spells as essentially interfering; that is to say, as discrete behaviors that erected unwanted barriers for her in her attempts to present specific material to the rest of the class. As far as his pills were concerned, she viewed the responsibility for his taking them as a matter of concern for Tommy, his parents, and his doctor. It was not within the scope of her definition of her professional responsibilities to become involved in a problem that was distracting in nature and took time away from her teaching duties. This being the case, and because she was unable to materially reorganize her perceptions of the situation, she was content to allow Tommy to use the nurse and her office as the appropriate setting for such interactions. This removed Tommy from her classroom during his periods of stress and, at the same time, enabled her to maintain her firm position regarding the limited and relevant areas of responsibility for a teacher.

From this point on Tommy began spending more and more of his time at the nurse's office, and it was here that we first met him. According to the nurse, whenever Tommy was in school — his absence rate for the months of September and October were extremely high — he would come to her office to take his pill or "whenever he felt a spell coming on." They would spend these periods of time talking and Tommy would describe vividly his feelings and tell her about the "things he saw." Often when his crying and trembling subsided she would call his mother, talk with her at length, and eventually have Tommy taken home. Although the nurse knew about the incident with the dog, Tommy himself soon brought it up during one of his particularly difficult days. They spoke about it at some length and the nurse, in the context of sharing and understanding his fear, related to him several other such incidents involving other children. It was during the next day that we met Tommy. On that occasion Tommy had come to the nurse's office and wanted to go home. He was sobbing uncontrollably and seemed extremely nervous when we came into her office. After he calmed down a bit we all sat around while Tommy told us about "the little man I saw in my class who was coming to put bad things in my head." Once more he spent a good deal of time talking about the past summer, but finally he began speaking of the terrible difficulty he had whenever he felt a spell coming on and would have to ask his teacher about letting him go out of the class to take his pill. He ended by informing us of his desire not to come to school any more. After speaking with Tommy's mother and the teacher we decided eventually to change his class, and, for the interim, we put him on half days, both to minimize his anxiety-arousing contact with his teacher and to enable us to have the time to search for an appropriate second-grade teacher. During the time that he was attending school only in the afternoons he spent most of his time doing his schoolwork in the nurse's office after his teacher had given him his assignment. We were, as yet, relatively new in the school. Although we felt the need to have Tommy's class changed, we wanted time to get a better idea of exactly which teacher would be most appropriate for him. Since neither Tommy's current teacher nor the school nurse minded his using the nurse's office as his interim "classroom," everyone agreed to this arrangement. This enabled the nurse and ourselves to utilize that period of time to search for, become acquainted with, and brief whoever was to become Tommy's new teacher.

The following week we were in the lunchroom during a time of the day when the school nurse usually is not in her office. Tommy entered the lunchroom looking obviously upset and a bit bewildered. He was grasping his bottle of pills tightly in his hand as he looked around for his teacher. Before we could reach him or he could see us he turned to another teacher and hesitatingly began asking her permission to take his pill. The teacher, noting his degree of upset and the air of panic pervading his speech, immediately took his hand and accompanied him out of the lunchroom. They proceeded down the hall to a fountain where she helped Tommy take the pill. Once this was accomplished the teacher took Tommy to her room where he calmed down in a relatively short period of time. With her arm draped gently around his shoulders she then took him back to the lunchroom where he sat at her class's table for the remainder of the period. In this very short time we knew that we had found Tommy's next second-grade teacher.

This teacher was a young and attractive woman who was relatively inexperienced in terms of the number of years she had been teaching. Her class was generally a bit more noisy than others but always jumping with activity. She was an extremely warm and accepting person who seemed most effective and efficient when she became intimately involved with and in the ongoing activities of her children. Although she never lost control of her class there was a pervading atmosphere of disjointedness in the sense that many activities might be going on at the same time. This looseness quickly subsided whenever she raised her voice a bit above the well-modulated tone in which she usually addressed individual students. Her lessons were not always totally prepared and sometimes were lost in organizing particular events. She was extremely patient with the children and utilized well both verbal and nonverbal cues to communicate her feelings to them. More than anything else she seemed to enjoy teaching and being with her children, and this enjoyment appeared to be reciprocal.

We immediately met with the nurse and the "new" teacher to consider the transfer of Tommy to her class. We discussed Tommy's difficulties and the reasons we felt she might be helpful. The teacher, in turn, communicated her desire to have him placed in her class and informed us that, indeed, she had a great affection for him and hoped she would be able to help him. It was decided that the school nurse would be the most appropriate person to handle the transition in the sense that she would both help to present the idea to Tommy and would remain the available resource whenever he felt the need to leave the classroom for any reason relating to his difficulties. It was also decided that the teacher would meet with us on a weekly basis to discuss Tommy's progress or lack of progress.

Tommy was transferred to his new class and immediately placed on a full-day schedule. During the first day the teacher spoke with Tommy about his difficulties and communicated to him how important it was to her that he get better and take his "spell pills." They established a procedure whereby he would not have to make any public statement in class prior to the granting of permission to leave the room to take his pill. Whenever Tommy was absent the teacher immediately called his home and spoke with him and his mother. Although Tommy was informed of the availability of the school nurse the teacher made it clear to him that his health, as well as his school work, was now also a joint venture between him and herself. To Tommy this meant that she very much wanted him to be able to talk with her about his feelings and his symptoms, and that her interest in him was as a "little boy" and not just as a "little student."

Tommy's progress after entering his new class was speedy and marked and was manifested in virtually all of the areas in which he had been experiencing profound difficulties. For purposes of clarity we describe these areas separately, although the reader should note that his behavior in each of these areas was influenced by, and interrelated with, his experiences in the others. Tommy's absence rate from school decreased almost immediately after he was placed in his new class. In terms of academic performance, Tommy rose to be one of the top five students in his class. According to his grades as well as his teacher's observations, he was beginning to fulfill the above-average potential noted in the first grade. Although before his shift he was unable to concentrate, had difficulty maintaining attention, and was unwilling to work at anything but his reading material, he was now actively involved in the varied projects occurring in his classroom. In general, his over-all academic performance, as well as his social adjustment, was at a higher level, occurred in a context relatively free of the debilitating effects of undue loss of attention or the inability to concentrate, and appeared to have become more inner-directed and self-satisfying than externally imposed.

Of greatest import were the changes that occurred in Tommy's symptomatology and schedule of medication. The week before his transfer was particularly difficult for him. His symptoms (fearfulness, phobic reactions to loud noises, periods of fitful crying, and apparent hallucinatory experiences) were quite pronounced, and the occasions necessitating his approaching his teacher to request attention for his "spell pills" seemed to exacerbate these symptoms. At that time he was on phenobarbital. During the time after his transfer to his new class he showed evidence of a steady and progressive reduction in the intensity and duration of his psychotic symptomatology. Soon after entering his new class the periods of fitful crying accompanying his pill-taking behavior subsided. He was gradually able to tolerate loud noises, although this aspect of his difficulty has been only recently eliminated. His hallucinatory experiences became less frequent and frightening, the more he spoke about them with his teacher. They, too, have not been reported for some time. In mid-December, approximately one month after his transfer, his medication was decreased to every other day, and by late January was further reduced. At present, all medications have been discontinued. In a recent meeting of the school nurse, the teacher, and ourselves, the teacher informed us that she had not noticed any changes since Tommy has been off medication. Tommy's mother reported similar progress at home and except for the fact that "he occasionally has nightmares and wakes up crying," felt that "the worst is over." Our latest classroom observations and information would support this point of view.

As far as Tommy's relationship with the nurse was concerned, this soon underwent a change. Although we made it clear to Tommy that the nurse was available to him whenever he felt he needed her, the frequency and duration of his visits to her decreased steadily after mid-November. Although he had been in her office virtually every day that he was in school and had remained there for significant periods of time, subsequent to his shifting of classes he began showing up less often and would remain for shorter periods. This change was a gradual process and occurred over a long span of time. By late December the nurse observed that Tommy "still comes to see me about little things and many times just to say 'Hello!' " Her most recent report indicated that, "Tommy has not visited my office in almost three weeks, except to look for a hat in the lost and found box!"

This case was described long before mainstreaming was in the air and also before there were classrooms for emotionally disturbed children. Today, the chances are high that Tommy would not be in a regular classroom but in a "least restrictive alternative." The presence of such alternatives, together with Tommy's behavior and blatant psychopathology, would probably effectively short circuit thinking of alternative ways to maintain him in the regular classroom. We are not asserting that all children can be maintained in the regular classroom. We are asserting three things:

1. No teacher (no human being) is equally effective with all kinds of children. It may sound like an extreme statement but we have never seen a child labeled as a serious classroom problem who could not be effectively managed by another teacher in that school if one disregarded grade levels. Just as we have emphasized that some parent-child relationships founder because of a mismatch be-

tween the child's and parents' characteristics or vulnerabilities, the same principle holds between pupils and teacher. To resort to a least restrictive alternative without considering and acting on this principle is to subvert the intent of mainstreaming. The first question is not what is the least restrictive alternative, but how seriously has one attempted to match a child to a regular classroom teacher.

2. Also illustrated by Tommy's case is the significant role of the consultant whose task it is to support both teacher and child, but who essentially acts as an advocate for the child.

3. When least restrictive alternatives are not available, necessity can truly become the mother of invention. Although not all such inventions are successful, the rate of success has been quite encouraging. What we have observed about mainstreaming is that it has led to procedural and administrative inventions that, obviously, are quite different than the inventions described in Tommy's case.

But Tommy's case is significant for another reason, and it has to do with the Yale Psycho-Educational Clinic that was in existence from 1962-1972.[6] Clinic personnel worked in the schools and the classrooms. To further understanding of the rationale for the role of the clinic member in the school and the significance of the rationale for mainstreaming, there is given part of the introductory comments of a clinic member to the faculty of a school before any relation between school and clinic was consummated.

> One of the most staggering problems facing our society concerns the degree of serious maladjustment in many people. One has only to look at the size and number of our mental hospitals, psychiatric clinics, reformatories and the like to begin to grasp how enormous a problem this is. We are talking about millions of people and billions of dollars. What needs to be stressed is that in the foreseeable future we will have neither the personnel nor the facilities to give these troubled people the quality of treatment they need. In all honesty I must also say that for many of these people our knowledge and treatment procedures leave much to be desired.
>
> As a result of our experiences, we at the Psycho-Educational Clinic in the Yale Department of Psychology have come to two conclusions: first, far too little is being done either to try to prevent the occurrence of problems or to spot them at those points in the individual's life where, with a little effort, a lot may be accomplished. Second, if we believe what we say, we ought in a very limited kind of way to attempt to see what we can do. I do not have to emphasize to a group of elementary-school teachers the significance of a preventive approach to problems in the early grades. As I am sure all of

---

[6]For a fuller description of the clinic in relation to mental retardation, see Kaplan & Sarason (1970); Sarason (1972, 1974),; Sarason, Grossman, & Zitnay (1972); and Sarason, Levine, Goldenberg, Cherlin, & Bennet (1966). Tommy was one of many cases in the first book describing the activities of the clinic. It also must be noted that most of the schools with which the clinic was affiliated were in the ghetto or central city.

you know as well as, if not better than I, you are faced daily with children whose behavior, learning difficulties, and interpersonal relations (with you or other children) arouse in you concern, bewilderment, anger, and a lot of other reactions. On the basis of all the talks and meetings we have had over the years with teachers there would seem to be in any one classroom of 25 children anywhere from three to six children about whom the teacher is concerned, in the sense that she has questions about their academic learning and personal adjustment in the school setting.

What do we propose to do? It is easier for me to tell you what we do not intend to do. For one thing, we do not intend to come into a school in order to see how many problem children we can refer out to various agencies. There is no doubt that you know a lot of children who could utilize the services of a child-guidance clinic or family service society. To come in with the intent of referring them out is both unfair and unrealistic because these agencies, particularly the child guidance clinics, are overwhelmed with cases and generally have long waiting lists. Even if the child-guidance clinic could take the child on, it would take them quite a while to get to first base with the child, and in the meantime you still have that child in your class. Treatment procedures are neither that quick nor effective to allow you to expect that your difficulties with the child are over once you know he is being seen in a clinic. The question we have asked of ourselves is how can we be of help to the teacher in the here and now with whatever questions and problems she raises with us? In short, we want to see how we can be of help within the confines of the school.

It is not our purpose to come into a school to sit and talk to teachers, however helpful and interesting that might be. When we say we want to be helpful in the here and now within the confines of the school, we mean that in addition to talking with the teacher about the child we have to be able to observe that child in the context of the classroom in which the problem manifests itself. For help to be meaningful and practical it must be based on what actually goes on in the classroom setting. For example, it is in our experience of no particular help to a teacher to be told that a child needs individual attention, a need which differentiates him not at all from the rest of us. What a teacher wants to know is when, how, and for what goals this "individual attention" will occur, and this requires a first-hand knowledge of what is going on.

We do not view ourselves in the schools as people to whom questions are directed and from whom answers will be forthcoming. Life and the helping process are not that simple. We have no easy answers, but we have a way of functioning that involves us in a relationship to the teacher and the classroom and that together we can come up with concrete ideas and plans that we feel will be helpful to a particular child. We are not the experts who can come up with solutions even though we have no first-hand knowledge of the context in which the problem has been identified.

I hope I have made clear that when we say we want to help it means that we want to talk to the teacher, observe in the classroom, talk again to the teacher, and together come up with a plan of action that with persistence, patience, and consistency gives promise of bringing about change. It is not a quick process and it is certainly not an easy one.

I cannot state too strongly that we are not coming into the schools with the intent of criticizing or passing judgment on anyone. We are nobody's private FBI or counterintelligence service. We are not the agent of the principal or some other administrative officer. In fact, we are in no way part of the administrative hierarchy or power structure of the school system. We have no special strength or power except that which flows from our being able to establish a situation of mutual trust between teachers and ourselves. To the extent that we can demonstrate to you by our manner, gesture, and verbalization that we want to help, to that extent we make the development of this mutual trust more likely and quickly to occur.

The thrust of the clinic's operations was, obviously, to keep children in the regular classrooms. There were some special classes for the mentally retarded but none for any other type of handicap. Children were not placed in special classes because they were retarded but because they were troublesome, and if state regulations did not set a limit to the size of these classes they would have been crowded to the extreme. Those were the days when pressure was mounting from within and without the schools for more types of special classes and more community facilities to deal with children with school problems. The clinic's aim was to see if the pressure to segregate within the schools and to refer to outside agencies could be blunted. Those were the days when suspensions and expulsions were frequent and not subject to the legal, civil rights procedures of today.

In early 1977, we interviewed Mr. Murray Rothman, long the Director for Special Education in the New Haven schools, to discuss what was being done about mainstreaming. What is relevant to the present discussion is that for several years before P.L. 94-142 was enacted he had been able to place in each of nine schools a person whose major function was to be of whatever help possible to classroom teachers in regard to their pupils. He had fought for and carried out this plan, he said spontaneously, because, as a result of his close working relationship with the Yale Psycho-Educational Clinic, he had witnessed first-hand how the role of a clinic member in school helped teachers to maintain handicapped children in the regular classroom. He then reported that in comparison to the schools that had no person functioning in the clinic-like role, the nine schools that did referred significantly fewer children to "least restrictive alternatives" (e.g., resource centers). It was his opinion that if he were able to have such a person in each school, the need for these alternatives would not be eliminated but discernibly diluted in strength.[7]

Summary

Mainstreaming (more correctly, *more* mainstreaming), in terms of both its current conceptual, substantive status and possible consequences, must be seen from a historical perspective that brings together long-standing educational practices and attitudes (in schools, colleges, and universities) that reflect the larger society, on the one hand, and the nature of and forces for social change, on the other. Up until relatively recently, the conflict between the forces for tradition and change had little impact on segregation practices within schools, which is another way of saying that educational segregation of the mentally retarded, by far the most segregated group, went unchallenged. However, as the conflict gathered strength, and as that conflict began to be manifested in schools, segregation of other "handicapped" groups became much more frequent.

The forces against educational segregation practices came primarily from outside the schools. P.L. 94-142 is the culmination of their efforts. However, these forces may have vastly overestimated the power of legislation to change either the structure and practices of schools in ways that are appropriate to the intent of mainstreaming or the hearts and thinking of school personnel. This situation must be understood not in moral terms (school personnel are not less moral or ethical than other groups) but in light of the weight of long traditions. Preliminary observations suggest that many school systems are unprepared to deal with mainstreaming, or they are approaching it in ways that only minimally begin to meet the intent of mainstreaming: to avoid the negative effects of stigmatizing labels, and to foster tolerance and mutual understanding between handicapped and nonhandicapped youngsters. These preliminary observations also suggest that school personnel are perceiving mainstreaming largely in terms of nonretarded, handicapped pupils. It appears that, in the future as in the past, children stigma-

---

[7]The idea of mainstreaming had long been congenial to Mr. Rothman. Although he understood well that referrals to special classes frequently said more about the inadequacies of schools and teachers than about children, he also understood and was sympathetic to the forces powering these referrals. That is to say, he did not see the problem in personality terms but as a reflection of how teachers were prepared (ill-prepared) for the realities of the urban classroom. This conclusion hit him full face when he began to teach one of the first special classes in an urban high school. In judging Mr. Rothman's conception and implementation of the clinic-role in the nine schools, the reader should know that he chose as his assistant a teacher (Irene Kaller) whom clinic members regarded as coming as close to being effective with any kind of child as they had ever seen. If these two people were, as they reported, influenced by the clinic it was because they independently had arrived at an outlook similar to that on which the clinic was based.

tized with the label "mentally retarded" will benefit least from the intended benefits of mainstreaming. But, as one school administrator in a large urban setting said, "Why not say that the mentally retarded will be harmed the least from the coming chaos!" Such a comment may well be unduly cynical but it reflects the mixture of anxiety, impotence, puzzlement, and pressure felt by school personnel in our urban settings. To overlook such feelings is to do injustice to both school personnel and the people who fought for mainstreaming. Between enactment of a law and adoption of practices consistent with the law is the whole, poorly understood problem of how to effect institutional change.

It is remarkable how many school personnel, especially those on an administrative and special services level, are totally uninformed about the existence and implications of P.L. 94-142. A director of a training program in school psychology had not heard of the law and had to have the concept of mainstreaming explained to him. One guidance counselor, an unusually creative and hard-working educator, was quite surprised when we told him about the law. He works in a suburban school district, with a largely white, middle-class population. "No," he said, "I have not heard about the law. In fact, last week I spent an hour observing a special class for the mentally retarded in our junior high. There were nine students: eight blacks and one Spanish-speaking person. Frankly, it was an upsetting experience. Such boredom! Such a waste of potential and money!"

The Sunday, May 1, 1977, edition of the *New York Times* contained a special 28-page section on "Spring Survey of Education." Aside from one brief article in which there was parenthetical reference to P.L. 94-142, special education was given short shrift. Less than two weeks later, on May 11, that newspaper contained an equally brief article with the heading, "Schools are forced to pay more attention to disabled," by Gene I. Maeroff. Here is the article:

> One of the most remarkable turnabouts in the nation's schools involves the change in attitude toward mentally and physically handicapped students, who for years have been relegated to the basements of educational concern.
>
> Out of sight and out of mind, the handicapped were supposed to be grateful that the schools let them in the doors. In fact, only now are some schools getting around to admitting many of the most seriously handicapped children, whose parents were told to keep them home or to find private facilities.
>
> A string of court decisions and a state-by-state legislative campaign, underpinned by the passage of a landmark bill in Congress, are compelling schools to pay more attention to the country's 3.5 million to 4 million handicapped youngsters.

Two Controversial Requirements

> The pendulum has swung so far so fast that already a mild reaction is developing against the extensive overlay of regulations that

will be fitted into place this fall.

Perhaps the two most controversial provisions of the Federal Government's law on behalf of the handicapped are those encouraging the "mainstreaming" of the handicapped with normal children and mandating the preparation of a specific program for each youngster.

Failure to comply with the directives can make a state ineligible for Federal aid, and officials in some places are uneasy with the pressure being exerted by Washington.

In Florida, for instance, the Legislature's House Committee on Federal-State Appropriations recently voted to refuse to accept Federal assistance for the handicapped unless the law was modified to give states more leeway in determining policy.

One Problem Cited

"Although the intent of the Federal act is a laudable attempt to address the unmet educational needs of our nation's handicapped children," the committee stated, "the current legislative and regulatory language forces those states with established on-going quality programs to either compromise their laws and existing programs or to refuse money which is badly needed."

The question of whether to isolate the handicapped in classes of their own or to integrate them into the regular programs — mainstreaming — is dealt with by language in the law that says children should be included in regular classes "to the maximum extent appropriate."

Albert Shanker, the president of the American Federation of Teachers, who says that the new law is "generally good, necessary and important," is fearful that without some changes the support for mainstreaming could have some unfortunate results.

"Given the fact that all school districts are facing fiscal problems," Mr. Shanker said, "it is easy to see them opting to place most handicapped children in regular classrooms rather than in more costly special education programs."

Also, there is concern in some circles about the time and expense involved in tailoring the educational program for each handicapped student — something that is not done, as a matter of course, for all normal pupils.

Reversal of Attitudes

In New York, the state law related to this provision allows the parents of a handicapped youngster to have a hearing if they are not satisfied with their child's program. These appeals are to be handled by the school board in each district, and some officials are worried about being deluged by appeals.

Jack Jones, who handles liaison with the states in the United States Office of Education's Bureau of Education for the Handicapped, is optimistic about the new Education for All Handicapped Children Act.

"People are agonizing a good deal about the complexity of the task they are confronted with," Mr. Jones said. "They realize the law represents a substantial challenge. But whenever we have a

> chance to explain the law to them and work with them, they are no longer as alarmed."
>
> A key element in the new climate regarding the handicapped is that no longer will school districts be as likely to give preference in the spending of funds to those who are not handicapped.
>
> It had been the policy in many locales to support programs for the handicapped only after all of the normal children had been accommodated. If anything, the handicapped may start getting the edge. (p. A20)

The article is noteworthy in several respects, not the least of which are the source and nature of the opposition to the law. The statement that "the handicapped may start getting the edge" in terms of money and attention expresses clearly what many individuals and groups within school systems have feared to say. One superintendent of a large city school system said, "I have to lay off 100 regular class teachers, at the same time I have to hire a fair number of special class teachers and personnel. How do you think these regular teachers feel? I can tell you first hand that my teachers are polarized and feeling is running high." Finally, on May 19, 1977, on the CBS national radio network, Nicholas Van Hoffman came out not only against mainstreaming but against the billions of dollars that implementing the laws for the handicapped would require. One senses that the backlash has started and that all the arguments, principled and unprincipled, advanced over the decades against mainstreaming will be resurrected. But we are a nation governed by law, not people, and it is most unlikely that the laws will be changed, although it is likely that the level of funding will be scaled down. What is not unlikely is that these arguments, reflecting as they do some dominant features of our history, practices, and culture, will power reactions that will effectively dilute the appropriate expression of the spirit of P.L. 94-142. Rhetoric aside, mainstreaming challenges the very nature of our society and it would be foolhardy to face the future as if that challenge will not be met by efforts to blunt it. Society and its dominant institutions do not change quickly.

A MAJOR DEFICIENCY OF P.L. 94-142.

We have already said that the law can be construed as criticism of what our schools have been.

> Handicapped and nonhandicapped students are human beings, not different species, and their basic make-up in no way justifies educational practices that assume that their needs for social intercourse, personal growth and expression, and the sense of mastery are so different that one must apply different theories of human behavior to the two groups. If we respond to the handicapped as if they are basically different we rob them and us of the experience of similarity and communality. We can no longer allow schools to segregate children from each other, and one kind of educational per-

sonnel from another, based on conceptions that are invalid and morally flawed.

That is the implied message of P.L. 94-142. But where did school personnel learn such conceptions? There are two answers, one general and one quite specific. The general answer is that they learned these conceptions, and justified them morally, from being born into and growing up in a society in which these conceptions and moral precepts were seen as valid, right, and proper. In short, they learned in the same ways and places everybody else learned. The contents of and the processes by which school personnel learn do not set them apart from other groups! The specific answer is that school personnel are graduates of training centers in our colleges and universities. It is there that they learn that there are at least two types of human beings, and if you choose to learn to work with one type you render yourself *legally* and conceptually incompetent to work with the other. As we pointed out earlier in this chapter, what we see in our public schools is a mirror image of what exists in colleges and universities. One of the clearest implications of P.L. 94-142 is that the gulf between special and regular education must be bridged, yet the law requires no change in our college and university training centers. Therefore, we have the situation in which the law mandates changes in our schools and changes in the attitudes, thinking, and practices of school personnel; at the same time, our training centers educate school personnel in the traditions of the "most restrictive alternative." An educational administrator in Milofsky's article was quoted as follows:

> "It's fine to pass laws," he says, "but it's the teachers who are stuck trying to implement them. Nothing in the law requires in-service training on a systemic basis and a lot of the teachers have no experience in dealing with handicapped kids. We think 766 should require major changes at the undergraduate level. If there are going to be laws like this, they should be taken into account during a teacher's educational training."

At its root, mainstreaming is a moral issue. It raises age-old questions: How do we want to live with each other? On what basis should we choose to give priority to one value over another? How far does the majority want to go in accommodating to the needs of the minority? The emergence of mainstreaming as an issue raises but does not directly confront these questions. To the extent that we put discussion of mainstreaming in the context of education and schools, we are likely to find ourselves mired in controversies centering on law, procedures, administration, and funding. These are legitimate controversies because they deal with practical, day-to-day matters that affect the lives of everyone. But the level of difficulty we encounter in dealing with these matters ultimately will be determined by the clarity with which the moral issue is formulated. This clarity will not "solve" the practical problems but, at the very least, it will make us more aware of two things: (a) so-called practical matters or problems always reflect moral issues, and (b) differences in moral stance have very practical consequences.

References

Bailey, S. K. *Congress makes a law*. New York: Columbia University Press, 1950.

Blatt, B. *Exodus from pandemonium*. Boston: Allyn & Bacon, 1970.

Blatt, B. *The revolt of the idiots*. Glen Ridge, N. J.: Exceptional Press, 1976.

Blatt, B. *Souls in extremis*. Boston: Allyn & Bacon, 1975.

Blatt, B., & Kaplan, F. *Christmas in purgatory*. Boston: Allyn & Bacon, 1966.

Children's Defense Fund. *Your rights under the Education for All Handicapped Children Act*. Washington, D. C.: Author (1520 New Hampshire Ave., N. W.), 1976.

Kaplan, F., & Sarason, S. B. *The Psycho-Educational Clinic*, 1970. Papers and Research Studies. Available from S. B. Sarason, Institution of Social and Policy Studies, Yale University, 70 Sachem, Street, New Haven, Conn. 06520.

Maeroff, G. I. Schools are forced to pay more attention to disabled. *The New York Times*, May 11, 1977, A20.

Milofsky, D. Schooling for kids no one wants. *The New York Times Magazine*, Jan. 2, 1977, 24-25, 28, 33.

Reynolds, M. C. *Trends in education: Changing roles of special education personnel*. Columbus, Ohio: University Council for Educational Administration. (no date)

Sarason, S. B. Community psychology and the anarchist insight. *American Journal of Community Psychology*, 1976, **4**, 243-261.

Sarason, S. B. *The creation of settings and the future societies*. San Francisco: Jossey-Bass, 1972.

Sarason, S. B. Jewishness, Blackishness, and the nature-nurture controversy. *American Psychologist*, 1973, **28**, 962-971.

Sarason, S. B. *The psychological sense of community*. San Francisco: Jossey-Bass, 1974.

Sarason, S. B., Grossman, F., & Zitnay, G. *The creation of a community setting*. Syracuse: Syracuse University Press, 1972.

Sarason, S. B., Levine, M., Goldenberg, I., Cherlin D., & Bennett, M. *Psychology in community settings*. New York: John Wiley, 1966.

Pirandello in the Classroom: On the Possibility of Equal Educational Opportunity in American Culture[1]

R. P. McDermott[2]

The Rockefeller University

and

Jeffrey Aron[2]

Brooklyn College

For some people, the history of American education is marked by valiant attempts to offer equal opportunity to all children. One has only to consider the introduction successively of compulsory education, standardized testing, racial integration, compensatory education, and, most recently, the placement in regular classrooms of children labeled as physically or mentally handicapped to appreciate the deep commitment to equal education by both the government and most citizens. Although the innovations most often have been phrased in ideological terms, it would be a mistake to dismiss them as merely ineffectual democratic altruisms;

---

[1] Much of the research reported in this paper was supported originally by predoctoral research grants to McDermott from the National Institute of General Medical Studies, National Institute of Mental Health, and the National Science Foundation. McDermott's writing time was financed by grants from the Carnegie Corporation to Michael Cole and the Laboratory of Comparative Human Cognition, The Rockefeller University. Members of the Laboratory also have supplied much needed intellectual input. Ken Gospodinoff helped immeasurably in the film analysis. Kate Anderson, Bruce Balow, Harumi Befu, Jack Bilmes, and Lois Hood supplied helpful comments on portions of a previous draft and, in his generous summary of the paper, Nicholas Hobbs helps to circumscribe the topic by pointing to some issues not handled in our discussion. Most important, the paper would not have been written without the help of George D. Spindler, who asked the question to which the paper, we hope, is a partial answer; he also supplied the encouragement and the forum for our efforts. To all of them, we extend our appreciation.

[2] Both authors are anthropologists; they work with psychologists, linguists, and behavior analysts in interdisciplinary research on children and social relations. Both authors have taught grade school in New York City.

rather, they can be understood as reasonable adaptations by people who primarily want the most for themselves in a modern technological society. It has been argued that this type of society is marked by the overall rational effort to get the best people to do the most important jobs and, accordingly, by educational efforts that begin with equal opportunities for all. In this vein, we can look sympathetically upon American education as "the embodiment of the fundamental value of equality of opportunity, in that it places value both on initial equality and on differential achievement" (Parsons, 1959). Historically, it is exactly this initial equality that reform efforts have been directed toward. Questions remain, however, on whether they have succeeded and whether it is possible that they can succeed.

Although the equalizing efforts of educational reform in America may appear to be, at first glance, both reasonable and for the good of all, each has been attacked severely. Each has been seen as the effort of people who have access to political and economic resources to limit that access to themselves. Compulsory education, for example, does not necessarily bring equal education to all. Making sure that all children go to school, and then failing some and passing others, can be interpreted as a means to justify and give credence and credibility to the socially fabricated fact that some people are more deserving of the rewards of our society than others (Tyack, 1976). In this interpretation, it is not an accident but, rather, a reflection of class power that our schools reproduce generations of upper classes that do better than the lower classes, and generations of whites who do better than blacks, and so on (Berg, 1969).

Take a second example. The testing services originated in traditional democratic motives. However, it has become horribly apparent that the excesssive assumption of "standardized" conditions in testing, given the reality that such an assumption is seldom warranted, works against efforts to bring equal education to any child different from the test maker's (and test giver's) limited social milieu (Orasanu, McDermott, Boykin, & The Laboratory of Comparative Human Cognition, 1977). People with resources have ways of keeping them. This truism operates even for democracies (e.g., America and Japan) that have insisted on universal testing for a rational egalitarian sorting of the population into occupational slots. In Japan, for example, where a much less diversified population than in America feeds into the schools, the affluent have erected a defense against a universal testing system. They have taken their children out of the public schools and sent them to the more exacting private schools that more efficiently prepare the children for the competitive testing controlling entrance to prestigious high schools and universities (Rohlen, 1977).

More recent reform efforts also have been attacked. Racial integration in American schools has been claimed to be a racist solution to a racist problem. The failure of compensatory education has led to speculation by majority educators about the genetic inferiority of some minorities, and also to charges of paternalism and cultural imperialism from the minorities the programs theoretically were designed to help (Levin, 1977). Whatever the arguments, equalization of opportunity is not an obvious trend in our schools. In fact, the lack of success by minorities in schools has helped to give rise to strong ethnic movements in the last two decades. Observation of these developments caused Parsons (1975) to add the "redifferentiation" of ethnic groups as a counterpoint to his earlier description of the equalizing and rationalizing trends of modern industrial societies. Apparently, there are reasons to be cynical about the possibility of initial equality in American education.

A New Reform in an Old Context

It is not clear which interpretation of our educational history, visionary or cynical, ought to carry more weight, and it is difficult to use the past as a guide to the future. Public Law 94-142 now mandates the inclusion in regular classrooms, insofar as possible, of all the children who have been classified previously as in need of special educational facilities. Many children who were originally removed from regular classes in order to receive the extra help they needed to keep up with their peers apparently have been stigmatized in the special programs; and the new law has been passed in the name of the children's right to an equal and nonstigmatized educational opportunity. When placed against the background of past efforts, the optimism of the supporters of the new law must pale before the cynical interpretations of reform efforts. Yet the recurrence of reform efforts to bring the vision of equality into practice is by itself an impressive dimension of American life (J. McDermott, 1976). To achieve its potential, we must learn to better equip our optimism with the fighting tools of dedicated social change agents.

The integration of special education children into regular classrooms is within the educational reform tradition. Teachers may help children to learn some particulars in school, but children get their fundamental education from the total community in which they are immersed. The value of classroom integration is that it will bring all the children into full view of each other. This is crucial for us all if we are to maintain some sense of community — of shared problems (Arensberg & Kimball, 1965) — in our everyday lives. Further, it may also cut down on the excesses of mislabeling, overlabeling, and stigmatizing children (Hobbs, 1976). Finally, the new law may offer us a potential victory (although temporary, and contradictory to its spirit) by making the pupils who are presently failing in our classrooms look more like average kids in comparison with those who are now excluded.

Unless, however, observance of the law is accompanied by massive institutional changes that can alter the allocation of interactional resources for teachers to maximize the development of their pupils, there is little reason to think that the integration of handicapped children will help us to make educational opportunity more equally available (Weatherly & Lipsky, 1977). At the present time, we know of only one serious proposal for such institutional changes (Church, 1976). Without such an effort, it is difficult to imagine how the new reform will have a different fate from the preceding inspiring, but unsuccessful, equalizing movements.

We present here some reasons for this conclusion. Our position is neither negative nor fatalistic, although we offer no hopeful predictions as long as the school system retains its present structure. To support our position, we offer a characterization of how schools work, not just to back a claim that reform most likely will not change the stratifying practices of our schools but, rather, to suggest how a move like integrating the handicapped might help considerably if it were accompanied by other forms of change.

Basically, we suggest that American schools are designed to produce and stratify differences in the intellectual achievements of different children. Culture can be taken as a set of interrelated propositions about the world, propositions which the members of the culture consistently use with (and on) each other in the demonstration (and enforcement) of the common sensibility of their own behavior (D'Andrade, 1976; Murphy, 1976). In America, at the core of the propositions that make up our cultural resources for dealing with one another are evaluations of the worth and potential of persons on the basis of their supposed natural, inherited, and unalterable intellectual abilities (Henry, 1963; Spindler, 1959). Almost all cultures have ways of distinguishing people by the speed and level of mastery with which they pick up different skills (Edgerton, 1970; Nerlove, Roberts, Klein, Yarbrough, & Habicht, 1975).

American culture, however, and perhaps most other Western cultures, are marked by an excesssive attention to (a) the location of minor differences in a person's behavior as representative of differences in natural ability, and, more specifically, (b) the measurement of these proposed natural abilities on the basis of the persons's performance on a limited set of intellectual tasks in school tests. We do not have to follow these practices. In our attempts to sort children efficiently into the occupational roles of our market place, we may be doing more harm than good.

In other cultures, people do not necessarily interpret each other's behavior in terms of inherent characteristics; among the Zapotec of Mexico, for example, it has been claimed that the people understand and act upon each other's behavior as if it consisted of sensible adaptations to the limited social circumstances that each must deal with at any given time (Selby, 1974, 1975). And even in cultures in which a child's personality and cognitive make-up are made explicit and taken to be the source of consistency in the child's behavior across time, there is generally much less concern with measuring personality and cognitive make-up on the basis of situation-specific tasks, such as school tests.

In American culture, however, our preoccupation with locating the natural intellectual skills of our children is so great that we accept the flimsiest of evidence during the first days of school. Once we have categorized the children as more or less able, we then, by way of self-fulfilling prophecies, arrange to have the children designated as less able actually accomplish less than the others. Every school must have its failures, whatever the long-range potentials of the children who are to be sorted out. Our communities and our economy demand such variation. If our schools were completely fair, we suspect that there still would be differential achievement because of the children's different experiences in the social world, both within and beyond the classroom. Ideally, such differential achievement is recognized across subject matter rather than across children. However, because our schools are presently organized with a heavy emphasis on sorting the able from the less able, the question we all face is whether the present perceived distribution of differential achievement by children in school is necessary or fair. Do all children get an equal chance at achieving their potential from the start of the school experience? We suspect not. We have organized our schools to sort children into achievers and nonachievers, and that is what we get. If we organized our schools for the maximally rich development of all our children, we could get something quite different.

What are the criteria our schools use to sort children initially? At best, the children are sorted by their differential preparation for school. For whatever reasons, some children enter school with more developed skills, both intellectual and social interactional, than other children. This differential should have little to do with what they eventually learn. But if they enter a class in which they are handled unequally, if they are given less adequate learning environments on the basis of their less developed entering-school skills, the chances of their catching up or even fitting in will be minimal. We present some details on such a case. We do not discuss schools at their worst, in which children are sorted on the basis of even more arbitrary markers of natural abilities, such as skin color, ethnicity, or ways of speaking or dressing; this kind of evil is visible, and we all can do battle with it. We are more interested in how the vast majority of us, as people of good will, still can create the circumstances for inequality in our schools.

This paper is organized as follows: (a) We elaborate on our position on how inequality is induced in the early school years. (b) We try to elaborate on how the self-fulfilling prophecies at work in our classrooms actually do the job of preserving inequality. We indicate, for one classroom at least, the nature of these prophecies and the environments in which they are embedded, and we suggest a play by Luigi Pirandello as a metaphor for how self-fulfilling prophecies work in this classroom. The contrast, of course, is Rosenthal and Jacobson's (1968) use of Shaw's "Pygmalion" as a metaphor for how schools induce differential achievement unfairly. Also, in this section, we offer some data to support our stand. (c) By way of conclusion, we claim that by itself the integration of handicapped children into regular classrooms will do little to alter the stratifying tendencies of our schools, and we point to some additional organizational changes that could help to make a difference.

How Schools Induce Inequality in Educational Opportunity

Increasing evidence is accumulating that, given an appropriate learning environment and enough time, almost everyone can do well on basic school tasks. It is unlikely that school tasks are generally harder than mnay tasks people normally work on in everyday life. No doubt, school tasks are unique in demanding certain kinds of mental activities in particular combinations; the combinations take much practice, and they are cumulative. It is not easy to pick up a skill in an advanced subject matter without a mastery of various prerequisite skills. In this way, school skills are similar to most other skills developed in daily life.

It is questionable whether proficiency on school tasks is superior to and more generalizable than proficiency on other complex tasks, long an assumption in various literatures dealing with the relation of schooling and the development of various competencies. In fact, some recent empirical work on the effects of schooling in different cultures has led to the conclusion that early school learning is good for later school learning and certain kinds of bureaucratic jobs that demand similar skills, but it is not uniformly generalizable to other tasks demanding elaborate intellectual operations (Cole, Sharp, & Lave, 1976; Lave, 1977). This work has been complemented by the documentation of the conceptual complexities underlying the behavior of various unschooled peoples who are faced with environmental challenges, such as the navigation of boats across thousands of miles of open sea without the aid of mechanical instruments (Lewis, 1972, in press). School learning is essential to more school learning, but it is not special in the sense of a superior and more generalizable form of learning.

How, then, is it that so many of our children do not make it in school? Alternatively phrased, why do we so persistently perceive and document such differential performances on school tasks by children who, in everyday life, are judged to be intellectually quite normal? The answer to this question lies in the fact that learning in school is primarily an organizational phenomenon. Success in learning is best understood in terms of the time a child spends on a task; some may learn faster than others but, with time, almost any child can learn what has to be learned in school, if the proper organizational constraints for getting the child on task are present (Bloom, 1974). The question of why some children achieve more than others should be approached as a question about the environments in which some children are consistently organized to attend to school tasks in classrooms while others are not.

Classroom environments often are the contexts for a negative self-fulfilling prophecy. Certain children, who, for whatever reasons, come to school behind their peers in the development of classroom skills, frequently constitute both pedagogical and interactional problems for most teachers. Teachers say that these children are harder to teach; part of this reaction stems from the fact that *they need more of the teacher's time if they are to catch up to their peers*. In addition, *they must learn under the pressure of knowing that they are behind*. This pressure results from a classroom situation that allocates status on the basis, in part, of the children's intellectual ranking in the classroom (at least until puberty, at which time the peer groups in many classes appear to get their revenge by awarding status on the basis of how bad children are, that is to say, on how good the children are at achieving school failure [McDermott, R. P., 1974]). For these reasons, and for some others that are elaborated later in terms of a specific case, the children in the bottom echelons of the classroom hierarchy are organizationally more difficult to get on task. These are the children who generally need to spend extra time on task. If they were already in possession of reading skills adequate for achievement independent of the teacher, then the various pressures of classroom organization would not fall so hard on them. However, if they are starting school without reading skills, the teacher is their primary resource. Without the teacher, they can make progress only by solitary effort.

Thus, for every day in the classroom, the children who are less skilled and often considered less able fall further behind their contemporaries and, consequently, provide the teacher with additional reasons to handle them differently. The small differences among children in the early years of school expand quickly to the drastic forms of differential performance that become obvious in later years. At the root of these differences is not so much the extreme complexity of the school tasks, nor the differences in the learning potentials of the different children, but the differential environments we offer the children for getting organized and on task so that learning can take place.

Notice that in evoking a self-fulfilling prophecy as a mechanism for the widely differential performances of children on school tasks, we did not invoke the teacher's attitude. We do not believe that teachers constrain their pupils' performances simply as a result of negative attitudes. We suggest that self-fulfilling prophecies consist of something more durable and far more hidden. The problem, generally, is not with teachers but with school systems that insist that children be measured against each other and differentially rewarded and degraded for both what it is that they know and how fast they came to learn it. To understand this problem more fully, we need to know more about self-fulfilling prophecies and how teachers and children are entrapped by the prophecies presently in use in our schools.

Self-Fulfilling Prophecies at Work in Classrooms

In their controversial little book, Rosenthal and Jacobson (1968) used G. B. Shaw's play, "Pygmalion," as a metaphor for some important points about the acquisition of social structure in schools. The play is about, among other things, how members of the upper social classes consistently elicit what they believe to be inadequate behavior from members of the lower classes by expecting less of them in various situations. Rosenthal and Jacobson (1968) argued that much the same thing occurs in schools. In other words, teachers consistently elicit inadequate behavior from some children by expecting less of them. Whether the much maligned research was adequate to prove the case is not an issue here; but three interesting points follow from the writers' argument. We have reason to agree and disagree with each.

1. Success or failure in school is a matter of a self-fulfilling prophecy. Teachers evaluate the learning potential of children in their classes and then offer the differential learning environments in which the children can live out the teachers' evaluations by behaving as expected.

2. Underlying many of the teacher's self-fulfilling prophecies that lead to school failure are negative attitudes or expectations for certain kinds of children (children with brown eyes instead of blue, to make the case ridiculous but possible; children with black skin instead of white, to make the case more realistic). In a later work, Rosenthal (1976) elaborated on how such attitudes are fostered in different environments. Teachers do more for the students they consider more likely to learn: They "create a warmer socio-emotional climate for their 'special' students," give them "more differentiated feedback," teach them "more difficult material," and give them "greater opportunities for responding" (p. 466). In order to discern how some children and not others are picked out as special and how particular kinds of teachers so discern particular kinds of children, Rosenthal, Archer, DiMatteo, Koivumaki, and Rogers (1976) developed an elaborate test to measure the sensitivity of children

and teachers to the nonverbal dimensions of interpersonal communication. But even with this empirical focus there is an assumption by Rosenthal (as there has been throughout a decade of stimulating work) that attitudes and expectations are at the root of the self-fulfilling prophecy. Negative expectations are the cause of children's falling behind in school because teachers offer differential instruction and differential positive feedback for equivalent work according to their expectations for children. And it is in terms of such differential instruction and feedback that the children not only fall behind but, eventually, stop trying.

3. Arising from the Pygmalion experiment, at least by inference, is the point that social change follows from changes in people's attitudes or expectations. For experimental purposes, it may be possible to manipulate such attitudes or expectations in the manner of Rosenthal and Jacobson; they changed the records of failing children to make them look brighter. For longer term results, it may be possible to change the education of our teachers to open them, perhaps through training in nonverbal sensitivity, to the amazing potential of all children.

AN ALTERNATIVE TO ATTITUDES AS SELF-FULFILLING PROPHECIES

We are in sympathy with the work of Rosenthal and Jacobson. However, we would like to propose a significantly different approach to the issues raised by the Pygmalion experiment. Our first argument, which was suggested both before and after the Pygmalion effort by many analysts (Cicourel & Kitsuse, 1963; King, 1967; McDermott, R. P., 1976; Rist, 1973; Spindler, 1959) is that success or failure in American classrooms represents the self-fulfilling prophecy of a system rather than of the attitude of a particular teacher. This argument does not make school unique.

Socialization for any institution is necessarily the product of a self-fulfilling prophecy (Church, 1973; McDermott, R. P., & Church, 1976; Spindler, 1973; Wieder, 1974). How could it be otherwise? The established members of any group constitute the environment with which a newcomer must make sense. They constitute the environments or contexts or systems of relevancy for the choices which newcomers are forced to make. And it is the responses of the established members that inform newcomers about the adequacy of their choices.

Schools necessarily work by self-fulfilling prophecies. The question is whether we can construct more useful and more egalitarian self-fulfilling prophecies to socialize our children. At the present time, there is no doubt that different children are handled differentially, and they achieve different levels of learning in the schools accordingly. For this reason, we are all concerned about the consequences of integrating children who are negatively labeled as "special" into regular classrooms.

The self-fulfilling prophecies currently in use in our classrooms are particularly rough on children who are different from their teachers' expectations. Children from special education programs who are integrated in regular classrooms are likely to be caught in this system and to be sorted into unsuccessful and even ineducable categories, and treated accordingly. Although Rosenthal and Jacobson may concur with this observation, our alternative description of and solution to the problem differs from theirs.

Thus, our second argument is that the mechanisms for self-fulfilling prophecies in classrooms are only incidentally people's attitudes or expectations. If only things were that simple! Sometimes, in order to understand how some children will do in a class, all we need to know are the teacher's attitudes, as, for example, in the case of minority children in the classroom of an avowed racist. But our problem is that teachers with positive attitudes toward and great sensitivity to the different kinds of children in their classrooms also can create inadequate learning environments for some of them.

More powerful factors than teachers' attitudes appear to be at work. Although these factors often are revealed in people's attitudes (e.g., the many positive correlations cited by Rosenthal, 1976, in his review of the expectancy research), they can remain hidden below the level of attitudes and exist in the organization of classroom learning. It is the structure and demands of the system as a whole that create and maintain learning problems. As part of our daily practice, we create children who are pedagogical and organizational problems. Once created, we respond to them differentially on the basis of how much of a problem they are. This issue is greater than that of individual students and individual teachers. It is true that a child at the bottom rung in one class may find a special relationship with a particular teacher to be just the right formula for progress (see the case history in Sarason's paper). However, the time given to one student means less time for others. In addition, it is no accident, but rather a built-in feature of classroom organization, that certain children get less time year after year. Thus, most classrooms are organized for both success and failure; most teachers expect and are required to find and certify some children to be better students than others.

Our third argument is that the source of social change is in the resources we offer teachers for organizing sustained learning environments. We do not have to change people's attitudes in order to change our educational system. Our job is, in fact, much more difficult than that. What we have to do is to change the everyday pressures on our teachers to produce, as if from a cookie cutter, children of uniform skill levels by certain dates. Certainly we can write laws that mandate teachers to treat everyone fairly. And we can train teachers to see the strengths of different kinds of children. But until we free teachers from the relentless pressures of sorting children into those who can make it from those who cannot, most children will have little chance to actually reach their potentials. We must de-emphasize the consequences of not achieving in the prescribed manner. The learning process, which may be very difficult to measure and sort, must be affirmed even, if necessary, at the expense of an easily sortable product.

It will not be easy to reverse this sorting tendency. Our communities demand the sorting of children. Our educational language pits child against child, smarter against dumber, achievement-motivated against nonachievement-motivated, advantaged against disadvantaged, and so on. Our testing services give a pseudoscientific credence to the sorting practices. And the market place that eventually employs the children continues to assume, against considerable evidence, that schooling is the best measure of the value of most personnel. All these conditions generate the self-fulfilling sorting practices of teachers. We can turn now to a description of the environments that embody these dictates to sort.

SIX CHILDREN IN SEARCH OF A LEARNING ENVIRONMENT

Rather than Shaw's "Pygmalion," we consider Pirandello's (1952) "Six Characters in Search of an Author" (written in 1922) as an ideal dramatic metaphor for how inequality is arranged in our elementary schools. The play is about six characters who have been written into a script that remains incomplete. The unfinished and emotionally wounded characters walk out of the script, take human form, and show up at a theater looking for an author to complete their story. The story is ugly; it involves various kinds of marital intrigue and incest, and most of the characters have been deeply hurt by most of the other characters. All of them would like to have the play rewritten with a decent ending. They want to have their story told in the way they feel it should be told. At the theater, they meet a director and some actors, and they tell the unbelieving crowd what they want. As they bare their lives with each other in front of the actors and the director, they relive their story; that is, they recreate the environments that occasioned their original struggles. With every step, they relive the hate, the embarrassments, the identity struggles, and their battles with each other. At the end of the play, there is the realization that their lives, as they have created them, have made this conclusion inevitable. The only course of action for the characters is to leave this stage in search of another author to rewrite their story. It is not a nice play; it is dramatic and amusing in the same way that theater-of-the-absurd dramas often are. To us, it speaks very much to the point of what is happening in our schools. We hope to demonstrate this parallel in the rest of this paper.

For the past two years, we have been studying two films of children in a first-grade classroom: one classroom, one day, one hour; one top group of readers, one bottom group of readers, around the same table. One film is of the bottom group, the other of the top group. As we watched the films, it became clear to us that the groups were much like the characters in the Pirandello play. They come to a classroom every day in search of an adequate ending to their story. They come to school to learn as their mothers and fathers have told them to do. In particular, they come to school to learn to read. They put tremendous attention and work into getting each other organized in order to get down to the page, in order to get some reading done. Yet, only the top group manages to stay down on the page. The children in the bottom group keep struggling to write an appropriate ending to their story. Somehow, they never quite make it. Somehow, it takes them longer to get down to the page and, after they are there, they do not last very long.

Much like the characters in search of their author, the six children in the bottom group keep creating the environments for each other that keep them from their desired ending. Because they come to school reading less well than the children in the top group, they need more time on task. But it is the children in the bottom group who get much less time on task, one-third as much time, in fact, as the children in the top group. If we could understand how this situation is arranged, we would know what we are up against in calling for equal opportunity in the schools.

Before offering some of the details of this real-life drama, we must consider some methodological asides and reservations. Although we may seem often to be considering a reasonable sample of all schools in the country, our discussion is limited to the one classroom in which McDermott spent hundreds of hours during the 1973-1974 school year. Even more specifically, we concentrate on the films of the two reading groups. What is lost in range, we hope to compensate for in the detail of the analysis.

The problems with which our classroom teacher must deal in these two reading groups — children with diverse backgrounds and diverse beginning reading skills — probably can be found in every classroom. The teacher opts for certain solutions to these problems, and the solutions seem to function to enhance the differences in the children's reading skills. Other teachers may choose different solutions but, given the constraints of most American classrooms, no one solution is uniformly better than another. Thus, this one classroom can be regarded as representative, not because every classroom is not different but, because of the problems which must be solved, classrooms across the land are similar enough to allow a detailed analysis of one excellent teacher's problems and solutions to speak to all of us for the time being. Few classrooms are free of the problems generated by children of diverse backgrounds and learning paces in school systems that expect and demand uniform progress.

We have mentioned only one way in which our study might be read as incomplete. Not only have we limited ourselves to one classroom, we have considered only the kinds of constraints which the teachers and the children put on each other while at their reading table. Obviously, a great deal is being left out. The culture that brings all these persons to this particular classroom with their particular sets of skills, desires, hangups, and the like is a more pervasive influence than what we can see at the reading table. This omission is a problem to the extent that various parts of our argument hinge on the reader's assuming along with us that certain dimensions of this culture are rampantly present and observable in most schools. For example, we offer no proof of the pressure on teachers to sort children for administrative reasons into the more and less capable. We do not want to rely too heavily on such an assumption. We are trying to avoid such statements as "American society forces teachers to sort children out" until we have some adequate description of such a development in the kind of detail offered (in part) in our account of the reading group. We have been looking for American culture and society for a long time, but we have found only people. People are hard to describe, but worthy of our efforts, even if they do not offer us the key to a complete description of American culture and society. For us to detail the pressures on our teacher from her school system and community and the influence of these pressures on the performance of the reading groups would involve us in another extensive research effort. For the time being, we are content to offer a social science of American education one step at a time, and we ask the reader to rely on accounts of the pressures on other teachers in other schools across the land, now well documented by Lortie (1975) and Wolcott (1973, 1977).

We have referred to the teacher as excellent. The only evidence for this claim is that her peers consider her excellent and, as a result of many days in the classroom, our agreement with them. Experienced classroom observers no doubt could find fault with her performance and could offer some helpful suggestions. By referring to the teacher's excellence and, at the same time, suggesting that her performance is inadequate, we do not mean to imply that nothing more can be done for these children or this teacher. Rather, we are simply trying to stop readers from refusing to consider the details of the case because they assume that the teacher is no good. Better teachers may exist in every school, but we cannot expect them as a matter of course. The problems of this classroom run deeper than those a single teacher can deal with in a year, and it is not until we join in the solution of these problems that the positive efforts of teachers, no matter how considerable, will have their full effect. It is important to make these points because, difficult as it may be to teach a first grade that includes children who do not know how to read, it may be even more difficult to learn to read in such a classroom. We are blaming no one; we simply are trying to describe the problems that are forced upon children and teachers and result in their performing so badly in school.

There are considerable differences in the behavior of our top and bottom groups because different environments are provided for the children in the two groups in which to work at learning to read. The top and bottom groups are faced with different problems to solve during their time at the reading table.

Since the teacher is the only person participating in both groups, her perspective on the tasks facing the groups is an important source of contrast. By her own account, the children in the top group represent less of a management problem. They appear to have already mastered the basics of reading. When they are sitting at the reading table, the teacher establishes a sequence in which they read and she lets the length of the reading assignments dictate the pacing of the sequencing. After the first child is called on, the teacher counts the pages of the story and the number of children at the table, and the normative order is thereby made available for all to see. In Figure 1, it is clear that the children act out that order rather perfectly: first one child reads a page, then the next child, and then the next. The accomplishment of this order requires constant monitoring and interactional work by everyone in the top group. However, for present purposes, it is possible to claim that the order achieved leaves most members of the top group considerable freedom. After the teacher calls on one of the children, they all move down into the book. After the reading turn is in progress, different children look around the room or whisper to each other until the turn ends. At the end, the members must attend most carefully to the group as the teacher assigns a new turn to a new child. In terms of reading, the children must attend carefully only to the sections they read, and the teacher must attend carefully only to the occasional problems the children run into in reading their pages. The children's problems in reading their pages constitute the topics of the reading lesson. Occasionally, the children create problems by word calling instead of reading for meaning, and the teacher's main pedagogical task is to convince the children that there is living language on the page. Thus, one child reads monotonously, "But Ricky said his mother . . .," and the teacher corrects her: "Let's read it this way, 'But Ricky, said his mother.' "

With the bottom group, the teacher has rather different problems. Accordingly, the teacher and the children constitute rather different environments for each other in the different groups. The children in the bottom group do not read as well as the children in the top group, and the teacher attends less to the language on the book's pages and more to the phonics skills needed to interpret any given word in the text. Thus, there are many more stopping places in the children's reading, and the story line, which could help to hold the lesson together, is seldom alluded to and never developed.

In addition, the teacher does not order the sequence of reading turns in the same way that she does in the top group. In the bottom group, each turn to read is negotiated on the basis of who calls for a turn, who is able in the teacher's eyes to read the page in question, and who has already had a turn to read. In Figure 2, it is clear that the different procedures have their effects on the order of who gets a turn.

There may be various reasons for the teacher's proceeding in this manner with the bottom group but only one is made apparent in the film record. Some children in the bottom group do not read too well and they can only read a page after it has been read by someone else. By putting each turn up for grabs, the teacher picks the child who can do the best job. This strategy of not calling on the children in the bottom group in a fixed order is used by many

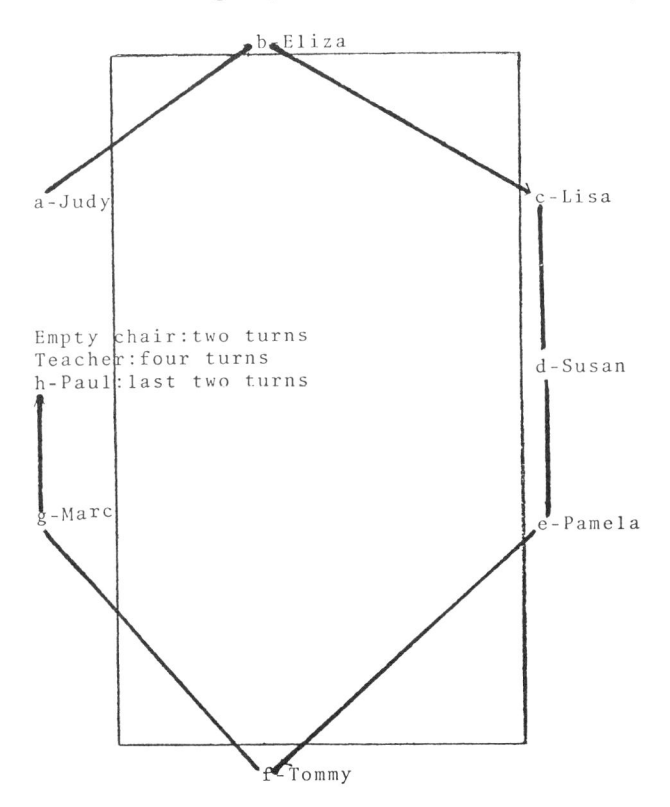

Sequence: a,b,c,d,e,f,g,h.   All read once.

Fig. 1. Taking turns to read in the top reading group.

teachers as a device for keeping the potentially disorderly children constantly attentive (Cazden, in press). In fact, this attentional device is built into the design of reading programs for the problem reader (Bartlett, in press).

This procedure has the consequence of giving no one, neither teacher nor children, any time out from monitoring each other for some idea of what to do next. Thus, it has the dual function of focusing everyone's attention on a particular activity, in this case reading, and keeping the social order of the group dependent upon the uninterrupted functioning of the focused activity. And often it is successful. But with each turn to read hanging on the teacher's attention to the details of each child's call for a turn, every interruption by the teacher leaves the group without a procedure for moving into the reading task.

Now consider the important information that the bottom group is interrupted for procedural, not pedagogical, reasons almost 40 times in its 30 minutes at the reading table, as compared with only 2 interruptions for the top group in its 23 minutes at the table. What is the source of these interruptions? Shockingly, almost two-thirds

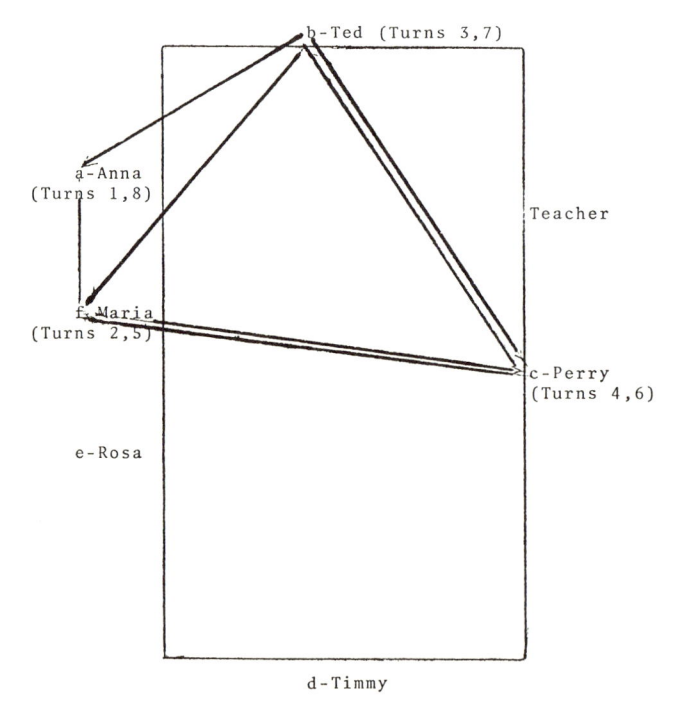

Sequence: a,f,b,c,f,all,c,b,a. Jimmy (d) and Rosa (e) do not read in this lesson. Both are called on once and both turn turn it down. All others read twice.

Fig. 2. Taking turns to read in the bottom reading group.

of the interruptions come from the members of the top group who go to the reading table while the bottom group is there, and from the teacher who deals with members of the top group as they busy themselves, or try to look as if they are busying themselves, with the individualized seat work the teacher has organized. (For some suggestions of how this pattern develops, see McDermott & Gospidinoff, in press.)

With all the procedural interruptions, the children in the bottom group get little chance to read. Not only do they spend time calling on the teacher for a turn, they also spend time waiting for the teacher while she attends to some members of the top group who have interrupted the time on task of the bottom group. Almost two-thirds of the time in the reading lesson is spent in either getting a turn or waiting for the teacher to attend to the group.

Perhaps the most disturbing interruptions of the bottom group come from the teacher herself. On one occasion, for example, she organizes the children to call for a turn to read their new books, "Raise your hands if you can read page 4." The children straighten themselves up in their chairs, form neat lines along the sides of the reading table, and either raise their hands for a turn or at least look at their books or the teacher. As their hands reach their highest point, the teacher looks away from the reading group to the back of the room. She yells at first one and then another child in the top group. The three children in the bottom group who had raised their hands, lower them to the table. One little boy who had not raised his hand pushes his chair away from the reading table and the teacher and balances on its two back legs. The other two children in the group simply look down at their books. The teacher returns and says, "Nobody can read page 4? Why not?" Eventually, the children recover, and someone gets a turn. But it all takes time. And worse, it cuts off the possibility that the teacher and the children will achieve trusting relations, that is, it cuts off the possibility that the teacher and the children will come to understand their working consensus about who they are and that what they are doing with each other is in their best interests. Such trusting relations appear to be an essential component of learning in groups (McDermott, R. P., 1977).

The children in both groups started the year using the ITA (Initial Teaching Alphabet) system of reading. The children in the top group moved off the ITA onto the regular alphabet around January. The movie under analysis was taken in May. The children in the bottom group still had not made the move from the ITA, which is a disaster, considering that the second grade is not equipped with ITA material.

This account of the self-fulfilling prophecy at work is ugly. The children in the bottom group (a) enter the first grade behind in the development of their reading skills; (b) they get about one-third the amount of time on task in their reading lesson; and (c) they get little instruction that will be useful to them in the second grade. Everyday in the classroom the children of the bottom group fall increasingly behind the children in the top group.

Although we suspect that there is no reason to talk of any of the children in the bottom group as organically or socially impaired, by the end of their second year in school, three of them were assigned to special education classes (labeled, respectively, as brain damaged, emotionally disturbed, and slow). What is special about these children is that they were trapped early in school in a maladaptive learning environment. There is reason to think that placement in a special, but stigmatized program will not help the children to catch up to their peers (Hobbs, 1976). On the other hand, to return them to the classrooms in which they experienced their original school failure may prove to be a cruel hoax, unless we understand and transform the dynamics of failure in our regular classrooms.

Culture Against Kids

What is driving this whole system? How is it that both the children and teacher in the bottom group have such a difficult time staying on the reading task? Together, they face both pedagogical and interactional problems not faced by the top group. Pedagogically, there is no doubt that it is easier for the teacher to practice reading with the children in the top group than to struggle with the process of teaching decoding to the children in the bottom group. Interactionally, there is the pressure of competition between the groups and the scarred identities of the children in the bottom group. Not only do the children in the bottom group come to school not knowing how to read, but they have a teacher who expects them to know how to read and who cannot teach them to read while she has 20 other children walking around the room. And it is in this difficult situation that they must overcome the pressure of having the other children taunt them for their performances. Even within the bottom group we hear claims of one child against another. ("Oh, you can't read." "Better than you!") Or we can point to a child in the bottom group who constantly calls for turns to read but, at the same time, appears to arrange her requests in ways that make it difficult for the teacher to call on her. Such anxiety is not visible in the behavior of the children of the top group.

In response to all these problems, the members of the bottom group make various adaptations. The one adaptation discussed here is that the teacher makes sure that no child is asked to read something too difficult. So the teacher uses the two different turn-taking systems with the two groups, and this adaptation has the consequences, already described, of keeping the bottom group off-task for more than half their time at the reading table. Part of the self-fulfilling prophecy drive in the classroom is the teacher's honest attempt to adapt to the needs of the children in the face of the competitive and sorting tendencies of that classroom and the school in which it is immersed.

The details of this story are specific to this classroom. But the story should be familiar to us all, and the outcome in most other classrooms apparently seldom varies enough to make a difference. The six children of the bottom group can continue their search for a more successful ending, but it is going to take a considerable reorganization of the problems with which they have to deal in order for them to achieve it. For it is difficult to stay on task, that is, to learn to read, when the major efforts of the children are directed to protecting their identities from being sorted into the less-able pile.

In this brief excerpt from a far longer and more complex analysis of the behavior of children and teacher in two reading groups (McDermott, R. P., 1976), we have been trying to make three points.

1. Schools initiate inequality in the performance of different children on school tasks by self-fulfilling prophecy.

2. Given the incessant pressures on any teacher to sort the children once and for all by natural ability on the basis of performance on certain school tasks, the self-fulfilling stratifying practices at work in our schools arise out of realistic evaluations of the problems different children present to the classroom teacher.

3. In the face of the social organizational and cultural roots of the self-fulfilling prophecies that lead to school failure, the possibility of using the schools as a vehicle for social change seems slim.

To establish initial equality in the schools, we will have to pay greater attention to controlling the stratifying practices that operate throughout our communities. Nonetheless, we can try to initiate changes in the classroomm and in the organization of education in the hope that they will be a starting point. There may be opposition to both the methods and the values of the transformations we are suggesting. If there is a risk of confrontation or even a risk of failure, it is no less dangerous at this point than the conditions which we are now generating.

Conclusion

We have been making the case that our schools foster inequality. How might we change the schools to allow all children at least an initially equal chance to achieve competence in math and reading? We are not sure of the answer to this question so we applaud any attempt to make a difference. We applaud the movement of children out of special education programs into regular classrooms, for it is proper in spirit and direction. Our only warning is that we should not expect to make a difference by fiat. Changes proclaimed from on high may alter the particulars of the problems with which teachers are asked to deal. However, until we make it possible for teachers to have the time and interactional resources for handling each child according to need, changes in school may serve only to make the teacher's job more difficult (Weatherly & Lipsky, 1977). Until we know how to make schools more egalitarian, we cannot ask the teachers to do the job for us by themselves.

Adults in every culture constrain the behavior of their children differentially throughout the life cycle. The scheduling of these constraints and the behaviors constrained differ from one culture to the next (Spindler, 1959, 1974). In American culture, adults heavily constrain the behavior of children around the age of 6 by sending them to school and insisting that they learn to read. Although there is considerable evidence that this is not the only or even the best time for the children to learn to read (Downing, 1973; Rohwer, 1971), we have generally allowed little room for variation in the children's behavior, and we inflexibly measure every child against every other child, both within the classroom and across the land. It is not easy to discern the virtues of this system, and we ought to take seriously alternatives that do not pit children against their peers.

How can we remove the pressures on our teachers to misappropriate the potential learning time of the children considered behind? How can we remove the pressures on the children so that being behind becomes a learning problem to be solved in due time by concentrated effort instead of an identify problem to be hidden from onlookers? We may have to consider making our educational system less competitive, particularly at the lower age levels. Competition can be healthy in some learning situations, but not when it leads to the degradation of the losers. Recent research has made it clear that competition is a useful strategy for organizing the practice of already acquired skills, but it is less useful than cooperation in the organization of activities in which children must develop new skills (Johnson & Johnson, 1975). Accordingly, the heavy reliance on competition in our classrooms may contribute to the problems of children who are behind in the development of particular skills when they enter school. The goal we must work for, and a goal which an emphasis on cooperation over competition may help to achieve, is the organization of classrooms to allow children who are behind the time and freedom from degradation to catch up with their peers.

The cross-cultural record offers us some astounding learning achievements in noncompetitive settings, as in music (McPhee, 1955), technology (Lewis, 1972), and even reading (Conklin, 1949). On the American scene, we have some accounts of minority children who fail in public schools but who achieve competence in traditional school subjects when they are transferred to schools run on a noncompetitive basis by members of their own ethnic groups (Collier, 1973; Hostetler & Huntington, 1971). There is reason to believe that noncompetitive classrooms also could work to the advantage of Native American children (Erickson & Mohatt, 1977; Philips, 1972).

Competition appears to be at the core of our cultural predilections and it will not be easy to reduce its role in our classrooms. This is no reason for not attempting battle with the beast. Consider the Japanese, who run a fiercely competitive society, but who make an effort to control competition in the normal classroom. On the level of everyday life in Japanese institutions, members work hard to overcome competition and to create the conditions for harmony and cooperation (Befu, 1971; Rohlen, 1973). In the long run, there are some institutional rewards for the people who cooperate (Befu, 1974). In the classroom, children are encouraged to work together in the name of their school and community. Rivalry among peers is concentrated on, if not successfully limited to, national tests in which everyone competes with everyone else, a strategy that has made the Japanese "examination hell" world famous (Vogel, 1972). As pointed out, this system has its pathologies, including social class inequities (Rohlen, 1977), but high rates of early school failure and functional illiteracy are not among them (Sakamoto & Makita, 1973). We do not want to follow the Japanese model in its details, but we can use it to guide our own efforts to appreciate the difficulties and rewards of creating conditions in which cooperation becomes a more dominant mode than competition for relating in the classroom.

Learning can be accomplished in isolation or in conjunction with others. The classroom social structure described here encourages individual students to learn basic skills for their own purposes. But it is clear that this method is failing to educate large numbers of students as either readers or individuals capable of making meaningful use of the contents of their education. We need to create classroom situations in which learning is a positive social achievement and individual identity is enhanced through contributions to group performance. In conjunction with efforts of this type, a move to integrate all children into regular classrooms could help us to release the powers of the children now held back and alienated in the early school years.

References

Arensberg, L., & Kimball, S. *Culture and community*. New York: Harcourt, Brace, & World, 1965.

Bartlett, E. Curriculum, concepts of literacy, and social class. In L. Resnick & P. Weaver (Eds.), *Theory and practice in early reading*. Hillsdale, N. J.: Lawrence Erlbaum Associates. (In press)

Befu, H. Japan: *An anthropological introduction*. San Francisco: Chandler, 1971.

Befu, H. Power in exchange: Strategy of control and patterns of compliance in Japan. *Asian Profile*, 1974, **2**, 601-621.

Berg, I. *Education and jobs: the great training robbery*. New York: Beacon, 1969.

Bloom, B. Time and learning. *American Psychologist*, 1974, **29**, 682-688.

Cazden, C. Learning to read in classroom interaction. In L. B. Resnick & P. A. Weaver (Eds.), *Theory and practice in early reading*. Hillsdale, N. J.: Lawrence Erlbaum. (In press)

Church, J. *Understanding your child from birth to three*. New York; Random House, 1973.

Church, J. Psychology and the social order. *Annals of the New York Academy of Sciences*, 1976, **270**, 141-151.

Cicourel, A., & Kitsuse, J. *Educational decision-makers*. Indianapolis: Bobbs-Merrill, 1963.

Cole, M., Sharp, D., & Lave, C. The cognitive consequences of education. *The Urban Review*, 1976, **9**, 218-233.

Collier, J. *Alaskan Eskimo education*. New York: Holt, Rinehart, & Winston, 1973.

Conklin, H. Bamboo literacy on Mindoro. *Pacific Discovery*, 1949, **2**, 4-11.

D'Andrade, R. A propositional analysis of U. S. American beliefs about illness. In K. Basso & H. Selby (Eds.), *Meaning in anthropology*. Albuquerque: University of New Mexico Press, 1976.

Downing, J. *Comparative literacy*. New York: Macmillan, 1973.

Edgerton, R. Mental retardation in non-Western societies. In H. C. Haywood (Ed.), *Socio-cultural aspects of mental retardation*. New York: Appleton-Century-Crofts, 1970.

Erickson, F., & Mohatt, G. *The social organization of participation structures in two classrooms of Indian students*. Unpublished manuscript, Harvard University, 1977.

Henry, J. *Culture against man*. New York: Vintage, 1963.

Hobbs, N. *The futures of children*. San Francisco: Jossey-Bass, 1976.

Hostetler, J., & Huntington, G. *Children in Amish society*. New York: Holt, Rinehart, & Winston, 1975.

Johnson, D., & Johnson, R. *Learning together and alone*. New York: Holt, Rinehart, & Winston, 1975.

King, A. R. *The schools at Mopass*. New York: Holt, Rinehart, & Winston, 1967.

Lave, J. Tailor-made experiments and evaluating the intellectual consequences of apprenticeship training. *The Quarterly Newsletter of the Institute for Comparative Human Development*, 1977, **1**(2), 1-3.

Levin, H. A decade of policy developments in improving education and training for low-income populations. In *A decade of federal antipovery programs*. Madison: University of Wisconsin Press, 1977.

Lewis, M. *We the navigators*. Honolulu: University of Hawaii Press, 1972.

Lewis, M. Mau Piailug's navigation of Hokule'a from Hawaii to Tahiti. *Topics in Culture Learning*. (In press)

Lortie, D. *Schoolteacher: A sociological study*. Chicago: University of Chicago Press, 1975.

McDermott, J. *The culture of experience*. New York: New York, University Press, 1976.

McDermott, R. P. Achieving school failure. In G. Spindler (Ed.), *Education and cultural process*. New York: Holt, Rinehart, & Winston, 1974.

McDermott, R. P. *Kids made sense: An ethnographic account of the interactional management of success and failure in one first grade classroom*. Unpublished doctoral dissertation, Stanford University, 1976.

McDermott, R. P. Social relations as contexts for learning in school. *Harvard Educational Review*, 1977, **47**, 198-213.

McDermott, R. P., & Church, J. Making sense and feeling good. *Communication*, 1976, **2**, 121-143.

McDermott, R. P., & Gospodinoff, K. Social contexts for ethnic borders and school failure. In A. Wolfgang (Ed.), *Nonverbal behavior*. Toronto: Ontario Institute for the Study of Education. (In press)

McPhee, C. Children and music in Bali. In M. Mead & M. Wolfenstein (Eds.), *Childhood in contemporary cultures*. Chicago: University of Chicago Press, 1955.

Orasanu, J., McDermott, R., Boykin, W., & The Laboratory of Comparative Human Cognition. A critique of test standardization. *Social Policy*, 1977, **8**, 61-67.

Murphy, W. P. *A semantic and logical analysis of Kpelle proverb metaphors of secrecy*. Unpublished doctoral dissertation, Stanford University, 1976.

Nerlove, S., Roberts, J., Klein, R., Yarbrough, C., & Habicht, J. Natural indicators of cognitive developments. *Ethos*, 1975, **3**, 265-295.

Parsons, T. The school class as a social system. *Harvard Educational Review*, 1959, **29**, 297-318.

Parsons, T. Some theoretical considerations on the nature and trends of change of ethnicity. In N. Glazer & D. Moynihan (Eds.), *Ethnicity*. Cambridge: Harvard University Press, 1975.

Philips, S. Participant structures and communicative competencies. In C. Cazden, V. John, & D. Hymes (Eds.), *Functions of language in the classroom*. New York: Teachers College Press, 1972.

Pirandello, L. Six characters in search of an author. In E. Bentley (Ed.), *Naked masks*. New York: Dutton, 1952.

Rist, R. *The urban school*. Cambridge: M. I. T. Press, 1973.

Rohwer, W. Prime time for education. *Harvard Educational Review*, 1971, **41**, 316-341.

Rohlen, T. "Spiritual education" in a Japanese bank. *American Anthropologist*, 1973, **75**, 1542-1562.

Rohlen, T. Is Japanese education becoming less egalitarian? *The Journal of Japanese Studies*, 1977, **3**, 37-70.

Rosenthal, R. Interpersonal expectancy effects. In R. Rosenthal (Ed.), *Experimenter effects in behavioral research* (enlarged ed.). New York: Irvington, 1976.

Rosenthal, R., Archer, D., Di Matteo, M. R., Koivumaki, J. & Rogers, P. *Measuring sensitivity to nonverbal communication: The PONS test*. Unpublished manuscript, Harvard University, 1976.

Rosenthal, R., & Jacobson, L. *Pygmalion in the classroom*. New York: Holt, Rinehart, & Winston, 1968.

Sakamoto, T., & Makita, K. Japan. In J. Downing (Ed.), *Comparative reading*. New York: Macmillan, 1973.

Selby, H. *Zapotec deviance*. Austin: University of Texas Press, 1974.

Selby, H. Semantics and causality in the study of deviance. In M. Sanches & B. Blount (Eds.), *Sociocultural dimensions of language use*. New York: Academic, 1975.
Spindler, G. D. *The transmission of American culture*. Cambridge: Harvard University Press, 1959.
Spindler, G. D. *Burgbach*. New York: Holt, Rinehart, & Winston, 1973.
Spindler, G. D. The transmission of culture. In G. Spindler (Ed.), *Education and cultural process*. New York: Holt, Rinehart, & Winston, 1974.
Tyack, D. Ways of seeing. *Harvard Educational Review*, 1976, **46**, 355-389.
Vogel, E. *Japan's new middle class* (2nd ed.). Berkeley: University of California Press, 1972.
Weatherley, R., & Lipsky, M. Street-level bureaucrats and institutional innovation. *Harvard Educational Review*, 1977, **47**, 171-197.
Wieder, D. L. *Language and social reality*. The Hague: Mouton, 1974.
Wolcott, H. F. *The man in the principal's office*. New York: Holt, Rinehart, & Winston, 1973.
Wolcott, H. F. *Teachers versus technocrats*. Eugene, Ore.: Center for Educational Policy Management, University of Oregon, 1977.

Special Education and the Future: Some Questions To Be Answered and Answers To Be Questioned[1]

Reginald L. Jones[2]
University of California, Berkeley

The point in studying the future is not to speculate and predict; rather it is to clarify the present and to project needed redirection.

(Rubin, *The Future of Education*, 1975, p. 199)

Numerous social and technological changes have occurred in the past decade, and some of them may influence special education. For example, we now have or soon will have the power,

Through human engineering, to modify indefinitely the bodies of selected individuals, for reasons ranging from scientific curiosity to prolonging life;

Through genetic engineering, to modify the characteristics of the human race and to shape the course of evolution; . . .

To alter to unlimited extent man's mental and emotional characteristics including intellectual abilities, motivations, affect, personalities, and character . . . (Harman, 1969, cited in Rubin, 1975, pp. 24-25)

Other provocative projections have been made as well. One reads, for example, of the imaginative uses of technology in the service of education, plastic substitutes for human organs, and various techniques for manipulating conception, fertility, and death.

---

[1]In addition to formal and informal comments by participants at the Minneapolis working conference, the paper has benefited from the suggestions of Drs. Oris C. Amos, Wright State University; William Banks, Janet Jamison, and Arthurlene Towner, University of California, Berkeley; Samuel Guskin and Melvyn Semmel, Indiana University; and Donald MacMillan, University of California, Riverside.
[2]Chairman, Afro-American Studies, and Professor of Education.

There is also considerable thinking about the future among educators (Bundy, 1976; Epps, 1973; Galtung, 1975; Gores, 1975; Rubin, 1975). It is not surprising, therefore, that special educators have turned their attention to future matters, too.

One of the most comprehensive discussions of the future of special education was presented by Schipper and Kenowitz (1976). Using the Delphi technique, they asked 121 school administrators to respond to 60 special education future events and to record the values which they attached to the events. Among the more interesting results are the respondents' predictions that between 1980 and 1995 (the dates are the median years of occurrence) due process procedures will be guaranteed and all exceptional children will be receiving educational services. More extended and comprehensive administrative alternatives were predicted. The administrators also predicted that severely handicapped children increasingly will become recipients of educational benefits, progress toward de-institutionalization will increase, and parental participation in school matters will expand.

Among instructional trends, there were foreseen expanded uses of technology and instructional media services to reduce or remediate particular handicapping conditions. However, the respondents also predicted that acceptance and implementation of the mainstreaming concept as well as more extensive use of individualized/prescriptive instruction will be in effect by 1985.

There were also predicted shifts in the preservice and inservice training of teachers. It was predicted, for example, that by 1985 general education teachers will need a minimum of 6 credits in child exceptionalities for certification and that performance-based criteria, rather than credit hours earned in a subject area, will be the basis for teacher certification. Once teachers were certified, continuing education as a requirement for certification renewal was predicted, with inservice education given by state and local education agencies.

Because the 60 statements were culled from an initial group of 800, it is possible that the statistically infrequent and more creative statements were eliminated. This speculation aside, it is clear that many respondents saw in the next decades an acceleration and extension of developments already underway, not the introduction of the exotic and farfetched notions we are capable of imagining. The respondents probably were in agreement with Rubin (1975) who noted that,

> The immediate tasks before us are sufficiently compelling that in conceptualizing the schools we need, it would be prudent to constrain ourselves to those evolutions already patently in process. It is not that radical changes for the long run are not necessary; rather it is that because those of the short run will heavily condition what comes later, to leap prematurely would be to waste motion, or

worse, to stumble. It is probable, moreover, that only a small number of ideas in the social forecasting stockpile are genuinely significant to educational planning. (p. 197)

Societal Trends, Educational Developments, and the Future

In the light of Rubin's analysis, a reasonable concern is the nature of the evolutions that are in process. Within the special education context, there are pressures to broaden the range of individual differences in schools, especially in relation to race, social class, and handicap. Increasingly, oppressed groups are tending to press vigorously for social and educational change. Thus, people who deviate in ability, physique, or emotional state, and racial, cultural, or linguistic background will insist that schools make nonrestrictive provisions for their education, either by busing, individualized instruction, or other curricular modifications and/or practices.

Although changes are being mandated by law and demanded by certain groups (e.g., oppressed minority groups and parents of handicapped children), by no stretch of the imagination should we believe that the accomplishment of the changes will be easy. Potentially, the most inhibiting factor is that many of the changes call for the fuller integration of racial and cultural minorities. To a significant degree, particularly in large cities and their surrounding suburbs, the efforts to integrate handicapped populations and racial minorities will be joined. By itself, the issue of racial integration is potentially explosive. During the past few years, for example, we have witnessed violent reactions to racial integration in Boston, Louisville, Los Angeles, and a number of smaller communities. There have been riots and schools have had to be closed.

It should be noted that activities directed toward the full integration of handicapped pupils also are the result of coercion and legal mandates. The strategy may be the only means of effecting change with any rapidity. At the same time, resistance should not surprise us.

It is apparent that handicapped persons are an undervalued minority group. They have been segregated in schools and isolated in communities. Their accomplishments and potential have been minimized and their limitations highlighted. They are victims of negative stereotyping. Although the fact is not generally known, attitudes toward racial minority groups are highly correlated with those toward the handicapped (Cowen, Bobrove, Rockway, & Stevenson, 1967; Harth, 1971). It has been speculated that these attitudes are linked by an hypothesized aversion to groups perceived as weak and powerless. If so, it is highly probable that powerful negative attitudes, in latent form at least, are held toward the handicapped. As with certain racial minority groups, through various segregationist practices we have accommodated society's attitudes by excluding handicapped persons from full participation in American life. Consequently, negative public attitudes may have had little opportunity for expression. With the movement toward mandatory integration, however, some stress and inconvenience may be created for nonhandicapped people, and it is possible that negative attitudes and behaviors toward the handicapped may become more evident.

For the preceding reasons and those discussed in the rest of this section (a. the growth of Third World populations, b. the advent of P.L. 94-142, c. medical advances, and d. militant parents) it is apparent that if a wider range of individual differences is to be accommodated in the schools, the educational system is likely to be in a state of tension for some time to come.

GROWTH OF THIRD WORLD POPULATIONS

In some instances, pressures will result from the sheer force of numbers. Consider the growth of the black population, for example. In the United States, the rate of increase in the black population is greater than the rate in the white population. For example, in 1970, the birth rate among blacks was 25.2 per 1,000, as compared with 15.5 among whites. Although rates for both blacks and whites are declining, the differential remains the same. Since 1920, the black birth rate has exceeded the white birth rate. Since 1930, the percentage and, hence, the number of blacks in the total population has shown a gradual increase, ranging from 9.7 per cent (11,891,143) in 1930 to 11 per cent (22,580,000) of the population in 1970.

As of 1976, 26 of the largest cities in the United States had black populations between 100,000 and 1,000,000, which represent from 71.1 per cent of the population of Washington, D. C. to 14.7 per cent of Milwaukee, Wisconsin.

In 1860, 92.2 per cent of the blacks lived in the South; the percentage has decreased over the years: in 1970, over one-half lived outside the South. This dispersion, combined with the enactment of civil rights legislation, has shifted the focus of race relations from the South to the entire country. Because of segregation and discrimination practices, just about every major city faces serious problems in the areas of *de facto* segregated education, inadequate and segregated housing, and unemployment in black communities (Pinkney, 1975).

There is evidence that other low-status populations (Puerto Ricans, Mexican Americans, American Indians, and lower class whites) are beset by similar problems of birth rate, housing, education, unemployment and medical care. Health, employment, housing, and education are interrelated in a potentially explosive mixture. With the increased growth of Third World populations, we can expect that the pressures on the mainstream to accommodate the styles and preferences of diverse groups will continue far into the future.

P.L. 94-142

The Education for All Handicapped Children Act, by now, is well-known to most educators. The law will have a profound impact on schools. Of special concern in the present context is the law's requirement that all handicapped children, some of whom are misclassified and others of whom are classified undeservedly, be provided with education in the least restrictive environment. A consequence will be that larger numbers of children will receive specialized educational programs than do now. The need for seeking out handicapped children, both among students already in schools and those who have not received previous formal schooling, will increase the numbers as well as the range of differences among pupils in schools and classrooms.

Enactment of P.L. 94-142 has led to some optimism — in special education circles at least — that widespread support for the improved education of handicapped persons will result. A model of linear change is implicit in the law, that is, that the movement from legislative enactment to funding to implementation will occur smoothly. It may, but, as with many programs of change in which the people charged with implementation have had only minimal involvement in their development, there is also a high probability that it will not. We will need to give more attention than we have to the potential system stress and backlash that may result from the introduction of P.L. 94-142. For example, the law's due process provisions, which require parents to participate in the decisions on their children's educational placements, will create system stress because the parents of children who require such decisions are most likely to be hostile to the educational system and its practices because they see them as racist and/or discriminatory. In contrast, many educators seem ill-prepared to communicate with Third World people and people of lower socio-economic classes whose attitudes, values, and language they do not either understand or accept. Workable procedural safeguards will be needed but they may take some time to develop.

> Kirp, Buss, and Kuriloff have pointed out some ways that educational systems in the past have evaded the spirit, if not the letter, of the law in implementing due process provisions . . . . In California, where due process provisions similar to those outlined in 94-142 already existed, the due process practice of five California districts were studied. They found that parental permission was often secured without parental knowledge of what they had consented to. In some cases permission for placement was obtained during the same visit as permission for testing. In three of the five districts studied, it was found that decisions regarding placements were made in-

formally and that the formal hearing merely ratified informally reached decisions. Furthermore, the study revealed that although parents had the right to attend the placement meeting, the right was rarely exercised. In these districts, an average of only two-and a-half minutes was taken to present and ratify each case. In the two other districts studied, the admission committee attempted a more thorough and systematic view. (Chiba & Semmel, 1977, p. 22)

We anticipate P.L. 94-142's requirement — that testing and evaluation be conducted with materials and procedures that are not racially or culturally discriminatory — will create considerable strain on the educational system as well; unless there are heroic strides in the development of assessment instruments, testing and evaluation will not be accomplished with appropriately developed instruments and procedures. Currently, one hears of attempts by school people to circumvent or bypass the provisions requiring the use of nondiscriminatory testing procedures, and outright resistance also has been reported. The arguments supporting these positions are that existing *instruments and standards are appropriate* and if the diverse groups want to be successfully integrated into American life they must be held to mainstream standards. On the other hand, some groups, Third World people in particular, will insist upon the development and/or adoption of pluralist standards, including the use of racially and culturally appropriate instruments in testing and assessment.

For several reasons then (e.g., due process requirements, emphasis upon racially and culturally relevant assessment, pressures for racial integration, the common problems of race and handicap, and the overarching objective of increasing the range of individual differences in schools), the potential for backlash should not be underestimated. The forces of change unleashed by P.L. 94-142, which represents the culmination of more than a century of activity on behalf of handicapped children, are running head-on into the entrenched attitudes, values, and practices — many of our own making — of both school people and the lay public which are at variance with the thrust of this historic legislation.

MEDICAL ADVANCES

Infant mortality has decreased dramatically over the years. For example, there were 99.9 deaths per 1000 live births in 1915, 55.7 per thousand in 1935, 26.4 per thousand in 1955, and 19.8 per thousand in 1970. These figures mask the differences in birth rates by race and the fact that while larger numbers of infants live, many do so with crippling conditions that, in most instances, will last a lifetime. With P.L. 94-142, all such children now must have appropriate educations; they cannot be excluded from schooling, as was once permissible. As a result, we should be seeing many more severely handicapped children in schools in the future.

MILITANT PARENTS

There was a time when parents accepted school policies unquestioningly. If certain handicapped groups were excluded as uneducable, the parents acquiesced and placed the children in institutions or kept them at home. If children were seen as incorrigible, the parents simply kept them out of school. If children were seen as slow learners, they were permitted to drop out at an early age. In the early years of this century, racial minority groups accepted segregated schools without concerted opposition. But no more.

Parents who are racially and culturally oppressed and parents of handicapped children have become increasingly sophisticated about educational matters, and they are unwilling to accept schools without question. Among the changes demanded are (a) the acceptance of all kinds of heretofore unacceptable students and (b) bringing up to normal or better achievement levels children who have been erroneously labeled "EMR" or "disadvantaged." Many parents reject the notion that learning problems reside in children; they blame the system and its structures. There is every reason to believe that these parental attitudes will continue (Gorham et al., 1975; Jones & Wilderson, 1976; Morton & Hull, 1976).

Educators Respond

Reaching the goal of accepting an expanded range of differences in schools is likely to be quite difficult because the forces of stability and those of change appear to be on a collision course. While parents and civil rights groups press for the integration of handicapped and minority group children in the regular classroom (Jones & Wilderson, 1976), some school administrators, teachers, and teachers' unions are resisting the idea (Melcher, 1972; Sosnowsky & Coleman, 1970; Young, 1976).

To accommodate the expanded ranges of differences in the schools, which have been or will be occasioned by mandates and pressures, and in response to the resistance in the school systems, special educators are moving vigorously in several areas: (a) the individualization of instruction, (b) the modification of teacher and student attitudes toward handicapped children and racially, culturally, or linguistically different children, and (c) the development of programs of inservice education. These areas are all critical to any future of special education that might be projected and, consequently, must be examined carefully. In the rest of this section, therefore, the following key topics are discussed: (a) teacher attitudes toward innovation and change, (b) assessment and modification of attitudes toward the handicapped, (c) individualization of instruction, and (d) delivery of inservice training. These four areas do not exhaust the range of considerations attendant to effecting future change in special education, to be sure, but they are important as starting points.

It may be argued that the approach taken here is pedestrian and reductionist because insufficient attention is given to system factors and to the impact of social trends and developments upon educational practice. People subscribing to such a view are quick to point out, with some support for their contention, that schools mirror social trends and, consequently, if the future direction of special education is to be understood correctly, the trends and other developments must be given attention. To concern oneself with factors such as teacher attitudes and inservice training, it is further argued, is merely to tinker, because the factors do not exist independently. However, given the enormity of the problems we face, we will have to proceed simultaneously on macro (systems) as well as micro levels. This paper presents a micro-level analysis.

My strategy is to critically evaluate some of the literature in our four areas of interest. We are too prone in special education to overgeneralize with too much certainty. There is the danger, of course, that my picture will be too pessimistic; that the prospects for change will be made to appear too bleak. Special education researchers are not only narrow in their studies, and the methodology of their investigations often far from perfect, but, also, they have left many important questions unanswered. Moreover, the research-based model — research, development, diffusion, and adoption — is subject to some question. Some observers argue that movement from research to development to diffusion to adoption simply is not the way that things are changed (Erlandson & House, 1971; Hilgard, 1969; House, 1971). Nevertheless, an analysis of research on the strategies for change in special education can be valuable because, in most instances, future practices are built upon present knowledge.

ATTITUDES TOWARD INNOVATION AND CHANGE

It is unlikely that any educational change or innovation, regardless of how well conceived or rigorously tested it may be, can survive without the active participation and support of teachers and administrators. An understanding of the attitudes of these groups toward change and innovation is of considerable importance, then, in our assessment of the likelihood that any vision of special education will come to fruition in the future. We need information about teachers' and administrators' attitudes toward innovation and change. We also need information about which features of innovations offer the best prognosis and, contrariwise, which inhibit change. In summarizing the educational change in 1971, Goodlad wrote,

> The processes of change have been haphazard and, insofar as knowledge about change is concerned, virtually noncumulative. We are only slightly better off today with respect to knowing how change is wrought and how to spend our human resources dollar wisely to effect change than we were twenty years ago. (p. 157)

In 1975, Stern and Keislar painted a similar pessimistic picture of the correlates of the acceptance of educational innovations.

> ... these efforts have been rather fruitless. Under a wide variety of conditions, correlational studies have shown no consistent association between any of a number of demographic variables and the active acceptance or rejection of a major educational change. Neither age, sex, grade level taught, type of training, nor years or type of experience could be used as a basis for prediction. There are no clear-cut features which differentiate the innovative from the traditional teacher. It is the same with setting. Size of local educational agency, number of schools involved, geographic location, or type of community, make little difference so far as installation of an innovation is concerned. (pp. 106-107)

Finally, Lilly (1973), who summarized a number of studies of educational change, concluded that two important but often neglected factors must be considered in examining the dynamics of innovation: "(1) personal characteristics of the initiators and, most important, of the instructional personnel involved in conceiving and carrying out the innovation, and (2) the political situation in, and surrounding, the system in which the change is to be made" (p. 214). Indeed, Lilly believed that decisions to adopt innovations are based more on these factors than on technical considerations (e.g., objective evidence that one approach is superior to available alternative approaches). If he is correct, and considerable impressionistic and analytical writing supports his premises, it is clear that our perspectives on the range of factors influencing the adoption of innovations must be broadened; and we must reckon with variables which are not yet clearly understood but, nevertheless, are critical to our understanding of how the adoption of innovations is influenced.

Because teachers and school administrators are so important to educational innovation and change, we have tended to overlook other influential groups. For example, resistance (or support) can come from parents, students, and community groups as well. Children are a particularly neglected source of data; for special education, the children would be the handicapped. Too often we proceed as if we alone know what is best for the students we serve. Future studies of educational innovation and change would be better rounded if information and reactions from students, parents, and community groups were incorporated into program planning and evaluation.

ATTITUDE ASSESSMENT AND CHANGE

> We must recognize that helping teachers to deal with the uniqueness of children is an attitudinal problem. . . . It is our feelings with which we must deal: our attitudes, fears, and frustrations about the handicapped, about something that is a little different. We can give skills and competencies, but our attitudes affect the delivery of them. In the design of training programs we must look at the attitudes of everyone involved. . . . and make those attitudes the focus of our change efforts. (Martin, 1976, pp. 5-6)

Martin's comments summarize a major problem with which we must deal in conducting present or future special programs. Until recently, little systematic attention was given to attitudes toward the handicapped; but the current interest in this subject is high; in 1976, editors of the *Exceptional Child Bibliography Series* introduced compilations of publications on attitudes toward the physically and mentally handicapped. Covering a period of 10 years (with a few earlier exceptions), these bibliographies contained over 150 entries that quite accurately reflected the research and literature on attitudes produced during this period. The majority of entries were descriptions or measurements of attitudes toward the handicapped. Relatively few were studies of attitude change.

It was thought that the studies should be evaluated by attending to such considerations as age of subjects, sampling, type of exceptionality, experimental design, and evidence of author familiarity with psychometric and social psychological theory. Inasmuch as the studies were found to be very general, such a detailed analysis was thought to be unnecessary. Methodological features of the studies can be summarized as follows. (a) Work in the assessment of attitudes in special education, whether attitudes of teachers toward concepts such as mainstreaming or toward groups of exceptional children, or attitudes of non-exceptional children toward the exceptional, are best described as "primitive." The same can be said for research in the area of attitude change. (b) With only a few exceptions, prior work in attitude measurement, such as attitude scale construction, was all but ignored. (c) The validity and reliability of instruments were almost never reported. (d) The sociological and social psychological literature on attitudes and attitude change were rarely cited. (e) Populations were small, nonrandom and often non-representative. (f) There was excessive preoccupation with assessing attitudes toward the handicapped with relatively little attention given to attitude modification. (g) Many studies employed an attitudinal treatment with pre and post tests but no control group. (h) None of the studies seemed to be guided by theory, nor did they build upon one another. (i) Virtually all studies, whether in the area of attitude assessment or attitude modification, were "one shot"; insofar as can be determined, there has been no replication of the results of any one study. (j) Even within a given area of handicap, subjects were often at different age levels. (k) Rarely was there instrument comparability across studies. In addition, there was (1) a failure to recognize that attitudes toward the handicapped are complex, and (m) that there is no one-to-one correspondence between attitudes and behavior.

Attitudinal complexity

In the majority of the studies on attitudes toward the handicapped in which teachers, school administrators, or peers have participated, the attitudes have been treated as unidimensional. Rarely (Efron & Efron, 1968; Gottlieb & Corman, 1975; Jones, 1974; Jones, Gottfried, & Owens, 1966; and Siller, 1967) was there recognition that attitudes toward any object or group tend to be multidimensional rather than unidimensional, and that attitudes toward any special education group or concept may differ as a function of the handicapping condition, age and status of the respondent, situation, or interactions among these and other variables. Fortunately, these facts have not escaped all researchers. For example, when Gottlieb and Corman (1975) factor analyzed attitudes toward the mentally retarded, they found four underlying factors: positive stereotype, segregation in the community, segregation in the classroom, and perceived physical and intellectual handicap. Siller (1967), who analyzed attitudes toward amputees and the blind, found seven virtually identical factors: interaction strain, rejection of intimacy, generalized rejection, authoritarian virtuousness, inferred emotional consequences, distressed identification, and functional limitations. Jones's (1974) work suggested that there may be commonalities as well as differences in attitudes toward various exceptionalities.

By studying attitudes in their multidimensional context, their nature can be clarified and the basis for programs of attitude change can be made sounder. It is not feasible to attempt the modification of attitudes in any global sense. Attitude change programs must be tailored to precise attitudinal components (McGuire, 1968). Indeed, as Scott (1968) reminded us, "The construct has become so complex that one can no longer clearly talk about measuring an attitude. Rather, one must restrict discussion to procedures for measuring a particular property of an attitude as conceptually defined" (p. 265).

Attitude-behavior consistency

The essence of the notion of attitude-behavior consistency is simply this: Most people operate on the assumption that when a person states that he believes in or feels a particular way about a person or object he will, in fact, behave in a way that is consistent with his statements. Thus, for example, when regular teachers and other personnel complete interviews, questionnaires, or scales on their attitudes toward various types of exceptional children, mainstreaming, instructional innovation, or other groups or concepts, we assume that their behavior will reflect these attitudes. Similarly, when children express attitudes toward their handicapped peers, we expect their behavior toward their peers to reflect their verbal statements. Regrettably, expectation is not matched by reality. The inconsistency between attitudes and behaviors is the stimulus for much contemporary sociological and social-psychological research (Gross & Niman, 1975; Schuman & Johnson, 1976; Wicker, 1969). Indeed, Schuman and Johnson cited 160 references to this problem alone, and reported that their working bibliography was well over 300 items!

Wicker (1969) reviewed 46 studies in which the participants' verbal and behavioral responses to attitudinal objects were obtained on separate occasions. The researchers used a wide range of verbal attitude measures (Thurstone and Likert Scales, the semantic differential, interviews), and several specific behavioral measures. The participants came from diverse populations (maternity-ward patients, labor union members, oil-field workers, and college students). On the basis of his analyses, Wicker concluded that measured attitudes were often unrelated or only slightly related to overt behavior; rarely were the attitude behavior coefficients above .30. Schuman and Johnson (1976), in a more recent summary, were less pessimistic. Their more comprehensive review showed that most attitude-behavior studies yielded positive results, although the correlations were rarely large enough to suggest that attitudinal responses can substitute for behavioral measures, an informative observation for future special education attitude research.

Conceptual and methodological problems in the assessment and modification of attitudes are many and complex. Although it is unlikely that special educators who are interested in these areas will be directly involved in solving attitude-behavior mysteries, at the very least they ought to be conversant with the problems and issues and the large body of established facts and principles that guide activity in this area; otherwise special educators will not advance our understanding of attitudes toward the handicapped or of how to modify them.

Future studies

Current research on attitudes is flawed in many respects, but even greater flaws are found in attitude-change research, in which serious problems have been overlooked completely. At least three areas of future investigation seem promising, therefore:

1. There is a need for systematic attention to those factors, including the cognitive and affective components of attitudes, that *regular teachers* perceive as impeding their ability to work effectively with handicapped children. One sees occasional studies in this area but systematic efforts are needed.

2. We need studies of nonhandicapped children's attitudes toward handicapped children and their integration, and of the developmental course of these attitudes. For example, we need to know how nonhandicapped children perceive different disability groups and how they view the integration of these groups.

3. Given the massive effort to change attitudes toward handicapped children, it would be valuable to systematically explore strategies for *equipping the handicapped* with behaviors that could reduce strain in their interactions with nonhandicapped persons. Such a strategy does not mean that the prejudices of nonhandicapped persons will be catered to, only that handicapped children, by recognizing and taking into account the discomfort often experienced by the nonhandicapped, may do much to foster the development of positive attitudes. Insofar as can be determined, work in this area is nonexistent.

While we need to explore various avenues of effecting positive changes in attitudes toward the handicapped, we must be prepared to accept the possibility that the opposite may occur (Guskin, 1973; Siperstein, Bak, & Gottlieb, 1977).

Siperstein and his colleagues used photographs and videotape to assess sixth graders' attitudes toward normal and handicapped peers. The results indicated that individual attitudes toward an academically incompetent, abnormally appearing child became more negative after group discussions. But group discussion did not affect attitudes toward academically competent, normally appearing children. The negative shift in attitudes toward the handicapped child occurred for groups comprised of both friends and nonfriends.

Guskin's studies used simulation games and role playing with a variety of populations, including preservice and inservice teachers. His purpose was to sensitize regular and prospective teachers to the needs of handicapped mainstreamed children so that they would be more accepting of such children and more open to the development of required, specific teaching skills. After his analyses, Guskin reached these conclusions:

> One thing we have discovered from our experience with role plays and games is that if they are to maintain involvement, the developers must give up control of the outcomes, both in terms of narrowly defined outcomes of the activity and in terms of the broader consequences of play. People were enthusiastic about the role plays but their spontaneous comments indicated that they were not necessarily enthusiastic about mainstreaming. They all had a much better feel for what it was all about, in concrete terms rather than academic truths. However, some had started out overly convinced that mainstreaming was the answer. They now had second thoughts. Others had strong reservations about integrating handicapped children back in regular classes. They were now much more

responsive. In short we could say we attained our objectives only if we restate them as giving teachers a more realistic perspective of mainstreaming. (Guskin, 1973, p. 94)

It has yet to be determined whether the findings and observations of Sipperstein et al., and Guskin are unique to the populations studied, can be explained by the studies' methodological limitations, or, indeed, represent valid phenomena at all. However, their findings alert us to the real possibility that not all intended outcomes of intervention efforts are successful, as is true of interventions in many educational and social science areas.

It is apparent that much work is needed in the assessment and modification of attitudes but we have a number of quite promising strategies, principles, and tested methodologies to guide us. In future studies, we need to use these principles and methodologies to improve our research and intervention activities.

Individualization of Instruction

Individualization of instruction refers to the matching of instructional strategies to the individual learner's aptitudes, needs, motivations, learning styles, and background. It includes pacing, modification of objectives, and materials, and personalization of instruction (Frase, 1972). People who are concerned with expanding the range of individual differences see individualization as a major vehicle for accomplishing this objective.

This discussion of the subject is in no way intended to be definitive. Rather, it is meant to call attention to a body of literature that is often neglected: (a) teacher opinions of individualization, (b) individualized educational programs as they relate to P.L. 94-142, and (c) theory in special education. As a corollary, the notion of student-learning environment interactions is introduced as well as the need to expand educational objectives.

TEACHER OPINIONS ON INDIVIDUALIZATION

Many teachers do not perceive the individualization of instruction as all that wonderful. Regular teachers appear to hold positive attitudes toward instructional systems that are designed for individualization (e.g., IGE, IPI; Spears, 1973) but they are less enthusiastic about individualization as a concept. For example, in his survey of a random sample of 609 members of Phi Delta Kappa, Spears found that 74-75% of the respondents, respectively, saw Individually Guided Education and Individually Prescribed Education as having the potential to improve elementary and secondary education. On the other hand, when Stern and Keislar (1975) reviewed the literature on teacher attitudes toward individualization they reached the following conclusions:

When attitudes of teachers toward individualization as a general concept rather than a specific program are solicited, approximately half the teachers say they value consideration of the pupil as an individual. But only less than a fourth of all teachers surveyed by Bosco (1971) report that they apply this principle in their own classrooms. While teachers may feel that individualization is necessary for math and reading, they prefer to work with the class as a whole most of the time. (Stern & Keislar, 1975, p. 116)

The significance of these observations is not necessarily ominous for the advocacy of individualization as an instructional strategy. They suggest, however, that teachers have no natural proclivity to individualize, and any individualization activity probably should be accompanied by various support systems, including instruction in special individualization techniques, the provision of instructional support (e.g., aides, consulting teachers), and other forms of assistance.

INDIVIDUALIZED EDUCATION PROGRAMS OF P.L. 94-142

P.L. 94-142 has been described as a "bill of the future" (MacMillan, 1977, p. 2). At the heart of this future-oriented legislation is the individualized education program (IEP). It requires the development of a written plan of instructional activities for each identified handicapped child. The plan includes annual goals and short-term objectives, the provision of specific educational services, and evaluation (Torres, 1977). The notion of the IEP is laudable; however, it assumes that the craft of teaching handicapped children is much more advanced than it actually may be. There are many difficult problems attendant to the full development and implementation of IEPs, like the notion of diagnostic-prescriptive teaching, which probably will be seen as a key to the development of individualized education programs.

Diagnostic-prescriptive teaching simply refers to the process whereby, through various procedures, student-learning needs are diagnosed and educational treatment procedures prescribed. There are many assumptions underlying the procedures, including the view that children's strengths and weaknesses can be reliably diagnosed, that the instruments used for such purposes are valid, and that the measures and learning outcomes are related. A concept of some current interest in the diagnostic-prescriptive literature is aptitude-treatment-interaction, the matching of instructional techniques to (broadly defined) learner aptitudes. The notion is appealing in its simplicity. If students with certain aptitude levels learn best through one technique, and students with a different aptitude level learn best through yet other techniques, we need merely identify the instructional technique that is most effective for the aptitude level and prescribe instruction accordingly.

Ysseldyke (1973) conducted an excellent survey of the literature on the subjects of both diagnostic-prescriptive teaching and related concepts (e.g., aptitude-treatment interactions, gain score research, descriptive research, and various measurment problems). Following a review of representative studies and a critique of strategies used to support diagnostic-prescriptive teaching, he concluded that the concept has little empirical support. Moreover, very little special education research employing aptitude-treatment interaction designs was found, and in studies identified, none demonstrated the effect. A major difficulty was the absence of diagnostic measures with sufficiently high levels of reliability to be useful in identifying children's strengths and weaknesses.

THEORY

For the most part, there is an absence of theory or theoretical discussion in the literature on individualization, as is the case in special education generally. It is true that a number of pupil and teacher characteristics, as well as a variety of cognitive and noncognitive measures and instructional techniques, have been studied for their predictive value for various learning outcomes; however, they are typically chosen for their measurability, and under ad hoc and intuitive presumptions that the variables are related to student achievement or other outcomes. Seldom is the selection of variables guided by theoretical models that generate the basis for their selection, predict their contribution to some educational outcome, or explain how they function singly, or in interaction, to lead to an effect. In the context of a discussion of competency-based teacher education in special education, Semmel, Semmel, and Morrison (1976) stated the need for theory quite well:

> The requirements of theoretical work must be drawn from an integration of our knowledge of handicapped learners, the nature of curriculum content, and conception of teaching. To be maximally effective in guiding research in teacher behavior, theoretical conceptualizations must seek to identify those instructional and pupil characteristics which most probably relate to pupil growth. This implies more than the construction of hypotheses related to the effects of one type of administrative arrangement over another. What is needed are efforts to construct models which suggest that teachers with specified characteristics, who demonstrate specified observable teaching behaviors, with pupils having specified learning characteristics will produce desired pupil outcomes within the limits of specific educational contexts. The complexity of searching for functional relationships between presage, process, and product variables in the study of teacher behavior demands a sizable effort in order to prioritize variables for study and potential pay-off. Theory is a powerful tool for organizing such an endeavour. It is, to be sure, not the only promising strategy for uncovering meaningful relationships between teacher behavior and pupil growth. But it is, in our opin-

ion, a necessary component of a total effort. . . . (Semmel et al., 1976, pp. 200-201)

If greater attention is given to theory construction and the theoretical effects in special education, it may mean that funding agencies may need to give support to this kind of activity in addition to projects that lead to concrete products.

STUDENT-LEARNING ENVIRONMENT INTERACTIONS

It is not unreasonable, if the vision of more effective education in a pluralistic society is to be realized, for student characteristics to be matched with learning environments. Although very little matching appears to be done now, it is possible that alternative environments increasingly will become available to be matched with diverse student aptitudes and background characteristics. The possible alternatives are open schools, schools-without-walls, learning centers, continuation schools, schools-within-schools, which already enjoy some currency (Smith, 1974), regional state schools, federal regional schools, college- and university-related open schools, industrial demonstration schools, labor-union-sponsored schools, and army schools, suggested by Clark (1968). Such schools and environments will develop out of the emerging ideas of student diversity and education in a pluralistic society. There would be many ways to succeed and many goals from which to choose, and no particular way of succeeding would be necessarily valued over another. If such developments are to come about, performances in the settings that are more natural than traditional schools will require new measures of process and style, of cognitive and noncognitive development. Moreover, "success and achievement will need to be differently defined; and many more alternative ways of succeeding will need to be appropriately rewarded than is the case at the present time" (Glaser, 1975, p. 133).

EXPANDING EDUCATIONAL OBJECTIVES

It also will be necessary to expand educational objectives. The Coleman-chaired panel report of the Presidential Science Advisory Committee (1973) concluded that we are not at the stage when our responsibilities toward youth go beyond the provision of free public schooling that is designed to increase cognitive skills. Without endorsing the Advisory Committee's full report or the claim of historical uniqueness for some of their recommendations, a number of their objectives seem worthy of consideration for the present discussion. According to the report, educational objectives might be expanded to include the following:

Cognitive and noncognitive skills necessary for economic independence and occupational opportunities.

Capability for effective management of one's own affairs.

Capability as consumers, not only of goods but, more significantly, of the cultural riches of civilization.

Capability for intense concentrated involvement in an activity.

Experience with persons different from self, not only in social class and subculture, but also in age.

The experience of having others dependent on ones' actions.

Interdependent activities directed toward collective goals.

The development of a sense of identity and self esteem. (Presidential Science Advisory Committee, 1973, cited in Rubin, 1975, p. 185)

Inservice Education

It is certain that future educational activities will require changes in present practices. Innovations can be easily introduced to preservice curricula, but securing their acceptance by experienced teachers will be a major task. Most likely, inservice education will be the vehicle for exposing experienced teachers to new administrative arrangements and instructional development. Given the probability that inservice education will play an important role in the adoption of our discoveries and inventions, it seems important to review the literature in this area. The questions addressed are: What is the state of the art in inservice training? Are there well-developed and tested models of inservice delivery?

THE INSERVICE LITERATURE

A search of the Council on Exceptional Children's customized computer retrieval system yielded more than 400 entries under the headings of inservice education and inservice teacher education, a sizable number of which were actually related to the subject! These abstracts, one of the more popular books on the subject (Rubin, 1971), several issues of current journals devoted to inservice training, and scores of articles, led to conclusions very much like Rubin's; he summarized the thinking of a number of experts on the subject of inservice education when he wrote:

> I should acknowledge, at the outset, that I concur with most of the arguments presented by my colleagues: In-service education has indeed been virtually a lost cause. Taken in toto, the conception set forth in previous chapters leads to three fundamental conclusions: teacher professional growth has not been taken seriously, it lacks a systematic methodology, and it has been managed with astonishing clumsiness. It is not surprising, therefore, that teachers have grown accustomed to its impotence, and that administrators have come to regard it as a routine exercise in futility. (Rubin, 1971, p. 245)

It would be cavalier to suggest that nothing is of value in existing writings on inservice education. The value is there. We know something about teacher preferences for inservice activities (Brimm & Tollett, 1974; Sterns & Keislar, 1975) and our principles for guiding the development of inservice programs are intuitively sound (Brimm & Tollett, 1974; Edelfelt, 1972; Mauth, 1962; Rubin, 1971). However, difficulties arise when questions are asked about the existence of a direct link beween inservice activities and students' school learning and performance. Studies have not established such relations, which is not to say that the more conventional inservice programs, which are designed to accomplish educational goals that are based upon teachers' desires and preferences, have no value.

INSERVICE MODELS

There are many inservice programs and models both within and outside of special education, but those labeled "competency based" (CBTE) seem to show the greatest promise for effecting the kind of relation between inputs (teacher behavior, curriculum, etc.) and outcomes (student achievement, etc.) that many educators think are important. Briefly, the key elements of competency-based programs are that performance goals are specified for teachers or trainees in advance of instruction and the participants must demonstrate knowledge of the principles that promote the agreed-upon learning outcomes. Specific elements of a CBTE program include the following:

1. The knowledge, skills, and behaviors to be demonsrated by a trainee are derived from an explicit, public conception of the teacher's role, and they are so stated that the trainee's specific competencies can be assessed.

2. Criteria for assessing competencies are based on specified behavioral indicators and explicit levels of mastery, under specified conditions, and are made public in advance.

3. Performance is the primary source of evidence for assessing a trainee's competency.

4. The trainee's progress through a program is determined by demonstrated competency rather than the lapse of time or course completion (Elam, 1971)

CBTE programs have been used not only in preservice but inservice education as well, including inservice special education. Semmel et al. (1976), summarizing CBTE studies in special education preservice and inservice training, discussed the programs' difficulties and promise in the following terms:

> From a CBTE perspective the purpose of research on teacher behavior is to provide an empirical basis for the selection of appropriate competencies and for the assessment of "good" teaching for teacher training. The best criterion for judging the utility of specified observable teacher behaviors is the effect of such behavior on the growth of handicapped pupils. Hence an empirical base of CBTE in special education would constitute the identification of a set of teacher behaviors which have been demonstrated to have significantly interacted with the characteristics of handicapped pupils to

enhance the growth of objectives for such pupils. Our review of the literature clearly indicates the absence of such a body of empirically developed competencies in special education — or for regular education for that matter. Both pre and in-service teacher training throughout the United States are currently in various stages of developing facets of CBTE programs with virtually no objective basis for supporting the competency statements which serve to define their operational objectives. Hence, most existing training programs in special education are predicated on criteria from needs assessment which may be unrelated to pupil growth criteria (i.e., professional biases, philosophical commitments, perceptions of school administrators, etc.).

As we review the body of literature available in special education it is apparent that relatively few researchers have focused their attention on relating specific behaviors to the growth of handicapped pupils. Further, those few attempts to uncover relevant teaching behaviors have been for the most part unsuccessful. Research in teacher behavior has had, as a result, virtually no impact on the field of teacher training in special education generally — nor on CBTE specifically. (Semmel et al., 1976, pp. 199-200)

In summary, it can be said that a number of principles suggest how inservice activities can be planned and specific inservice programs can be structured according to several models. It would be a mistake, however, to believe that our knowledge is sound enough or the models developed well enough (including CBTE) to suggest that the prospects are great, particularly if pupil outcomes are our objectives, for soundly implementing any future programs that might be envisioned. This area is one to which special educators will want to give considerably more systematic attention than has been given to date.

Summary

In this brief paper, visions of the future of special education were projected and areas of research needed to secure the visions examined. Expanding the range of individual differences in schools is seen as a major future direction. We also need to understand matters related to race and social class and the increasing tendency of oppressed groups to press for social and educational change.

A review of the research and writing in the areas of (a) teacher attitudes toward innovation and change, (b) assessment and modification of attitudes toward the handicapped, (c) individualization of instruction, and (d) the delivery of inservice education reveals that much work must be done to further our understanding of how to make school people receptive to innovation and change, develop and validate techniques for individualization and inservice delivery, and improve our ability to assess and modify attitudes toward the handicapped. In several instances, a major problem is the failure to use existing facts and principles to inform our activities, a neglect that is quite evident in the areas of attitude measurement and change and the delivery of inservice education.

Several of the problems and needs highlighted here are not unique to special education, to be sure. The point of the exercise has been to draw attention to a body of literature that too rarely is cited but which is critical to the understanding of probable future directions in special education. Familiarity with this research and writing should enable us to plan for the future with greater confidence than we have now.

References

Bosco, J. Individualization: Teacher's views. *Elementary School Journal*, 1971, **72**, 125-131.

Brimm, J. L., & Tollett, D. J. How do teachers feel about inservice education? Teacher attitudes toward inservice education inventory. *Educational Leadership*, 1974, **31**, 521-525.

Bundy, R. F. Social visions and educational futures. *Phi Delta Kappan*, 1976, **58**, 84-90.

Chiba, C., & Semmel, M. I. Due process and least restrictive alternative: New emphasis on parental participation. In M. I. Semmel & J. L. Heinmiller (Eds.), The Education for All Handicapped Children Act (P. L. 94-142), *Viewpoints*, 1977, **53**, 17-29.

Clark, K. B. Alternative public school systems. *Harvard Education Review*, 1968, **38**, 100-113.

Cowen, E. L., Bobrove, P. H., Rockway, A. M., & Stevenson, J. Development and evaluation of an attitude to deafness scale. *Journal of Personality and Social Psychology*, 1967, **6**, 183-191.

Edelfelt, R. A. The reform of education and teacher education: A complex task. *Journal of Teacher Education*, 1972, **23**, 117-125.

Efron, R. E., & Efron, H. Y. Measurement of attitudes toward the retarded and an application with educators. *American Journal of Mental Deficiency*, 1968, **72**, 100-107.

Elam, S. *Performance-based teacher education*. Washington, D. C.: American Association of Colleges for Teacher Education, 1971.

Epps, E. Future of education for black Americans. *School Review*, 1973, **81**, 315-500.

Erlandson, D. A., & House, E. R. Theory and practice: Why nothing seems to work. *National Association of Secondary School Principals Bulletin*, 1971, **55**, 69-75.

Frase, L. E. The concept of instructional individualization. *Educational Technology*, 1972, **12**, 45.

Galtung, J. Schooling and future society. *School Review*, 1975, **83**, 533-68.

Glaser, R. The school of the future: Adaptive environments for learning. In L. Rubin (Ed.), *The future of education: Perspectives on tomorrow's schooling*. Boston: Allyn & Bacon, 1975.

Goodlad, J. I. Educational change: A strategy for action. *Journal of Secondary Education*, 1971, **46**, 156-166.

Gores, H. B. Future file: Schoolhouse 2000. *Phi Delta Kappan*, 1975, **56**, 310-12.

Gorham, K. A. et al. Effect on parents. In N. Hobbs (Ed.), *Issues in the classification of children*. San Francisco: Jossey-Bass, 1975.

Gottlieb, J., & Corman, L. Public attitudes toward mentally retarded children. *American Journal of Mental Deficiency*, 1975, **80,** 72-80.

Gross, S. J., & Niman, C. M. Attitude-behavior consistency: A review. *The Public Opinion Quarterly*, 1975, **39,** 358-368.

Guskin, S. Simulation games for teachers on the mainstreaming of mildly handicapped children. *Viewpoints*, 1973, **49,** 85-95.

Harman, W. W. The nature of our changing society: Implications for schools. Eugene, Ore.: ERIC Clearinghouse on Educational Administration, Oct. 1969.

Harth, R. Attitudes towards minority groups as a construct in assessing attitudes toward the mentally retarded. *Education and Training of the Mentally Retarded*, 1971, **6,** 142-147.

Hilgard, E. R. The problem of R and D within behavioral sciences. *Journal of Research and Development*, 1969, **3,** 37-48.

House, E. R. A critique of linear change models in education. *Educational Technology*, 1971, **11,** 35.

Jones, R. L. The hierarchical structure of attitudes toward the exceptional. *Exceptional Children*, 1974, **40,** 430-435.

Jones, R. L., Gottfried, N. W., & Owens, A. The social distance of the exceptional: A study at the high school level. *Exceptional Children*, 1966, **32,** 551-556.

Jones, R. L. & Wilderson, F. Mainstreaming and the minority child: An overview of issues and a perspective. In R. L. Jones (Ed.), *Mainstreaming and the minority child*. Reston, Va.: Council for Exceptional Children, 1976.

Lilly, M. S. The impact (or lack of it) of educational research on changes in educational practice. In L. Mann, & D. A. Sabatino (Eds.), *The first review of special education*. Philadelphia: JSE Press, 1973.

MacMillan, D. *Mental retardation in school and society*. Boston: Little, Brown, 1977.

Martin, E. Integration of the handicapped child into regular schools. In M. C. Reynolds (Ed.), *Mainstreaming: Origins and issues*. Reston, Va.: Council for Exceptional Children, 1976, 5-7.

Mauth, L. Psychology and the in-service program. *National Elementary Principal*, 1962, **41,** 13-16.

McGuire, W. J. The nature of attitudes and attitude change. In G. Lindzey & E. Aronson (Eds.), *The handbook of social psychology* (Vol. 3). Reading, Mass.: Addison-Wesley, 1969, 136-314.

Melcher, J. W. Some questions from a school administrator. *Exceptional Children*, 1972, **39,** 547-51.

Morton, K. A., & Hull, K. Parents and the mainstream. In R. L. Jones (Ed.), *Mainstreaming and the minority child*. Reston, Va.: Council for Exceptional Children, 1976.

Pinkney, A. *Black Americans*. Englewood Cliffs, N. J.: Prentice-Hall, 1975.

Presidential Science Advisory Committee. *Youth: Transition to Adulthood*. Report. Washington: U. S. Government Printing Office, 1973.

Rubin, L. J. (Ed.). *Improving in-service education: Proposals and procedures for change*. Boston: Allyn & Bacon, 1971.

Rubin, L. (Ed.). *The future of education: Perspectives on tomorrow's schooling*. Boston: Allyn & Bacon, 1975.

Schipper, W. V., & Kenowitz, L. A. Special education futures — a forecasting of events affectig the education of exceptional children: 1976-2000. *The Journal of Special Education*, 1976, **10,** 401-13.

Schuman, H., & Johnson, M . P. Attitudes and behavior. In A. Inkeles (Ed.), *Annual review of sociology*. Palo Alto: Annual Reviews, 1976, 161-207.

Scott, W. A. Attitude measurement. In G. Lindzey & E. Aronson (Eds.), *The handbook of social psychology* (Vol. 3). Reading, Mass.: Addison-Wesley, 1969, 204-273.

Semmel, M. I., Semmel, D. S., & Morrissey, P. A. *Competency-based teacher education in special education: A review of research and training programs*. Blomington, Ind.: Center for Innovation in Teaching the Handicapped, Indiana University, 1976.

Siller, J. *Studies in reaction to disability, XIII: Structure of attitudes toward the physically disabled; disability factor scales – amputation, blindness, cosmetic conditions*. New York: School of Education, New York University, 1967.

Siperstein, G. N., Bak, J. J., & Gottlieb, J. Effects of group discussion on children's attitudes toward handicapped peers. *Journal of Educational Research*, 1977, **70,** 131-134.

Smith, V. H. *Alternative schools. The development of options in public education*. Lincoln, Neb.: Professional Educators Publications, 1974.

Sosnowsky, W. P., & Coleman, T. W. Special education in the collective bargaining process. *Phi Delta Kappan*, 1971, **52,** 610-13.

Spears, H. Kappans ponder typical school procedures. *Phi Delta Kappan*, 1973, **54,** 615-618.

Stern, C., & Keislar, E. R. *Teacher attitudes and attitude change, Vol. 2: Summary and analysis of recent research*. Arlington, Va.: ERIC Resources Information Center, 1975.

Torres, S. (Ed.). *A primer on individualized education programs for handicapped children*. Reston, VA: Foundation for Exceptional Children, 1977.

Wicker, A. W. Attitudes versus actions: The relationship of verbal and overt behavioral responses to attitude objects. *Journal of Social Issues*, 1969, **25,** 41-78.

Young, M. E. Mainstreaming and the minority child: The Philadelphia experience. In R. L. Jones (Ed.), *Mainstreaming and the minority child*. Reston, Va.: Council for Exceptional Children, 1976.

Ysseldyke, J. E. Diagnostic-prescriptive teaching: The search for aptitude-treatment interactions. In L. Mann & D. A. Sabatino (Eds.), *The first review of special education*. Philadelphia: JSE Press, 1973, 5-32.

Life-Long Learning by Handicapped Persons[1]

Arthur W. Chickering[2]
and
Joanne N. Chickering[3]
Memphis State University

Most persons concerned with education for the handicapped have focused on the elementary and secondary school levels and on children whose problems include mental retardation and varied learning disabilities. The dominant orientation toward postsecondary and higher education, implied if not explicit, has been that if a person has the intelligence to do college-level work he or she also has the ability to enter and to manage traditional college and university environments and educational practices. It has been assumed that such persons need minimal help and that institutions need not make any special response to meet their needs. Now, greater opportunities for handicapped persons in the public schools and diverse "mainstreaming" efforts, are likely to lead substantially more handicapped persons to seek postsecondary and higher education than in the past. Furthermore, as we recognize the imperatives of the "knowledge society" and the need for "life-long learning," we also recognize that our concerns for the education of handicapped persons cannot stop at the elementary or secondary levels but must extend to higher education as well. This paper considers changes underway in higher education as they re-

---

[1] A number of Empire State College faculty members contributed examples and insights which substantially strengthened this paper. They were Nat Brod, Fernand Brunschwig, Robert Congemi, George Dawson, George Drury, Jogues Egan, Kurt Feuerherm, Cornelius Gallagher, Lloyd Lill, M. Scheffel Pierce, Rhoada Wald, Wilson Wheatcroft, and David Youst.
[2] Distinguished Professor of Higher Education and Director of the Center for the Study of Higher Education. Formerly, Vice President for Policy, Analysis, and Evaluation at Empire State College.
[3] Counselor, Student Development Center. Formerly, Director, Self-Help Environments, Plainfield, Vermont.

late to the needs of this expanding constituency and respond to new legislative imperatives.

Like major earthquakes, Public Law 94-142, *The Education for All Handicapped Children Act*, and the federal regulations implementing Section 504 of the Rehabilitation Act of 1973 are sending shock waves through the world of education. These waves have been most immediately felt at the elementary and secondary levels, but they will quickly reach the people who are concerned with postsecondary and higher education. Most existing structures will survive, of course, but the shake-up will cause the renovation and revision of educational facilities, programs, and practices.

Although these actions directly concern handicapped persons, they are not isolated events outside the general flow of social change. They are only one manifestation of the strong currents which are fed by political, economic, and cultural tributaries and have created an ever-widening "mainstream," not only in education, but also in jobs, recreation, community participation, and housing. Postsecondary and higher education respond to social changes, albeit slowly. Major changes already are underway which are consistent with the requirements of P.L. 94-142 and the regulations of Section 504. The primary consequences of the legislative earthquakes, therefore, will be to accelerate these changes.

Before considering the changes underway and their implications, we need to recognize some important ways in which postsecondary education and life-long learning differ from elementary and secondary education.

1. Moving from "secondary" to "postsecondary" is also moving from "compulsory" to "postcompulsory" education. That is, the legal requirement for school attendance no longer operates for students and their parents. Other requirements and incentives may create strong pressures to pursue further education, but the response to these pressures is voluntary rather than mandated.

2. As one goes up the educational ladder standardization decreases. With the transition from secondary to postsecondary schooling, the range of possibilities in content, educational processes, and learning environments increases sharply.

3. As persons become older and move through adolescence and young adulthood into the roles and responsibilities associated with family life, settling into a career, and participating in community activities, their aspirations, interests, attitudes, skills, and knowledge become more sharply articulated and solidly crystallized. Individual characteristics become more clearly defined. Consequently, individual differences in motive, learning style, sense of competence, skills, and knowledge acquire a significance they do not have at the elementary and secondary levels.

With the combination of voluntary responses to wide-ranging possibilities and significant individual differences at the postsecondary level, we can reasonably expect each student to assume substantial responsibility for defining his or her purposes; specifying desired kinds of knowledge, competence, or personal development; and identifying appropriate institutions, programs, educational activities, and resources. We also can expect that students will evaluate the learning offered and make judgments about the usefulness and personal significance of the activities in which they have invested time, dollars, and energy. To the extent that these expectations are valid, powerful forces are created for changes in our current systems, changes that give students access to wide-ranging alternatives and help them to establish more integral relations between work and study, living and learning, experience and abstraction, action and theory. Since these forces have been gathering strength during the post-Sputnik years, it is not surprising that the major changes underway in postsecondary and higher education are responsive to them and consistent with the intent of The Education for All Handicapped Children Act and the regulations of Section 504.

The domain of postsecondary education and life-long learning is large indeed. Most of it lies outside the boundaries of two-and four-year colleges and universities. Recent research on adult learning (e.g., Ontario Institute for Educational Studies) asked students to describe "learning projects" they had undertaken during the past 12 months. (A learning project was defined as a "highly deliberate effort to gain and retain certain definite knowledge and skill, with a clear focus, pursued for at least seven hours.") The study found that "out of 100 learning projects, 19 are planned by a professional educator and 81 by an amateur" (Tough, 1976, p. 59). This finding indicates that many more specific and systematic kinds of learning are pursued outside the institutions of higher education than within. So when we limit our focus to changes underway in higher education, we need to recognize that we are dealing only with a small piece of the total action. It is a significant portion of the action, nevertheless, and becomes more so as pressures for credentials and certificates escalate. Furthermore, colleges and universities are major recipients of federal support, completely subject to the Section 504 regulations, and likely to be strongly influenced by the Education for All Handicapped Children Act.

Changes in higher education occur in many ways and at many levels. Typically, change is nonlinear. Within single institutions and across higher education it occurs by fits and starts. Most institutions seem to operate programs on a LIFO principle — Last In, First Out. When a cost squeeze or hiring freeze is initiated, new young programs are usually the first to be nipped in the bud. But sometimes even well-established programs that differ from entrenched traditional practices can be cut down. Monteith College, a unique component of Wayne State University, for example, was eliminated after it had been well underway for about 15 years. Backlash also may occur in the absence of financial pressures, as when a new alternative becomes sufficiently strong to threaten or draw resources from other activities. The dynamics are like those that operate for minority groups: Prejudice and discrimination become apparent only when the group begins to command respect and attention. And, of course, some new programs are put out of business or wither away simply because they are unsound or ineffective.

Often, practices may precede policies. Quite frequently, groups of teachers and students will pursue nontraditional content through innovative educational processes without official blessing by any governing or administrative groups. As these innovative efforts gain widespread acceptance and understanding, policies are developed in which the new realities are recognized. Judgments about change will differ, therefore, depending upon whether we look at official institutional policies, the range of practices carried out under the institutional umbrella, or the numbers of students actually pursuing one or another kind of new program.

Assessing change across higher education is further complicated by variations among types of institutions and among subgroups within the types. Faculty members of selective research universities may not even be aware of curricular content and educational practices that are widely accepted among two-year community colleges. They may not even know that such institutions are included under higher education. Networks of small private colleges may have interdisciplinary and experiential programs that are unknown to most faculty members of large, public, four-year colleges. Within a large complex institution, the engineering school or a department in the natural sciences may have well-developed options for programed learning, personalized instruction, and hands-on apprentice relations that the humanities faculty never hear about. Thus, generalizations about changes underway in higher education are fraught with ambiguity and error.

Generalization is further complicated by uncertainty about a reasonable time perspective. We do not know what rate of change is normal for the complex we call higher education and we do not have any clear standards. Because we are considering the future of education for handicapped persons into the mid-1980s, perhaps it is reasonable to take the mid- or early 1960s as a point of departure. During those years the post-World-War-II and Sputnik eras came to a close. A small but hopeful turn toward peace seemed to have been achieved, and we were relaxing after the cold war tensions and the threat of nuclear war that peaked with the missile crisis in Cuba. It was before the turbulence of the late 1960s that triggered so many changes, some lasting and some already set aside, on campuses across the country.

It also should be clear that we are not suggesting that the changes described in the following sections are dominant in higher education or even in most institutions. Higher education is still dominated by print, lectures, and essay and multiple-choice exams, which are used in regularly scheduled classes on established campuses by full-time faculty members with typical academic backgrounds. Undoubtedly, this condition will continue to dominate for some time. Nor are we suggesting that the changes underway should replace or eliminate those traditional practices. Their significant contributions will be needed for many students and subject matters. Our argument is that they will be increasingly supplemented by the range of activities which have been developing in sophistication and frequency for more than 20 years.

From this perspective, we believe that a strong structure for lifelong learning by handicapped persons will be erected during the next 5-10 years. We are optimistic because the two solid cornerstones that are essential to sound building are currently being set: (a) the simple, but significant, fact that higher education is now taking seriously several principles that are critical for effective education, and (b) the rather remarkable fact that the major changes underway in higher education are consistent with these principles. Furthermore, these cornerstones are being set in a bedrock of current conditions and social changes which will permit little compromise or turning back. Most important for our purposes, both the principles and the changes are highly congruent with our views of optimal conditions for learning and development by handicapped persons.

Educational Principles

One way to point out the congruence between the key educational principles and our views of education for the handicapped, is to make a minor amendment to The Education for All Handicapped Children Act; we suggest the simple substitution of the word "persons" for the words "handicapped children." Some of the key clauses would then read as follows:

"Each *person* requires an educational blueprint custom-tailored to achieve his/her maximum potential."

". . . assurance of special education being provided to all *persons* in the least restrictive environment. . . . "

" . . . assurance of the maintenance of an individualized program for all *persons*. . . . "

". . . assurance of an effective policy guaranteeing the right of all *persons* to a free, appropriate education. . . . "

"The vital provisions . . . toward the guarantee of due process rights with respect to the identification, evaluation, and educational placement of all *persons* within each State are constructively refined. . . . "

" . . . to guarantee complete and thoughtful implementation of the comprehensive State plan for the education of all *persons* within the State. . . . "

"To terminate the all too frequent practice of the bureaucratic 'bumping' of *persons* from agency to agency with the net result of no one taking substantive charge of the *person's* educational wellbeing; to squarely direct public responsibility where the *person* is totally excluded from an educational opportunity;. . . . "

"P.L. 94-142 also orders the U. S. Commissioner to conduct an evaluation of the effectiveness of educating *persons* in the least restrictive environment and orders the Commissioner to evaluate the effectiveness of procedures to prevent erroneous classification of *persons.*"

How many of us would take the position that these educational principles and rights are valid, not simply for handicapped students but for all persons? Before we vote, let us speak to the major problem it presents to those persons who are strongly identified with handicaps. It is the problem that plagues every special interest group and is felt most sharply by those persons who have been treated as "special," "deviant," and "marginal": racial and ethnic minorities, emotionally disturbed persons, and those who are poor as well as those with other handicaps. It is the conflict between (a) supporting general changes that create more favorable conditions for the particular subgroup but still may leave that group at the bottom of the heap, relatively speaking, or (b) supporting principles and actions that are more sharply restricted and clearly targeted and leave general conditions largely unaffected while they improve the relative status and well-being of the special group. Usually, you cannot have your cake and eat it too.

The conflict, as it occurs for education of the handicapped, is set before us directly by Hobbs (1975) in the first two assumptions of his report.

1. *Classification of exceptional children is essential to get services for them, to plan and organize helping programs, and to determine the outcomes of intervention efforts.*

We do not concur with sentiments, widely expressed, that classification of exceptional children should be done away with. Although we understand that some people advocate the elimination of classification in order to get rid of its harmful effects, their proposed solution oversimplifies the problem. Classification and labeling are essential to human communication and problem solving; without categories and concept designators, all complex communicating and thinking stop. We shall address abuses in classification and labeling, but we do not wish to encourage the belief that abuses can be remedied by not classifying. In fact, we shall argue for more precise categories and for more discriminating ways of describing children in order to plan appropriate programs for them, and we shall advocate safeguards to decrease the deleterious effects of classification procedures that can, in fact, have many beneficial outcomes. . . .

2. *Public and private policies and practices must manifest respect for the individuality of children and appreciation of the positive values of their individual talents and diverse cultural backgrounds. Classification procedures must not be used to violate this fundamental social value.*

The richness and vitality of our national life will not be enhanced by increased uniformity, by the imposition on all children of the values and aspirations of the dominant, white, Anglo-Saxon, Protestant majority. To the extent that classification and labeling serve this end, as they sometimes do, they are suspect. Public policy should manifest a commitment to cultural pluralism, to the appreciation of enriching values to be found in the ways of life of people of diverse ethnic and racial backgrounds. Public policy should support the right of the individual to be different, and encourage not mere tolerance but a positive valuing of difference. (Hobbs, 1975, pp. 5-7)

There's the rub. How can we have public policy valuing the *individual* and individual differences, when it is the pressures of *groups*, special interest groups, that determine legislative priorities and funding? And how can we have educational practices that recognize and value individual differences if we begin by assigning students to various classes and categories? It is safe to say that the range of individual differences among all but the most severely handicapped persons on any collection of variables critical for learning (e.g., motivation, intelligence, perceptivity, energy, drive for self-actualization) approximates the range in the general population. How do we nourish that sense of wide-ranging individual differences among handicapped persons and their underlying similarity to others, while we recognize valid generalizations about both their special needs and special potentials?

We do not pretend to have any solution to this fundamental problem. And the difficulty with the amendment is that in the context of hard realities and finite resources, it calls for a *Yes* or *No* response, when most of us would want to vote *Yes* and *Yes*. For we recognize that the basic principles for educating handicapped persons underlie all effective teaching and learning. We recognize that education of the handicapped will be most effective when each educational system, each school teacher, and each college professor recognizes the significance and social value of individual differences.

The basic point here is that when it comes to educational principles, those embedded in the legislation concerning education for handicapped persons are entirely consistent with fundamentally sound principles for the education of all persons. It is interesting that these principles are now moving into the mainstream of higher education. Here are some of the current formulations that are being recognized by increasing numbers of institutions, faculty members, and students:

- Learning occurs more fully and efficiently, and is retained better, when it is rooted in the purposes and needs of each learner.
- Teaching and learning are more effective when individual differences in personal background, prior competence and knowledge, cognitive styles, and rate of learning are recognized.
- Learning is more effective when it occurs at a time and in a place appropriate for the learner.
- Most learning is enhanced when it integrates concrete experience, application, and active experimentation with observation, reflection, and abstract conceptualization.
- Different subject matters, areas of competence, and knowledge require different approaches to teaching and learning.
- Significant learning can occur on the job, at home, and in the community, as well as on the campus and in the classroom.
- Learning that occurs as a result of non-school activities and responsibilities is worthy of academic recognition and credit.
- Evaluation is central to learning; self-evaluation is central to self-directed and life-long learning.
- The educational standards of an institution, a program, or a teacher should be appropriate to the constituencies served and should recognize individual differences within general expectations.
- Credit should be granted for knowledge and competence gained, not simply for time served.
- Institutions, programs, teachers, and students should be evaluated on the basis of the learning that occurs, of the "value added" by participation, not solely on the basis of credits awarded, degrees granted, or student status at graduation.
- College-level learning and degrees granted should encompass a wide range of knowledge and competence: diverse professional and vocational skills; disciplinary, interdisciplinary, area, ethnic, and problem-oriented studies; and major dimensions of personal development.
- Equal opportunity means equal access to higher education.

Prior to the early 1960s, the principles concerning access, individual differences, experiential learning, and evaluation were taken seriously by only a few institutional mavericks outside the general flow of higher education: Antioch, Berea, Black Mountain, Goddard, and Meikeljohn's Experimental College, for example. But now these ideas are becoming accepted by many two- and four-year colleges, supporting major developments that will permanently expand the range of alternatives for higher education.

The annual meetings of the American Association for Higher Education document this change. Their meetings and subsequent reports focus on "Current Issues in Higher Education." The title for the 1970 report, as things began to simmer down after the turmoil of the 1960s, was "The Troubled Campus": It had subsections such as "A Troubled Society," "Conflict and Priorities," "Campus Governance," and "Freedom and Control." But Part Three of that report signaled some of the changes now underway. It was called "New Directions" and included papers on curricular reform, alternative models, and preparing college teachers. By the 1971 meeting, a major shift had occurred toward new students and new alternatives, which has gathered momentum since. Entitled "New Teaching, New Learning," the report has major sections on "New Teaching Contexts," "New Settings for Learning," "Exits and Entrances," and "Reinterpreting Higher Education." "The Expanded Campus" was the theme for 1972, with sections on "Women and Blacks," "Breaking Time-Space Patterns," and "Curriculum and Instruction," which gave attention to improving college teaching. In 1973, "The Future in the Making" dealt with problems of human scale, college environments, new students, and "New Perimeters." "Lifelong Learners" were the focus of the 1974 meetings, and discussions were held on "New Ways to Meet New Needs," with presentations on learning contracts, modules, performance-based education, newspaper courses, open university approaches, and credentialing innovations, such as regional examining institutes and the educational passport. In 1975, "Learner Centered Reform" was the theme and major sections dealt with "Shaping a New Tradition," the "State of the Art," and measuring success. The general orientation of 1975 was carried into 1976 at a more general level under the rubric, "Individualizing the System"; questions of scale, financing, and faculty development were dealt with as they related to the major concerns with access, individualization, experiential education, and life-long learning. The theme for 1977 focused on education and work and carried forward issues of integrating experience and learning, competency-based education, access, and individualization.

This steady flow of speeches, papers, and pronouncements all wrestled in various ways with the educational principles presented previously and others associated with them. As we academics are wont, these papers examine pros and cons, problems and potentials, strengths and weaknesses, and short-run consequences and long-range implications. A few describe actual programs in action.

Now, even the novice Boy Scout knows that smoke does not necessarily mean fire. In fact, large amounts of smoke often signify that, although the potential may be there, there is not much real combustion underneath; the problem may be green wood, limited oxygen, little tinder, or no spark. A good, hot, well-burning fire does not give off much smoke, but it does cook the beans. But most fires start off smoky. Even a raging forest fire begins with smudges from struggling flames and embers.

So the discussions and reports dominating the AAHE reports and higher education publications during the 1970s do not mean that there have been equivalent changes in educational priorities and practices. But changes are occurring which should warm the hearts of persons who are concerned with education for handicapped students.

Program Changes

The changes underway are not only congruent with an integrated set of educational principles, but also are internally consistent and mutually reinforcing. Thus a powerful synergy is at work among new developments. It is not wildly visionary to predict, despite the fact that changing higher education in the past has seemed to be more difficult than moving a mountain or a graveyard, that major transformations will occur throughout higher education during the next 5-10 years. This prediction is strengthened by the two elemental pressures that drive us all: (a) rising costs and reduced support, and (b) reduced numbers of typical college-age students concurrent with increased numbers of older students from diverse backgrounds. In large measure, the innovations underway are responses to these pressures, as well as to reinvigorated educational principles. Since cost and enrollment pressures are more likely to grow than subside, we can look for accelerating change. Their positive implications for life-long learning by handicapped persons are quite obvious.

BRINGING EDUCATION TO THE LEARNER

Undoubtedly the most significant recent move to bring education to the learner occurred with the opening of British Open University in 1971. The addition of 25,000 students doubled university enrollment in Britain with one stroke. Specially prepared courses with high-quality study materials, kits for scientific experiments in the home, and other materials are mailed directly to students. These materials are backed by television and radio programs that enrich the basic materials. New readings and assignments arrive periodically. Some student assignments are computer scored; other papers and essays are graded by tutors who send back written evaluations. A network of regional centers and smaller local units provide settings where students hold group sessions to go over difficult work or meet individually with tutors or counselors.

The system has become an international model. It has given new dimensions to correspondence study and other forms of mediated instruction. The University of Mid-America, operating from the University of Nebraska, Lincoln, is a current U. S. effort to serve a five-state consortium comprising Nebraska, Oklahoma, Iowa, Kansas, and Missouri. Coastline Community College, which boasts "a thousand-mile campus," is an analogous venture in California. Undoubtedly, alternatives like these, which use varied combinations of correspondence materials, television, radio, and human assistance, will continue to grow as increasing numbers of institutions create their own adaptations.

A second development that is bringing education to the learner consists of varied arrangements that extend the campus and put full-time faculty members, tutors, advisors, adjunct professors, and the like in locations close to students. Antioch College, for example, has six campuses and 18 centers across the United States. In addition there are "Programs," which are ad hoc responses to particular needs. In each unit, a small group of faculty members and support staff serve a particular educational constituency, working out objectives, resources, staffing patterns, experiential opportunities, standards, and office locations in response to the needs of the students and community. Empire State College, part of the State University of New York, has Regional Centers in Buffalo, Rochester, Albany, Manhattan, and Long Island. A Regional Center in the Lower Hudson area is half in White Plains and half at Rockland Community College in Suffern. In addition, there is a Center for Labor Studies in Manhattan. Each Center has smaller satellites where one or more faculty members are "on location" in settings like the Martin Luther King Health Center in the South Bronx, Creedmore Psychiatric Center, Sperry Rand Corporation, Bedford-Stuyvesant Restoration Complex, and community colleges and vocational training schools. Further, some faculty members "circuit ride," that is, they meet students in spaces provided by local libraries. The College also has a Center for Statewide Programs, based at its administrative headquarters in Saratoga Springs, which coordinates the work of 9 small units in urban and rural locations around the state, each staffed by one, 2, or 3 faculty members, and supported by additional monies to employ tutors, adjunct faculty members, and field supervisors. Some of these satellites are special purpose units serving particular constituencies; others are general in orientation, responding to a range of students limited only by the resources, tutors, and adjunct faculty members the unit has been able to identify and support.

Goddard College, based in Plainfield, Vermont, illustrates a somewhat different wrinkle with its Adult Degree and Master's Programs. Here, students work in six-month cycles. Each cycle begins and ends with a residency period. During these periods students are oriented to major areas of study and are helped to plan their courses of study for the subsequent months. In planning and carrying out these studies, students make use of resource persons, facilities, materials, and the like, which are available back home, and they maintain periodic communication with supervising faculty members by mail, phone, and occasional personal visits. In addition, the Master's Program has regionally based faculty members who serve as nearby resource persons and bring groups of students together periodically to review progress and share experiences.

Presentation and final evaluation of work accomplished occur during the concluding residency of each cycle. At that time, continuing students also plan their next study cycle.

The weekend college, although not as substantial a change as that signaled by the British Open University and the extended campuses, also is worth noting. An established institution typically sets up a full complement of courses and services, often separately administered and staffed, which are made available Friday evening, and all day Saturday and Sunday. This simple scheduling extension makes education available to students who, otherwise, might be able to squeeze in only a single evening course. Anyone who has struggled to a degree through the slow and painful accumulation of evening course credits at the rate of three or six per semester, will recognize what a boon the weekend college can be.

Other alternatives across the country are similar to these examples. Each aims to make higher education more accessible by reaching out to students, by reducing constraints of time and place; each aims to create conditions in which students can fit learning to their living by undertaking education while continuing to meet the demands and responsibilities of job, family, and community.

Our focus on these new alternatives should not obscure the fact that extension courses, continuing education programs, and evening divisions have served large numbers of students for many years by offering courses in convenient locations, like local high schools. Enrollments in these programs are leaping, and the whole range of possibilities for learning boggles the imagination. Better records of student performance are being kept. The Continuing Education Unit provides a kind of "credit" recognition that, in some cases, allows students to include their studies in degree programs. This solid foundation of continuing education programs and extension courses, with the new alternatives supplementing it, combine to make higher education much more accessible than before, significantly reducing the constraints imposed by limited course schedules, distant locations, and the costs in time, energy, and money required to pursue campus-based instruction.

RESPONDING TO INDIVIDUAL DIFFERENCES

Making higher education more accessible by reducing practical problems of getting to it does not mean that it is more accessible psychologically in terms of students' purposes, preparations, or backgrounds. The developments described in the preceding section are not necessarily accompanied by individualized approaches to what students learn and how they go about learning it. Using heavy reading lists and high standards with students whose last formal education was a shaky high school career 10 or 20 years ago may drive away more potential participants than are encouraged. Conversely, offering superficial generalities to thoughtful adults who have lived through complex realities may have the same result. Offering from 7-9 p.m. in the local high school the same Introductory Psychology or History of Western Civilization course that put students to sleep on campus from 8-10 a.m. may save some driving time and travel costs, but it does not offer much improvement in educational benefits. Sending identical course materials, on fixed time schedules, to be graded against common standards, to 5,000 students the length and breadth of Great Britain, is certainly efficient delivery, but it hardly recognizes the enormous differences among students from Cornwall to the Hebrides and from London to Belfast.

As the thrust of recent research, experimentation, and publication makes clear, higher education is finding that increased attention to individual differences must accompany the admission of more diverse students seeking life-long learning.

Responses vary in complexity and comprehensiveness. They can be described by the degree to which they individualize six major dimensions: purposes, learning activities, rate of learning, standards, structure, and control.

The "individualized major" has been with us for some time and now is a legitimate option in many colleges and universities. This option is useful to persons whose purposes are not well served by an existing predefined major. With the help and approval of a faculty committee, the student puts together a combination of courses or other activities that satisfies the faculty's expectations for breadth, depth, and internal coherence. The areas studied, the combinations, and the sequences are treated flexibly. But if this is the only level of individualization undertaken, each piece of the mosaic is the same as in a more standard pattern. The learning activities, the rate of learning, the standards held, and the locus of control are not typically modified for that individual. But in a large institution with numerous departments and courses, individualized majors provide openings to very creative and functional combinations that meet a wide range of intellectual concerns, career plans, and avocational interests.

"Personalized instruction," "computer assisted instruction," and other alternatives for programed learning and self-instruction typically are offered as supplements to regular courses, and sometimes as replacements. Rate of learning is the principle variable here. Complex programing, which provides branching to fill gaps in required information or skills, or to deal with typical misunderstandings, also recognizes differences in ability and prior learning. Individual differences in purpose or emphasis are not usually recognized. But increased "modularization" of larger courses is underway; it allows students to mix and match smaller units according to individual interests and priorities. Learning activities, methods of evaluation, and criteria for mastery are prescribed. Often, these materials are portable or available to students on demand throughout the day and evening to increase their accessibility. So far they are most numerous in various hard sciences, with psychology and other social sciences running a somewhat distant second. As yet, relatively few materials are available in the humanities. A very large array of self-instructional materials has been developed for numerous vocational training topics. Most, however, have been created by business and industry for their own training programs. As cooperation between the worlds of work and higher education increases it is likely that many of these materials will be recognized as "college-level learning" and baptized with an appropriate number of "credits."

Contract learning offers the most comprehensive and flexible response to individual differences. But whether its potentials are realized depends entirely upon institutional guidelines and expectations, and upon the flexibility and creativity of faculty members and students. A learning contract can recognize very complex combinations of individual variables, or it can ignore most of them. A competent and sensitive faculty member can help a student to clarify the immediate purposes for a particular contract in the light of past learning and future aspirations. Then student and teacher can collaboratively decide upon learning activities that combine concrete experiences, observation, reflection, abstract conceptualization, active experimentation, and application. These decisions can be made to suit the student's learning style and the requirements of the knowledge, competence, or personal development sought. Methods of evaluation and standards for performance can be norm-referenced, criterion-referenced, or designed to measure progress and learning rather than status, or they can include all three. The contract can be tightly structured, setting forth a clear set of deadlines and requirements, or it can be left open, to develop organically as initial learnings clarify the emphasis and directions for future work. It can aim to cover large amounts of ground and levels of difficulty in a short period of time, or the rate of learning can be moderated so a student functions with more deliberation and assurance. The teacher can leave most of the design, implementation, and evaluation in the hands of the student, only seeking enough interaction to make sure of a good beginning and final summative evaluation, or the teacher can carry much of the initiative in laying out the learning activities and prescribing methods and standards for evaluation. A good teacher can use all these possibilities flexibly and openly with students as they carry on the transactions involved in designing and carrying out a learning contract. And when learning contracts are the building blocks, the same sensitivity and flexibility can be used in designing the larger structure of a degree program.

At the other extreme, however, contract learning can be a caricature, a charade, in which individual differences are given less recognition than in a large lecture course. For there are some faculty members who have collections of "boilerplate" contracts and who function much like an automatic vending machine: Put in your dollar and out comes a cold sandwich, a hot cup of soup, or a TV dinner, all nicely prepackaged, and preheated. Often, those boilerplate specials are close approximations to student needs and learning styles, and if the faculty member has a large enough collection and uses them wisely, numerous tastes and dietary needs may be accommodated. So, although we may be restive when an overloaded faculty member uses such expedients, still they may represent a gain in individualization over the batch processing that has characterized so much of higher education in the past.

These varied responses to individual differences in purposes, rate of learning, prior knowledge and competence, learning styles, and self-determination make life-long learning more psychologically accessible. Furthermore, when used in the context of satellites and other extended campus arrangements that temper the constraints of time and place, and when they incorporate a large array of correspondence courses, programed learning materials, television courses, and other forms of mediated instruction, the total adds up to dramatically expanded opportunities.

Individualized education also can be more rigorous. When the methods and criteria of evaluation are set and acted on for each individual, and when each person's work or major program is directly supervised by a faculty member and a committee, then standards for performance can be established which are more difficult than when the student is simply one among 50, 100, or 300 students in a course or a major department. Individualized standards can be especially significant for handicapped persons; sentimentalism and formalism can seriously undermine the kind of tough-minded evaluation they need for realistic educational planning and achievement. We have already experienced the unfortunate consequences of open-admission policies coupled with limited assistance and slack standards.

The point, obviously, is not to drive persons out of the system and away from learning. It is to help students formulate goals that are based on understanding not only their potentials for learning and development but, also, the realities of their current status and the kinds of achievements necessary to develop their potentials and reach their goals. We serve neither the students nor society by glossing over those realities and passing them along to the next faculty member, institution, or certifying agency. The longer the realities go unrecognized, the more difficult the student's adjustment and recovery when they are confronted. We need the kind of stance taken by Annie Sullivan, Helen Keller's teacher, who was caring and challenging, not sentimental and protective.

In this discussion of individualized approaches, we should also recognize that higher education's favorite teaching method — solidly based in our pre-Gutenberg heritage and still very much alive and well — provides great opportunity for individualization. Indeed, perhaps the greatest play of individual differences occurs in large courses where 300-500 students are taught through lectures, textbooks, and final exams. We know how wide ranging the differences are among those hundreds of students: in what they study, when they study, how much time and effort they spend, what they learn, and what they may or may not retain. Perhaps there is no other instructional setting in which students have greater flexibility, autonomy, and freedom from supervision, in which there is less formative evaluation and the criteria for summative evaluation are looser and more abstract. Skillfull well-motivated students who know how to go after their own learning can make good use of such a system, especially if the teacher suggests supplementary readings, pertinent field experiences, and so forth. The problem, of course, is that no student gets much help in deciding what or how or how much to study, and when. So most students do not make such good use of the opportunities. They simply muddle along, conforming as best they can to formal assignments and whatever other signals they can get about what the teacher expects. For this reason, the added alternatives offered by varied self-instructional materials and contract learning represent a real gain.

EXPERIENTIAL LEARNING

There is nothing new or startling about the integral relation between experience and knowledge. For Socrates, the unexamined life was not worth living, and Sophocles observed, "one must learn by doing the thing; for though you think you know it you have no certainty until you try." Webster's dictionary gives "know" as the first synonym for "experience."

Many persons say that "experiential learning" is redundant, that all learning is "experiential." Fundamentally, they are right, but the term as currently used refers to higher education's increased recognition of direct experience and its implications. To define the term, we can begin with Webster's simple definitions of *learning* and *experience*: "Learning — to gain knowledge or understanding of, or skill in, by study, instruction, or experience; . . . *Experience* — the actual living through an event or events, actual enjoyment or suffering; hence, the effect upon the judgment or feelings produced by personal and direct impressions." These definitions are broad enough to include judgment and feelings as educational outcomes as well as knowledge, understanding, and skills. They include the educational processes of study, instruction, and experience, the actual living through of events. And they recognize that both joy and suffering accompany learning. Experiential learning, therefore, is not confined to such events as encounter groups, field observations, travel, or work experiences. And it does not reject the value of lectures, print, films, video or audio tapes, and other forms of mediated instruction or vicarious experience.

The elements of experiential learning have been variously described. Despite minor differences, the level of general agreement is high. Kolb and Fry's (1975) experiential learning theory is a useful formulation. According to the authors, experiential learning occurs through a four-stage cycle:

> Immediate concrete experience is the basis for observation and reflection. These observations are assimilated into a "theory" from which new implications for action can be deduced. These implications or hypotheses then serve as guides in acting to create new experiences. (pp. 119-120)

Experiential learning, therefore, has four ingredients, and each requires a different ability: (a) to enter new experiences openly and fully without bias, (b) to stand back from those experiences, observe them with some detachment, and reflect on their significance, (c) to develop a logic, a theory, a conceptual framework that gives some order to the observation, and (d) to use those concepts to make decisions, solve problems, take action.

Thus, the cycle involves two quite different types of direct experience: active experimentation and hypothesis testing which systematically apply general theories or propositions, and more open engagement in which prior judgements and assumptions are suspended or held in the background. And it involves two quite different cognitive processes: straight-forward recording of reflections and observations related as closely as possible to the direct experiences themselves, unfettered by pre-existing conceptual frameworks that might screen out or distort incongruous perceptions, and, then, analyses of the interrelations among the processes followed by syntheses that suggest larger meanings and potential implications. This approach has some critical consequences when it is well carried out.

1. Experiential learning attaches major importance to ideas. When ideas are used as hypotheses and tested in action, their significance and the attention given to them is greater than when they are simply memorized or left as unexamined abstractions. An idea taken as a fixed truth gives no cause for further thought. An idea as a working hypothesis must undergo continual scrutiny and modification which, in turn, creates pressures for accurate and precise formulation of the idea itself.

2. When an idea is tested for its consequences, it means that results must be accurately observed and carefully analysed. Activity not checked by observation and analyses may be enjoyable, but intellectually it usually leads nowhere, neither to further clarification nor to new ideas or experiences.

3. Reflective review requires both discrimination and syntheses to create a record of significant elements of the experiences. As

Dewey (1938/1963) put it, "To reflect is to look back over what has been done so as to extract the net meanings which are the capital stock for intelligent dealings with future experiences. It is the heart of intellectual organization and of the disciplined mind" (p. 21). For a fuller account of experiential learning, see Chickering (1977) and Keeton (1976).

Consider first the potential of experiential learning for student motivation. An apprentice, intern, or aide carrying responsibilities in an area of professional or vocational interest regularly discovers gaps in competence or knowledge that need filling. A volunteer helping in a community agency sees ways where further learning would lead to more substantial service. A concerned citizen actively tackling a social problem discovers complex issues requiring insights from several disciplines. When such engagements become part of college studies, clarity of purpose and strength of motivation are enhanced at the outset and sustained by the carrying power of the ongoing activities and responsibilities. The rewards that come from bringing order to experiences through reflection and abstract conceptualization, the excitement of seeing knowledge and skills effectively applied, and the sense of making real gains in working knowledge create a self-amplifying process that generates increased energy and commitment for further learning.

It is probably not simply coincidental that the growing interest in experiential learning has occurred at the same time that the percentage of adult and part-time students has increased sharply and open access has brought the increased enrollment of students whose prior learning has not been bookish or academic. The primary motivations of these students usually are in some immediate interest or in the desire to handle a job, family, or community responsibility more effectively. These students do not typically start out interested in ideas for the sheer pleasure of intellectual pursuit. Learning linked to pragmatic concerns and present realities provides a better grip on daily existence that, in turn, creates the perspective and space for more general studies.

Experiential learning also has the potential for improved learning itself. One of the principal ways learning improves is by strengthening the links between ideas and their applications. When ideas are translated into specific acts, when theories of practice are realized through concrete behaviors, and when abstract relations are turned into tangible or visible products, then the result is a strong and integrated system of working knowledge. If objects are not bound to symbols by action they tend to remain fragmented and incoherent; if symbols are detached from reality they remain hollow and limited. The "ivory tower," "absent minded professor," and walled-in university all reflect that detachment which, when carried to extremes, becomes counterproductive. We have almost mimicked the scholarly professor who, when given a choice between going to paradise or going to a lecture about paradise, chose the latter. Strong links between ideas and realities, between rich experiences and conceptual organizers of such experiences, increase retention; the information, principles, varied applications, and knowledge of strengths and weaknesses remain available for the future.

Another potential concerns more effective integration of professional/vocational training and general or liberal education. Barton (1976) put the problem well when he wrote as follows:

> People seem to be able to move smoothly within the system of education and within the system of experience, but not between them. For three quarters of a century, the linking mechanisms enabling one to move from high school to college and from one college to another have been honed through College Board scores, semester credit hours, standardized grading systems and comparable transcripts. At the same time, employers generally have recognized the preparation given by other employers; and if there was any doubt about how well the prospective employee performed before, the answer was there for the asking. But connections remain inadequate at the crossovers between education and employment and between employment and education. (p. 119-120)

Experiential learning can help to establish crossovers between the academy and the world of work. It can provide young persons with pertinent experiences to accompany their diplomas. The simple fact of sound performance on a job is often more important than the extent to which the experiences are directly related to the kinds of employment sought. One of the main reasons employers shy away from young persons is that they are skeptical of their stability, conscientiousness, and willingness to conform to the requirements of responsible functioning as subordinates. They question whether an unseasoned youth will recognize the importance of being on time, meeting deadlines and production targets, taking directions and acquiescing to authority, working harmoniously with others, and exercising initiative judiciously. Once a young person has demonstrated these capacities in one job, his or her future prospects markedly improve. Experiential learning, therefore, has very practical pay-offs for young persons competing for jobs in a tight market.

The crossover possibilities can be especially rich for older persons whose ongoing activities include not only varied responsibilities on the job but, also, at home and in the community. Often these responsibilities, the environments in which they are pursued, the relations involved, and the diverse persons encountered are themselves resources for learning. They offer events and activities for observation and reflection, settings for application and active experimentation. Use of these built-in resources gives immediacy to academic studies and provides continued opportunity for relearning and re-examination. In addition, there are the practical advantages of ready access, established working relations, and convenience.

A final potential is more general but more fundamental. It occurs when students recognize that words in print are not absolute truths but one person's particular organization of reality, and, conversely, that experience alone can be a poor and misleading teacher, a distorted basis for belief. When students recognize that truth can only be approximated, that wisdom rests on multiple experiences perceived from diverse angles in varying lights, refracted through prisms of varying shape and composition, then the cornerstone for solid, active, and continued learning has been set. Then, ideas are held more tenuously and actions are taken with more openness and humility. Then the experiential learning cycle may be built into daily existence, making learning part of living, rather than apart from it and only pursued in and for some institution or credential.

Another innovative dimension of experiential learning, which greatly strengthens its potential contribution, are the procedures for granting credit for learning achieved prior to enrollment — "life-experience learning." Numerous institutions have developed processes to assess such knowledge and competence. The typical approach asks a student to prepare a portfolio describing and documenting prior experiences and the kinds of knowledge and competence which have been derived from them, and relating the prior experiences to current educational purposes or a degree program. In most cases the portfolio is reviewed by a faculty committee which makes a judgment about the amount of credit to be awarded. In some cases, the student may be asked to take an oral or written exam, carry out a performance, or create a product. The total process usually results not only in a statement on the amount of credit allowed, but also a general educational plan for completing the degree.

The task of evaluating experiential learning and allocating credits raises a number of complex issues: How much credit should be granted for what kinds of learning under what kinds of conditions? For traditional practices, these basic issues have been buried by a pile of conventions, such as the Carnegie unit: the typical formula stipulating one hour of academic credit for one hour of class time plus two hours of preparation, each week for about 15 weeks; and the understanding that a typical 3-credit course meets 3 times each week, or once each week for 3 hours. When the Carnegie unit was developed, there probably was a rationale for those particular divisions of hours and weeks and the values assigned to them, but today we can find no one who can articulate that logic, even though curriculum committees and course designers worry mightily about equivalencies whenever a new class offering or alternative is proposed.

The credit system was useful when universities and colleges were few in number and curricular offerings were limited and rigidly defined; a credit hour then had a specific meaning and utility. Today, however, higher education has become so diverse that the value of the credit hour fluctuates widely from institution to institution and one course to another; but the credit hour continues to be used because we have nothing to take its place. Thus, each of us works within this system, developing individual standards on how much can be reasonably expected from students. These individual standards are influenced by the implicit limits of each department or institution. Underneath these conventions the amount of work expected by different teachers, and the work and learning actually accomplished by students, varies greatly from person to person, department to department, institution to institution. The meaning and worth of a degree ranges widely, not only among institutions but within the same institution as well. One reason for the current emphasis on competency-based programs is the concern with that variability and the questions of quality control, credentialing, and equity which are raised thereby. We have come to recognize that "time served" does not adequately represent learning or provide a sound basis for credentials.

The problem with experiential learning is that as yet there are no conventions, guidelines, or even informal understandings to help a faculty member, a department, or an institution to decide how much credit should be granted for what. In the absence of new standards which can be applied to everyone, rationales and rationalizations must be developed in each case, which presents difficult problems of judgment. Yet, these judgments are probably the best we make, precisely because more systematic attention must be given to the process.

There are at least two institutions that focus solely on the credentialing of students and do not offer instruction: The Regents' External Degree Program of the New York State Education Department, and Thomas Edison College, in New Jersey. Both enable students to earn baccalaureate degrees by completing series of established examinations, or undergoing special assessments, which are individually designed.

The increasing momentum of these developments is perhaps best illustrated by the history of the Council for the Advancement of Experiential Learning (CAEL) which grew out of a project begun in 1973. This project coordinated the efforts of 10 two- and four-year colleges concerned with developing ways to assess and grant credit for prior experiential learning. The initial consortium is now an independent association of 250 institutions with two general purposes:

> (a) to foster the development of educational programs that better integrate experiential learning and theoretical instruction and to encourage more widespread use of such programs, and (b) to further

the understanding and practice of assessing experiential learning which has occurred prior to enrollment.

It is reasonable to predict that these two developments in experiential learning — increased incorporation into ongoing educational activities and credit for prior learning — will have a profound effect on higher education and its capacity to assist life-long learning.

COMPETENCY-BASED EDUCATION

In granting credit for prior experiential learning the focus is on the knowledge and competence acquired rather than how it was acquired. Competency-based education shares that orientation in that it gives primary emphasis to outcomes for students rather than inputs from faculties. Competency-based approaches seem to work best when they are used in relation to particular kinds of professional or vocational training, or in clearly defined disciplines in which needed skills and information can be defined and tested. But extending such an approach to complex kinds of professional development and abstract liberal arts and general education objectives is much more tricky. When such objectives are made explicit and concrete enough to be measured they seem trivialized. In addition, students may so focus on the limited samples on which they are evaluated that they neglect the more general kinds of knowledge and competence the samples are supposed to represent. But when objectives are left abstract it is hard to be sure that everyone agrees on what they mean and is evaluating performance according to reasonably similar criteria. Furthermore, the time, effort, tolerance, and patience required for a faculty to navigate safely between the Scylla of overgeneralization and the Charybdis of trivialization is more than most seem able to muster. So it is not surprising that despite a good bit of talk, fully developed competency-based programs in higher education are few and far between.

Alverno College instituted its program in 1971 when the president challenged the faculty in each discipline to justify its contribution to the undergraduate curriculum and the College purposes. That challenge led to the compilation of a list of desired "competencies"; by dint of sustained effort, well nourished by outside support, the framework for a curriculum was developed: eight major areas with six levels of competence defined for each. We report these definitions in some detail because it is the details, not the abstractions, that make competency-based learning difficult.

1. Develop effective communications skill
   - Identify own strengths and weaknesses as initiator and responder in communication situations of the following types, including a variety of audiences: reading, writing, listening, speaking, graphing and reading graphs
   - Analyze written and oral communication situations

- Communicate with clarity of message-exchange in communication situations of the following types, including a variety of audiences: reading, writing, listening, speaking, graphing and reading graphs
- Demonstrate sufficient understanding of basic concepts of at least 3 major areas of knowledge to communicate in terms of them
- Demonstrate understanding of communication as historical process involving development of meaning and form in relation to technological and cultural forces
- Communicate effectively through coordinated use of 3 different media that represent contemporary technological advancement in the communications field

2. Sharpen analytical capabilities
    - Identify explicit elements of a work (A work may be an article, artifact, or process)
    - Identify implicit elements of a work
    - Identify relationships in a work
    - Analyze the structure and organization of a work
    - In the interpretation and/or creation of one or more works, develop new hypotheses, new conclusions, or new relations of materials and means of production
    - Produce a single work that demonstrates facility in 3 types of analysis: elements, relationships, organizing principles

3. Develop workable problem-solving skill
    - Identify the process, assumptions, and limitations involved in the scientific method
    - Formulate questions which yield to the problem-solving approach
    - Apply the problem-solving process to a problem
    - Apply the problem-solving process to a new area of knowledge (area different from problem in Level 3)
    - Design and implement original research project of sufficient complexity to involve direction of or collaboration with others
    - Demonstrate that problem solving is an assumed approach in one's own search for knowledge and one's reflection upon experience

4. Develop a facility for making value judgments and independent decisions
    - Identify own values
    - Demonstrate understanding of philosophy, history, religion, arts, and/or literature as reflection of values
    - Demonstrate understanding of relationship of values to scientific and technological development
    - Make value judgments for which you (a) identify viable alternatives and (b) forecast and weigh consequences
    - Demonstrate understanding of the validity of value systems differing from culture to culture
    - Communicate value judgments effectively, either to defend them or to persuade others to them, and demonstrate commitment to them

5. Develop facility for social interaction
   - Identify and analyze own strengths and weaknesses in group situations
   - Analyze behavior of others within a theoretical framework
   - Evaluate behavior of self and others within a theoretical framework
   - Demonstrate effective social behavior in variety of situations and circumstance — both private and public, within one's own culture
   - Demonstrate effective social behavior in variety of situations and circumstances, beyond as well as on college campus, involving different cultures or subcultures and large as well as small groups
   - Demonstrate effective organizational activity
6. Achieve understanding of the relationship of the individual and the environment
   - Identify environmental components
   - Identify relationships between individual attitudes, beliefs, values, behaviors, and environmental components
   - Demonstrate an understanding of the interaction effects of cultural and physical setting upon individual and group behavior
   - Analyze alternative courses of action regarding a particular environmental problem on the basis of their feasibility, cultural acceptability, and technical accuracy
   - Assess the consequences of various courses of action in regard to a selected environmental problem and the likelihood that goals will be achieved
   - Defend a choice among solutions to a particular environmental problem
7. Develop awareness and understanding of the world in which the individual lives
   - Demonstrate awareness, perception and knowledge of observable events in the contemporary world
   - Analyze contemporary events in their historical context
   - Analyze interrelationships of contemporary events and conditions
   - Demonstrate understanding of the world as a global unit by analyzing the impact of events of one society upon another
   - Demonstrate understanding and acceptance of personal responsibility in contemporary events
   - Take personal position regarding implications of contemporary events
8. Develop knowledge, understanding, and responsiveness to the arts and knowledge and understanding of the humanities (Level 1 of this competence is to be achieved for a total of 3 arts and/or humanities including at least 1 of each)
   - For each selected art, express response and demonstrate understanding of elements, and for each selected humanity, demonstrate understanding of the elements characteristic of its method

- Express response to and demonstrate understanding of one of the arts in relationship to other arts, and demonstrate understanding of an artistic work as an expression of philosophy, religion, or history
- Express response to and demonstrate understanding of the arts, and demonstrate understanding of the humanities, in both cases as expressions of interrelationships between the individual and society.
- Demonstrate understanding of works of other cultures and their impact upon modes of expression of one's own culture
- Formulate independent judgments regarding the relative intrinsic and extrinsic values of artistic or humanistic expressions and persuasively communicate the significance of their worth
- Demonstrate facility of self-expression in one or more artistic or humanistic modes and commitment to their importance

These formulations describe a challenging range of learnings and succeed in capturing the liberal arts and general education values which are shared by many undergraduate institutions. Manuals for training assessment teams carry these definitions further; they explain the general orientation taken, identify additional subheadings, and provide illustrative examples. But there is more to do, as a recent report indicates.

> The continued refining of specific abilities associated with each level is work yet to be completed. It is at the heart of the development of assessment instruments and procedures necessary both for student appraisal and program validation. . . . Competence-based liberal learning in a management context, at this point in time, however, is still held within the parameters of the curriculum that preceded it — namely, the traditional liberal arts disciplines with strong professional programs in education and nursing. Now the entire set of curricular options (context) must be broadened just as the process of education at Alverno has been broadened by competence measured by achievement (CLU's) rather than accumulation of time exposures (credit hours). (Historical development of CBL at Alverno, 1976)

A few other institutions are working in the same direction. Metropolitan State University, in Minneapolis and St. Paul, Minnesota, defines six general competence areas, then, through "Individualized Educational Programs," it helps each student to design a degree plan that relates his or her purposes and the major competencies. The Community College of Vermont has a similar approach. Mars Hill College also has been tackling the competence definition problem with an orientation toward general dimensions of student development, such as those described in Chickering (1969).

All these efforts are promising. They have sufficient momentum so that it seems likely that they will persist and serve as good examples for others. But the task of developing one's own particular combination, which is required if competency-based education is to be taken seriously, remains formidable for most institutions. The generalization of the approach throughout higher education seems likely to be a long and painstaking task.

COMMUNITY-BASED EDUCATION

Community-based education aims to capitalize on these foregoing developments. It extends the campus through relations with other organizations and agencies by using community resources for experiential learning and direct instruction and delivering instruction through TV, radio, printed materials, classes, and individualized combinations. The Center for Community Based Education of the American Association of Community and Junior Colleges uses the following description:

> Course and activities for credit or non-credit, formal classroom or nontraditional programs, cultural recreational offerings specifically designed to meet the needs of the surrounding community and utilizing school, college, and other facilities. Programming is determined with input from the community being served. (Fletcher, Rue, & Young, 1977, p. 12)

Their survey of all two-year institutions in the United States brought a 65% response; 95% of the respondents reported a commitment to community-based education, and 90% of the Boards of Trustees had avoided inhibitory policies, with 60% formally encouraging such development.

Now the description leaves much room for interpretation; many comprehensive community colleges could claim to meet the conditions with their diverse day and evening, credit and noncredit courses. But increasing numbers of institutions are going further; the Community College of Vermont, for example. The average age of their students is 30, somewhat above the national community college average of 27. Only 25% of the students are bound for a degree and 10% are not high school graduates. The College has a network of regional centers that are resources, not only for students, but also for the community and various agencies within it. Counselors from vocational rehabilitation, the Department of Social Welfare, Manpower Training, and various community action groups come with their clients. Each college resource center tries to respond to the needs expressed by organizations and individuals. When the needs are identified, teachers are found in the community or among the college staff. The centers try to build bridges betwen theory and practice by employing practitioners as teachers who then add theory to their own experiences: accountants teach accounting, practicing psychologists teach psychology, lawyers teach law, and welders, welding. The initial interests of students and community agencies may not focus on traditional academic disciplines in the humanities, natural sciences, and social sciences, but studies in other areas often spark interest in more universal human problems and existential issues. Often, the need for more general knowledge and competence becomes apparent as a more specific bit of information and skill is mastered. A growing sense of perspective may reveal the value of studies in history, economics, political science, and human development.

The College has no buildings and few facilities of its own. Office space is rented in central locations and classes are held in available community facilities, often donated or made available at a nominal fee: libraries, church basements, convalescent homes, high schools, corporate meeting rooms, or governmental agency space.

Individual counseling is a cornerstone of the system; counselors make up one-third of the full-time staff. The counselors help students to identify past learnings and remaining gaps and to develop programs that fit their needs. Students who may be having difficulties with their classes are referred to counselors by the teachers. Counselors may be the principal point of interaction for students from half-way houses and drug rehabilitation centers and for students who are mentally retarded or physically handicapped, or have emotional problems or learning difficulties that made success problematic in the past. The counselors respond with whatever resources are at hand; they create student networks of peer counseling, develop telephone hotlines, and arrange for work with individual teachers.

At Adirondack Community College, an enterprising faculty member established a "buddy system" to help the isolated, discouraged, beaten, and unsuccessful students he encountered as he toured rural villages on his motorbike. He discovered the strength of pairs who can study, do field work, and pursue learning together, present joint reports and participate together in class discussions and projects. A collaborative rather than competitive approach to learning results, not only for the pairs, but for the classes, as they share information and skills. In the process, they provide useful human support and encouragement and they help each other to build the confidence and self-esteem necessary to work in other contexts where they are left more to their own devices.

A high value is placed on flexibility and responsiveness. Community-based education aims to avoid large numbers of full-time faculty and resident experts that then call for a curriculum to exercise that faculty, require special facilities, and make the institution difficult to change. Instead, it counts on linking students to human and material resources that are available in the community and on developing those relations so that resources are called upon only as they are needed. The object is to maintain a sound institutional core that can be managed flexibly in terms of staffing, curriculum, and the educational resources necessary to meet the needs of the particular community to be served.

This approach requires close cooperation with local industry, businesses, social agencies, job placement services, counseling and mental health centers, and health professionals. When a range of such collaborative relations has been established, the college not only has built a framework for effective service but it also has created a support network that both holds it accountable and delivers strong political support in case of outside attack.

Faculty Development and Educational Advising

All these major areas of change — bringing education to the student, responding to individual differences, experiential learning, and competency-based and community-based education — call for new faculty roles and responsibilities as well as new kinds of faculty competence and knowledge. None of these changes can proceed effectively without the explicit allocation of time, energy, and funds to professional development activities for faculty members, administrators, and supporting staff. That is one reason why faculty development has been a topic of special concern at the annual meetings of the American Association of Higher Education in recent years. See also the advertisements in *The Chronicle of Higher Education*; there are ubiquitous workshops and conferences on individualized education, personalized instruction, life-long learning, and adult development. Institutes and centers for improving college teaching have sprung up around the country and some long-standing activities have received increased support. The Danforth Foundation alone, under the leadership of Warren Bryan Martin, Vice President for Higher Education, has provided three years of support for the development of five such centers at Harvard, Stanford, Northwestern, Spellman, and Empire State. Microteaching and self-criticism of video-taped lectures and discusssions, which have been staples in training elementary and secondary school teachers for some time, now are being used by increasing numbers of college faculty members.

Once the base of competence has expanded to carry forward these new developments the resistance to them will taper off. Not only will there be a cadre of employed persons with a vested interest in their further development, but the anxieties of others, rooted in uncertainties about their abilities to function in these new ways, will diminish. Many faculty members will then become more open to the satisfactions that derive from these new ways of working with students, and they will value the security of serving an expanding constituency rather than a more limited and stable population of typical college-age students.

These new developments also create pressures for more effective educational counseling. As students have access to different institutions and alternatives, as individualized approaches let them design individualized degree programs and learning contracts, and as experiential learning opens a diverse range of possibilities, the needs for information, advice, and self-understanding increases sharply. High attrition and transfer rates attest to the difficulties of making sound choices, even when the available alternatives were limited. If waste motion is not to escalate as options expand, and if students are to assume greater responsibility for designing their own lifelong learning programs, then resources for personal counseling, educational advising, and career planning are required.

The need for educational advising and counseling is being met in two ways: (a) Colleges and universities are giving increased attention to this function by creating new units or shifting the emphasis of existing services. These changes do not come easily in the context of reduced financial support and budgetary belt tightening, but they are being made. (b) A new kind of institution has come into existence to help students to identify the opportunities for learning that are best suited to them. This institution offers advice and counsel about appropriate institutions, programs, or combinations thereof; it also may provide assessment services so that students can determine their current knowledge and competence in terms of their purposes and the entrance requirements of career programs. The current institutional forms vary from emphasis on evaluating and credentialing, with limited counseling, as at the Regents' External Degree Program and Thomas Edison College, to a heavy emphasis on counseling with limited evaluation, exemplified by the National Center for Educational Brokering in Syracuse, N. Y. Experiential learning fuels the need for a national network of such institutions. This need has been recognized by recent federal support for Educational Information Centers. Within 5-10 years, such centers will be established around the country.

Three Students

Three case histories illustrate how some of these changes come together for individual students.

CAROL[4]

Carol (a pseudonym) was 28 years old and legally blind when she enrolled. Her husband was a middle-management executive and they had a 5-year-old daughter. Carol had studied previously at several institutions and she wanted a baccalaureate degree so she could teach. Certain authors and poets and the fields of anthropology, psychology, and human potentials were her major areas of interest. In collaboration with a faculty member, she designed a six-

---

[4]Palola & Bradley, 1973

month contract for full-time study which included the following major elements:

1. Composition of a portfolio in the form of an intellectual autobiography under the heading, *What I Have Learned Related to What My Program Includes.*

2. Readings in Hermann Hesse, accompanied by a notebook of reflections and a paper examining his ideas in relation to her own thinking about human potentials.

3. The inauguration and development of a human potential group, together with a journal in which the experience and progress of the group were logged.

4. Consultation with the state education department on the requirements for certification, and the identification of appropriate summer courses.

5. Continued participation in developing a community college child-care center.

6. Completing a course in Law and Society at a nearby college.

The faculty member's evaluation of this contract, which is part of a discussion of Carol's achievements, follows:

> Student has radically reconceived the Hesse reading portion of her contract. On the one hand, reflections on Hesse's writings have merged with her thinking about the human potential group study and have contributed to her developing concept of "multiple man". . . . On the other hand, she sees this and kindred reading not as something to be finished here and now, but as a resource to be called upon and used as it becomes relevant to life. She has prepared a short paper in which she expresss these ideas.
>
> Student has kept a log on the human potential group project. She has likewise interviewed each of the members. She has prepared an evaluation of this experience.
>
> Exploration of possible fields of study resulted in a clarification of educational objectives. Teaching social studies in a secondary school is no longer a goal. During the summer term, student followed a course in "Social Movement." The course was taught by T. N. who awarded the student a grade of "A."
>
> The child-care center project for the local community college has reached a stage in planning where it is envisioned to be a joint effort with community-action groups. In the course on Law and Society, the student received a grade of "A."

On the basis of the learning and college credits documented in her intellectual autobiography, Carol received the equivalent of 100 credits of advanced standing; 72 credits were from studies at other colleges and universities, which included an Associate in Applied Science degree; the equivalent of 28 credits were granted for experiential learning. A report on her portfolio said,

> Carol's portfolio was remarkable because of its length, content, thoroughness, and richness. It consisted of five volumes, some 800 pages of documents, poetry, and essays on such topics as planning

and development of a child care center; impressions on her own childhood; the meaning of learnings from secondary schooling; post-high school activities and notes on a study of World War II, reflections on marriage, motherhood, and blindness; her attitude changes from racism to humanism; experiences and reactions to her work as a high-school guidance counselor and social worker in the inner city; her teaching activities and involvement with human services programs. (Palola & Bradley, 1973, pp. 6-7)

Carol's performance shows how a mature, bright, well-motivated woman can make use of the flexibility provided when higher education extends itself to meet the student through individualized contracts and experiential learning. She was given advanced standing that not only recognized her prior college credits but also took account of what she had learned from her experiences at work and at home. Her contract was addressed directly and practically to her areas of intellectual interest and professional aspirations. It included readings, writing, and investigation; it took advantage of appropriate courses at nearby institutions; it made use of ongoing community responsiblities; and it encouraged her to bring together a group of persons who shared her concerns for human potentials.

Note that the institutional processes and arrangements were basically no different for Carol than for other students. True, she used talking books and large type, and it was more difficult for her to get around so that she took a little longer than a sighted person to orient herself to the Learning Center where she met with her faculty member; otherwise it was "business as usual" for the institution and for her.

KEITH[5]

Of course, the new arrangements are no panacea. They often require more initiative, stronger motivation, greater self-discipline, and a sharper sense of purpose than traditional arrangements. "Keith," aged 35, was not as well prepared, energetic, and organized as Carol. On his admission application he wrote,

> I am a totally impaired hearing person but can read their lips if they talk slowly. I lost my hearing when I was one year old through spinal meningitis.
>
> Presently I am working full time in the Post Office here and am active in church work with deaf people. I like to major in Community and Human Service areas with a B. S. degree. Since I am working at the Post Office from 5:00 p.m. to 1:30 a.m. I like to study half time in my free time.
>
> I chose Empire State College because it will give me more flexible time and courses to meet my need to serve my deaf fellows. I am

---

[5]Based on materials and interviews supplied by David Youst, Genessee Valley Learning Center.

aware that there are openings to help my college education at night, but I cannot use them due to my working hours.

Keith brought with him 60 credits accumulated during 1957-1970 in an Associate in Arts degree course from a nearby technological institute. He was assigned to a faculty member who had elementary skill in manual communication. Together they designed a contract with specific purposes:

> . . . to obtain an introductory level knowledge and understanding of the theoretical and conceptual principles of sociology; to increase knowledge about community organizations and services available to deaf people; to develop a degree program outline which summarizes and documents prior learnings and to establish major topics to be studied in future contracts.

To accomplish the objectives related to sociology and community organizations, Keith worked with an adjunct faculty member who was fluent in manual communication. They met on a weekly basis and discussed the content and issues raised in the assigned textbook. In addition, Keith surveyed major community service organizations and wrote a paper answering questions about accessibility of services, the degree to which special needs of deaf persons were being met, and the groups of individuals who were involved in fostering the use of such services by the deaf. Keith worked with the full-time faculty member preparing his degree program, analyzing his prior experiences and documenting his learning achievements.

Keith's contract, like Carol's, included work related to both professional and intellectual interest and to his avocational interest in services to deaf persons. The faculty member and a tutor both had facility with manual communication and experience with other deaf persons. Yet the contract did not work out very successfully. It had been designed to be completed in four months on a half-time basis to yield eight credits. Keith actually took almost 10 months to complete it. He had difficulty studying independently and managing his time; he did not read quickly; and his papers had to be written two or three times. He withdrew for a period and then re-enrolled. Throughout this extended period, his faculty member and tutor kept in touch with him, and he with them, which sustained his courage to persist. But it was not easy for him to manage the multiple demands of study, job, and his academic limitations. In completing the contract he gained an added understanding of the community resources available for deaf persons and, therefore, he was in a better position to offer services through his church. And he did learn some sociology. Keith received approximately two years of advanced standing toward a B.S. degree for the courses he had taken earlier at a technological institute for a degree in printing and for some of the additional learning he had acquired on the job and in the community. But whether he will be able to complete a baccalaureate degree remains to be seen.

The changes underway, obviously, will not necessarily lead us to an educational utopia in which our colleges and universities are populated with model students, singing as they go, and learning by leaps and bounds. We will still have all kinds of students and our success, like theirs, will continue to be checkered.

PAULA[6]

One kind of student surely will persist: the person who is interested in typical academically oriented studies. Such a student can also take advantage of the new developments, although he or she may not feel the need to exploit all the possibilities. "Paula," for example, aged 30, has muscular dystrophy and has been confined to a wheelchair for more than 10 years. She was interested in literature and began by concentrating on Shakespeare. Her contract read as follows:

> Paula will study four areas of Shakespeare's work: his sonnets, tragedies, comedies, and histories. She will study the sonnets particularly from the thematic point of view, careful to chart how Shakespeare deals with the problem of the preservation of beauty. She will note Shakespeare's descriptions of beauty and his developing ideas on how procreation, love, and art may overcome time and mutability. She will read all of the sonnets, and add to her study of them some study of techniques. For instance, Paula should try to establish the dominant variations of the English sonnet form used by Shakespeare, as well as major developments in his use of stanza, line, image, diction, etc.
>
> Second, Paula will study the tragedies: *Macbeth, Hamlet, Othello, Lear, Antony and Cleopatra,* and *Romeo and Juliet.* She will focus on both general and specific questions. She will concern herself with the nature of Shakespearean tragedy, the public consciousness of Shakespeare, his English Renaissance cosmology, the relationship between great and flawed individuals and the society of people around them, etc. Also, she will seek to establish differences among the tragedies; analyzing, comparing, evaluating to find variations and significant development in Shakespeare's ideas and art. For instance, the early work of *Romeo and Juliet* must be compared to the mature work of *Lear,* in order to establish some sense of a living, growing artistic expression.

After describing the work to be done in relation to the comedies and historical plays, the contract continues as follows:

> As for writing, Paula will write four full-length papers on topics selected by her because of interest and significance. She should write on one topic from each of the contract's major sections. Em-

---

[6]From materials and interviews supplied by Robert Congemi, Northeast Learning Center, Empire State College

phasis will be on the completeness of her coverage, the unity of her work, its coherence, its intellectual "soundness," and compositional correctness of expression. . . .

Paula will be evaluated by her mentor through the modes of essay and oral examination. She will be rated on the details of her knowledge in each of the contract's major areas; on her ability to establish major meanings of the texts; on her skill in analysis, comparison, evaluation; on her ability to answer the general concerns enumerated above; and on her skill in utilizing an acceptable level of English expository prose. . . .

Here we have a straightforward study of literature. The contract is solidly designed and challenging. One suspects that the questions posed and comparisons asked for take life in the face-to-face exchanges between faculty member and student. We expect that Paula's reactions and ideas get thoughtful responses which connect with her own particular circumstances. But such work certainly could go on quite well in most traditional settings with a creative and conscientious teacher.

It is hard to estimate the value of the personal contact. In this case it may have had more meaning for the teacher than the student. He commented on their working relationship thusly:

> For our first meeting she came to my office. I met her on the first floor and helped her husband carry her up. I was immediately struck by her naturalness. Being singled out did not seem to bother her at all. She needed a metal clip for her wrist to hold a pencil, but I very quickly forgot about her handicap.
>
> Once we got started I worked with her almost entirely by phone. It was hard for her to get to my office. I thought I might have to go to her place and I did at first but it turned out to be unnecessary. We discussed the readings once every two weeks by phone. She sent her papers by mail and I read them, marked them up, and returned them the same way. She would have someone type them for her and her husband got the books she needed.
>
> Her problems were very much like the problems of my other literature students: getting her ideas clearly onto paper, seeing relationships among the varied works. Basically she seemed to me much like any other suburban housewife who was functioning very well at home, a together person who was a regular student.

Faculty Reactions

Reactions of this kind to handicapped students emerged time and again as we interviewed faculty members in environments in which education was reaching out, creating individualized programs, and using experiential opportunities. The following comment was typical:

> In reviewing the history of our unit I find I have worked with six students who have been handicapped to the extent of requiring extensive assistance through the Department of Vocational Rehabili-

tation. These are J———— S., a paraplegic, G———— D., who has muscular dystrophy, B———— W., who had a severe back injury and has limited mobility, M———— Y. and P———— M., who have serious paralysis from polio, T———— W., with a severe hearing loss. In reviewing the contracts written for these students there is no particular evidence of adaptation to their limitations. The contracts took into account the limited mobility or other problem, but except for having restricted options available the contracts are not different from those for other students. I hope this information will be of some help to you in your survey for adjustment of program to handicapped students. My own conclusion is that we recognize limitations, but they do not appear in the formation of the actual content of contracts. (Pierce, 1976)

Perhaps even more significant were the frequent descriptions of how much the teachers themselves had learned from students who had various sensory, neurological, or physical handicaps. First they commented on the stereotypes they had discovered in themselves. They had experienced awkwardness and embarrassment, wanting to help, wondering how to, but uncomfortable about calling attention to handicaps and asking about limitations. Or they had somehow found themselves speaking loudly to a visually handicapped person, or talking to a companion instead of speaking to the handicapped person directly. Most often they remarked on how much they learned about their own teaching styles, preferences, and prejudices. Most teachers are print oriented, like most of higher education. When a student must learn in some other way and cannot rely heavily on books, the teacher is forced to discover new resources, new approaches that rely on oral and aural communication. This expanded repertoire then becomes available for other students who can learn most effectively in other modes than reading. A teacher who may have come to depend upon a flair for language and rhetoric finds herself tongue-tied with a deaf person. New ways of generating interest and excitement, new ways of creating metaphors, analogies, paradoxes, and the like must be invented. A teacher who makes extended use of graphs, charts, pictures, and diagrams, may find himself confronted by a blind person. The approach, then, must be re-thought and new alternatives developed; however, they turn out to be valuable for other students who, though sighted, grasp certain concepts more readily when models to touch and manipulate are available. Thus teaching persons with various types of handicaps improves the perspective, the range of competence, and the resources faculty members have available for all students.

Implications for Postsecondary and Higher Education

The changes underway in higher education and the educational principles they express strongly support the key provisions of mainstreaming legislation concerning "least restrictive environments," "nondiscriminatory evaluation," "individualized programing," and "comprehensive personnel development."

1. They focus on the students as learner, as active agent, not as a tabula rasa, a vessel to be filled, a lamp to be lighted.

2. They recognize the acountability of colleges and universities to the individual student, the community and the state.

3. They embody a support system concept and provide increased access to a variety of new media, materials, and resources for experiential learning.

4. They recognize individual differences in goals, prior learning, cognitive styles, rate of learning, and standards for performance.

5. They make provisions for individual degree programs and learning contracts that shift the focus from particular shortcomings or handicaps to the person as a learner with a unique combination of strengths and weaknesses.

6. They extend the roles, responsibilities, and competencies of faculty members.

7. They create working relations among faculty members, practitioners, and specialists.

Of course, it will be some time before such changes become sufficiently widespread to be available throughout the United States. Handicapped persons, like most other students, usually will have to select among limited local alternatives, go elsewhere, or not go at all. But these new options are becoming increasingly available and legitimized for the students with sufficient initiative to seek them out. Some of these developments are occurring through the creation of new institutions but most appear in existing institutions as new options are added to traditional practices. Often, the new alternatives are not highly publicized and may be used by only a small proportion of the students currently enrolled..

Undoubtedly there will be backlash and periods of consolidation. Change is seldom linear. But we predict that, by 1984, higher education will have moved directly contrary to Orwell's forecast, that a host of alternatives will be regular and accepted practices in the colleges and universities in the United States.

These changes, the Education for All Handicapped Children Act, and the Section 504 Regulations have more immediate implications that need to be addressed. In some ways it may be easier for postsecondary and higher education institutions to respond than for elementary and secondary institutions. At the elementary and secondary levels, arrangements and practices that already are in place will have to be renegotiated. Postsecondary and higher education will require negotiations, but no renegotiation, simply because at this point there are no pre-existing policies, personnel, or political entities with vested interests in education for handicapped persons. Schools have special education staffs, special facilities and resources, special certification requirements and a panoply of associated structures; colleges do not. Therefore, in postsecondary and higher education institutions, it should be possible to initiate appropriate arrangements based on assumptions of mutual benefit rather than on adversary relations and political trade-offs.

Four major responses are called for. They will not only serve handicapped persons but, also, all other students who would pursue life-long learning. They are (a) broadened professional competence, (b) alternatives to existing practices, (c) services and support for part-time students, and (d) new planning strategies for life-long learning.

BROADENING PROFESSIONAL COMPETENCE

First priority goes to professional development and inservice training activities that help faculty members and administrators to acquire knowledge of and competence in the problems and potentials of handicapped persons and of the individualized and experiential learning programs that meet their needs. Ideally, these activities should occur at two levels. General information and training workshops need to be carried on throughout the institution. These activities would provide a background for more specialized work with individual faculty members and administrators or with departments in which handicapped persons are enrolled. The specialized activities would help those persons and their students to develop individualized programs, identify or create special resources, discover opportunities for appropriate field experiences, and establish criteria and methods of evaluation. Depending upon the size and location of the institution, such assistance might be provided by one or more faculty members with appropriate competence already employed, or by an itinerant teacher who serves several institutions.

While such inservice training activities are underway, the professional competence and resources of each institution also will need broadening. The definition of the faculty needs modification to include practitioners, experienced handicapped persons, mature and competent students, and other community resource persons who can offer technical assistance and special skills. As we move from universal secondary to universal postsecondary education, we must short-circuit our past reflexes whereby, as Sarason put it, "professionals define the problems so professional assistance is required, thus rendering the problems unsolvable." There is no way the expanding need for life-long learning can be met simply by increasing the numbers of full-time faculty members with Ph.D.s who, in the face of climbing student-faculty ratios, also are expected to advance knowledge through research and render community service. Existing faculty roles and responsibilities will have to be unbundled, new roles will have to be developed, and new kinds of professionals and paraprofessionals will need to become members of the academy. These changes will become especially pressing as increased numbers of handicapped persons puruse life-long learning.

This two-pronged effort to broaden professional competence will be carried forward best by small regionally based networks of collaborating institutions. Such networks could undertake demonstration programs stimulated by federal and local project support. In five years there would be sufficient experience with educational effectiveness and related costs so that a regularized basis for support and fees could be established.

ALTERNATIVES TO EXISTING PRACTICES

Most persons teach as they were taught. If the cliché holds true, and it seems to, then alternatives must be developed to existing practices that rely heavily on lectures and exams delivered to large groups. If lectures and exams are the major educational approach experienced through the undergraduate and graduate years, it is unlikely that significant progress will occur in individualized progaming, least restrictive environments, and nondiscriminatory evaluation. If undergraduate and graduate institutions preparing the teachers who staff our schools and colleges do not offer alternatives for learning which are consistent with the teaching practices required later, we are in a catch-up ball game; inservice training will be needed indefinitely. The need for alternatives that permit individualized and experiential learning is especially critical in teacher education programs. But most college and university teachers come from other disciplines and departments; thus such alternatives are needed in those areas as well.

If life-long learning is to be encouraged, then these alternatives must recognize the significant research and theory on the life cycle, adult development, and cognitive styles that are currently available. This literature suggests concepts of individual differences that apply to handicapped persons as well as to others and can help faculty members and administrators to recognize ways in which new alternatives must depart from the methods that are traditionally employed with late adolescents and young adults. Perhaps the most important variable is "locus of control." Systematic and sustained energy is invested in life-long learning when a person has the confidence and competence to articulate goals, pursue them, and evaluate progress. Educational institutions can help students to develop the necessary confidence and competence and the institutions can respond to them when they already exist. But most of our traditional practices were created to respond to younger and more dependent students. That is why new alternatives are required to serve the recurrent educational challenges faced by adults.

The "locus of control" variable is especially important for many handicapped persons who have had to depend heavily on parents, educational institutions, and governmental agencies. There is a critical need for educational practices that help persons to learn how to learn and to develop the ability to take charge of their own existence and continued development. The result can be not only fundamental human and social contributions but, also, significant savings in service costs for a more self-sufficient constituency.

SERVICES AND SUPPORT FOR PART-TIME STUDENTS

Most adults do not want to study full time and many who want to cannot. Handicapped persons are no different but they have additional technical and attitudinal barriers to surmount. Historically, our higher education system has been oriented heavily toward full-time study. A report on part-time students prepared by a Task Force of the State University of New York (Hall et al., 1976) calls attention to some pervasive practices.

> Part-time student access is constrained and frustrated by a complex of problems that begins with admissions and continues through registration and restrictions set for certain courses and programs.
>
> Admission forms typically request high-school transcripts, test scores, and information concerning participation in high-school activities, which are difficult for adult students to obtain and often are useless or misleading. Admissions judgments based on twenty-year-old grade-point averages or rank in class, and on outdated test scores may bear little relationship to the student's current ability to succeed in college. Once-sharp skills may have become rusty and dull, or significant deficiencies in ability or motivation may have been remedied. When adults are asked to take current admissions examinations their scores may be unduly depressed by anxiety and unfamiliarity with tests. The tests themselves, standardized on typical college-age populations and relying heavily on book learning, may not accurately assess the student's ability to learn. Admission processes often require commitment four or more months in advance of the enrollment date, but the family and work obligations of most part-time students often make it difficult or impossible for them to be confident about their situation that far ahead. Moreover, in many cases part-time students who want to pursue a particular course or two are required to complete lengthy matriculation procedures before registering for the courses that interest them.
>
> Part-time students have difficulty obtaining adequate advice and counsel concerning their educational plans, the academic program, and various institutional procedures and expectations. Faculty office hours usually are restricted in number and scheduled during the regular working day. (pp. 2-3)

Problems of access are not solved simply by extending to older persons arrangements designed for typical undergraduates. Admissions procedures, matriculation requirements, faculty availability, staffing patterns, and schedules all need re-thinking if access is to go beyond limited evening-course offerings. But even when problems of distance, time, and institutional arrangements are solved, financial barriers may remain. (The following comments concerning financial aid problems for adult students are essentially those of John Hall, former Dean of Student Services, Empire State College, now president of Goddard College.)

Many adults need financial aid but the forms and systems designed for typical undergraduates do not serve them well. The attitude of many financial aid professionals is one of the greatest obstacles. They refer to older students as "non-traditional" and see them as a "nuisance." Older students are entitled to financial aid but this attitude makes it difficult for them to get what is rightfully theirs.

The first problem is to obtain necessary information and forms. The distribution systems are designed to reach high-school seniors or students already enrolled in college. Little is done to inform adult students about the kinds of financial assistance available. Nothing is done to help them to cope with the numerous forms required by most federal and state programs. High-school and college students can obtain assistance from counselors and financial aid officers; but adults, especially those who go to school outside the usual 9 to 5 working day, have difficulty obtaining such help.

Obtaining the necessary information and forms only positions the adult to cope with more fundamental problems. The formulae used to determine eligibility are designed basically for young, dependent students. Even when they recognize the independent student, they seem to assume a young adult who has a high percentage of effective income available for educational purposes. The middle-income older person with dependents is discriminated against.

Program guidelines themselves often discriminate when they are designed to offer "four years of assistance to recent high-school graduates." Such guidelines obviously do not encourage adult students although, legally, the students are not prohibited from receiving such grants. College work-study programs, another source of financial assistance, also are designed for younger students. Adults employed full- or half-time, or who have substantial family obligations, find it next to impossible to participate, yet large amounts of financial aid monies are allocated to such programs.

Most of the financial aid programs require information concerning the income and resources of parents. Some require parents to sign a petition for the applicant. These requirements are incongruous for 30-50-year olds who may be parents themselves and contributing to their parents' support.

Most aid programs require that a student pursue a degree. Thus, a wide range of educational needs are not accommodated. Many older persons wish to change careers and update their skills. They may have a college degree. But, unless they enroll for another degree, they cannot receive financial aid.

Adult women experience complexities beyond these generalizations. A married woman usually needs to obtain her husband's support. Unless she has an independent income that is not crucial to her family's support, the husband must share his income or be willing to sign for a loan. He must participate in the complex processes of applying for financial aid and thereby admit to an implication of inadequacy as a provider. Only a married woman whose family income falls below the subsistence level can receive financial aid from a variety of federal, state, or private resources without her husband's signature (Durchholz & O'Conner, 1974).

As long as these institutional and financial barriers to part-time study remain, life-long learning by handicapped as well as many other adults will be difficult to achieve.

NEW PLANNING STRATEGY FOR LIFE-LONG LEARNING

All these piece-meal efforts can make a substantial difference. Undoubtedly, change will occur in institutions and agencies in a step-by-step fashion and haltingly. But the time is fast approaching when we need a new strategy for planning and resource management of post-compulsory education and life-long learning. This new approach must de-emphasize the importance of formal schooling, that is, the learning that happens on campuses and in classrooms, which has run away with us during the last 50 years; it will need to re-emphasize the teachers, resources, and learnings that are available on the job, at home, and in the community. So that a balanced approach to education for all is achieved, it will have to address tough questions concerning financial support and resource distribution to avoid disproportionate allocations to special groups.

The concept of individualized education provides a useful starting point. It is only a short step from individualized education to individualized development. We are almost ready to help each person so motivated to create individually designed plans that integrate career aspirations, life-style considerations, marriage, family, and community responsibilities, and to help large numbers of adults to conceptualize, act on, evaluate, revise, and up-date such plans. Many of the elements already exist or are being created: educational opportunity centers; careers and educational counseling centers; evaluation centers for degrees and certificates; individualized educational programs at many two- and four-year colleges and universities; inservice training programs provided by business, industry, and social agencies; educational benefits as part of collective bargaining agreements; and educational passports and credit equivalencies established by state and national organizations.

Moreover, we have the technical capacity to administer and support such individually designed developmental programs. Developmental work by a single institution or in a region could begin tomorrow. Essentially, we would generate a complex matrix of descriptors for each person. An IBM card, not surprisingly, would supply the visual metaphor. Each column would list an array of descriptors under a general heading. Some of the major column headings might be (a) major areas of competence and knowledge currently achieved, (b) further learnings desired, (c) services needed, (d) pertinent resources, (e) achievement criteria, (f) methods of evaluation, (g) prospective deadlines, and (h) estimated costs. Various conversion formulae would help to fit individually designed programs based on such a matrix to various classification and credentialing systems and to various requirements for promotion, job enrichment, transfer, or new careers.

As an institution or a regional learning services center accumulated experience with this matrix, individual educational demands and cost figures could be aggregated to provide a basis for planning, development and resource allocation. (This outline is a simple extension of a proposal by Nicholas Hobbs for planning individualized educational services for handicapped persons.)

Such a scheme may seem fanciful but it may be closer to implementation than we think. Indeed, a localized and limited model could be created in short order. And if we are to develop new planning strategies for life-long learning, some such approach will be necessary.

Perhaps we can best conclude this paper by returning to our proposed amendment to the Education for All Handicapped Children Act and suggest that such an amendment will come to pass. Arrangements for higher education and life-long learning increasingly are bringing education to students and recognizing individual differences; they are focusing more directly on desired competence and knowledge and less on institutional forms and places. Opportunities for experiential learning are helping students and faculty members to respond to strengths and weaknesses that range beyond the verbal skills emphasized by typical classroom instruction. Resources for learning are being developed that recognize the constraints of and exploit the possibilities in the student's daily existence.

Under these circumstances, life-long learning by persons with various sensory, neurological, and physical handicaps will become much like that pursued by non-handicapped persons who also bring various combinations of strengths and weakness. The legislative requirements of the Education for All Handicapped Children Act for least restrictive environments, nondiscriminatory evaluation, and individualized programing will become the educational arrangements available to all persons. Then, the mainstream of higher education will have become broad and deep enough to encompass all the diverse students who would pursue life-long learning.

References

American Association for Higher Education. *Annual Reports*. Barton, B. Learning through work and education. In M. Keeton (Ed.), *Experiential learning: Rationale, characteristics, assessment*. San Francisco: Jossey-Bass, 1976.

Chickering, A. W. *Education and identity*. San Francisco: Jossey-Bass, 1969.

Chickering, A. W. *Experience and learning*. New York: *Change* Magazine and Educational Change, 1977.

Dewey, J. *Experience and education*. New York: Collier, 1963. (Originally published 1938.)

Durchholz, P., & O'Connor, G. Why women go back to college. In *Women on campus: The unfinished liberation. Change* Magazine, 1975.

Fletcher, S. M., Rue, R. N., & Young, R. Community education in community colleges: Today and tomorrow. *The Community Services Catalyst*, 1977, **7**(1).

Hall, J. W., et al. *State University of New York and the part time student*, A report of the University Task Force on Part-time Students. Saratoga Springs: Empire State College, 1976.

Historical development of CBL at Alverno. Alverno College, 1976. (mimeo)

Hobbs, N. *Futures of children*. San Francisco: Jossey-Bass, 1975.

Keeton, M. (Ed.). *Experiential learning: Rationale, characteristics, and assessment*. San Francisco: Jossey-Bass, 1976.

Kolb, D., & Fry, R. Toward an applied theory of experiential learning. In C. Cooper (Ed.), *Theories of group processes*. New York: John Willey, 1975.

Palola, E., & Bradley, P. *Ten out of thirty*. Empire State College, 1973. (Based on materials supplied by George Drury, Genessee Valley Learning Center, Empire State College.)

Pierce, M. S. Plattsburg Unit, College Wide Division, Empire State College. Personal Communication, October 1976.

Tough, A. Self-planned learning and major personal change. In R. M. Smith (Ed.), *Adult learning: Issues and innovations*. Information Series No. 8, ERIC Clearinghouse in Career Education, July 1976.

Organizational Needs for Quality Special Education

James J. Gallagher[1]
University of North Carolina – Chapel Hill

The rapid expansion of special education programs and services in the United States after World War II is worth the attention of a competent educational historian. Because education is widely seen as a mirror of society, major changes in the educational system represent fundamental changes in the American society. We are witnessing today a serious effort to reintegrate handicapped persons in the social mainstream; additional funds are being spent willingly on new programs to further that effort. In the past, a number of observers (Caldwell, 1972, Dunn, 1968, Kirk, 1972) have pointed out, the willingness to spend additional funds seemed to be the price for insuring that handicapped persons would be segregated — in special classes, schools, or institutions — to keep them away from and out of sight of their normal contemporaries.

By 1972, state and local contributions to special education had reached the $2.3 billion level and the federal government had provided $300 million (Hensley, Jones, & Cain, 1975). This accelerated rate of growth was noted by Gallagher, Forsythe, Ringelheim, and Weintraub (1975): From 1966 to 1972, state funds for special education had increased 300 percent.

Such a growth rate created many problems in program implementation and quality, and a major period of reassessment resulted. For one thing, representatives of organized minority groups began to complain that school systems were using special education as a vehicle for excluding minority children from regular education programs (President's Committee on MR, 1970.) Also, research results on the impact of segregated special education programs were less

---

[1]Director, Frank Porter Graham Child Development Center; Kenan Professor of Education and Psychology. Dr. Gallagher was assisted by Ann Ramsbotham in the writing of this paper.

enthusiastic than expected (Garfinkel & Blatt, 1968; Goldstein, Moss, & Jordan, 1965; Karnes & Teska, 1975), which caused special education leaders to review their attitudes toward the value of special classes for mildly handicapped pupils.

Two different strategies have been successful in increasing resources for special education: (a) direct appeals to the legislature and (b) appeals to the legal system. Beginning with P.L. 85-926, which, in the late 1950s, authorized grants to universities for training leadership personnel, a cascade of legislation has strengthened the federal role in helping the handicapped (Martin, 1976). This legislative cornucopia culminated in the passage of P.L. 94-142, *Education for All Handicapped Children Act*, which contains sweeping requirements for total service to all handicapped children. Similar legislative activities at the state level resulted in the consistent increase of resources noted previously. Currently, 46 states have some form of mandatory legislation for the handicapped (Hensley, Jones, & Cain, 1975).

In the past decade, a new set of court challenges on the right to education for handicapped children has emerged. The challengers were clearly stimulated by the Civil Rights movement. Court decisions, such as the Pennsylvania Association for Retarded Children v. Commonwealth of Pennsylvania, Civil Action No. 71-42, established the right of handicapped children to an appropriate education and mandated the state to act to deliver needed services (Gilhool, 1973). More than 20 similar cases have been decided in courts across the country, most in the spirit of the Pennsylvania decision. These mandates have provided a powerful impetus at the state level to increase the resources channeled into special education. Many observers feel that the court actions were the impetus for the recent federal legislation and increased support.

In the midst of special education controversies over mainstreaming and desegregation, and the readjustments caused by the effects of various legislation and court decisions, it is sometimes difficult to sort out essential from extraneous needs. There appear to be two keys to insuring continuous quality in special education: (a) the generation of a comprehensive and widespread support system, and (b) the creation of organizational entities to move innovative and proven ideas and skills through that support system to the consumer. The elements of the support system are noted in Table 1.

The objectives behind these support elements are simple enough: to generate, transform, and deliver valid ideas and skills to the people who provide direct assistance to exceptional children and their families. When such a broad, complex purpose is directed to over 5 million children with diverse special problems across the United States, organizational strategy and planning of considerable magnitude is called for.

Table 1

Elements of the Support System

Research:	Discovery of new knowledge.
Development:	Synthesis of available knowledge to a specific product.
Demonstration:	Illustration and evaluation of exemplary or novel programs.
Personnel Preparation:	The training of new or retraining of experienced professionals or paraprofessionals.
Technical assistance:	Systematic consultation and short-term training resource systems.

There can be identified two other service support systems against which education can be measured. Medicine receives support through the extensive financing of medical school training and research from the federal government, and additional help through the design and development of other medical technologies. In agriculture, the tradition of federally supported university applied research and technical assistance through county field agents has brought forth major and measurable gains in farm output.

Support System Components

Legislation and court actions are highly legitimate tools to generate resources for exceptional children. However, unless we know what we want to achieve with the results of these actions and confrontations, special education will win only hollow victories. It will have acquired the power and resources to accomplish its goals without a clear perception of how to reach those goals. There follow brief descriptions of some of the important components of a comprehensive support system which can provide the essential strategies:

I. RESEARCH AND DEVELOPMENT

One of the most poorly understood components of an educational support system is research and development. In the classroom, the special educator is far distant from research, both geographically and philosophically, and, hence, often downgrades its utility. Nevertheless, a good case can be made that much of the improvement in special education over the past few decades has resulted from research activities. The research most useful to the educator has not been necessarily identified as "special education" research. For example, Freud, Skinner, Brown, Piaget, and Bandura were all scientists who were not noted for an interest in the problems of exceptional children, but their work produced knowledge which has been adapted to the needs of exceptional children by researchers interested in special education. Indeed, in practically all special education programs today, evidence of the ideas of these five seminal scientists can be seen.

The great distance between practitioner and researcher has led to a lack of enthusiasm and support for requests for research funds by powerful political teachers' associations (NEA, AFT). They much prefer to support the funneling of service money directly to the practitioner. Given its limited resources, consequently, educational research often has concentrated on small and inconsequential problems, which has further diminished its influence.

There is a striking contrast between limited educational research dollars and the medicine-agriculture enterprises. Levien (1971) reported that allied health fields spent $2.5 billion on research and development, representing almost 5% of the nation's total expenditure on health care. In agriculture, more than 1% of agriculture's contribution to the GNP is spent on research and development. Until a similar commitment is made in education, we will continue to be disappointed in the trivia and insignificant contributions of research and development.

For educators and decision makers looking for a quick "fix" from research to relieve the chronic problems of special education, there can only be substantial disappointment. Nevertheless, an organized effort to transform and synthesize information already available would be most helpful to them. Certain truths about the research process have not been adequately presented to the general public or the practitioner.

1. Research that will make a significant contribution to our understanding of exceptional children is going to take a long time and require major investments in personnel and resources. Exploring the nature of intelligence, environmental influences on the child and family, the developmental processes of language, and similar questions will require sustained and organized efforts that are measured in years, not months.

2. Research results are like valuable ore or oil removed from the earth: In their raw form they are not useful to consumers. This process of research refinement and transformation does not occur more often precisely because important institutional elements are missing from the support system.

3. It is impossible to predict in advance what research will be most valuable. While one can order curriculum development projects with some understanding of what the end product may be, one cannot say the same for research. More freedom of inquiry for investigators is necessary in knowledge discovery.

4. Research can be irritating to practitioners when it raises questions about well-accepted practices. In the process of the questioning, some of our favorite clinical or teaching techniques may be attacked. Questioning is an important function for research, but the researcher does not expect to win popularity contests in pursuit of this kind of truth.

In a comprehensive support system, research and development money should be allocated to insure both the continual discovery of new knowledge and the greater utilization of old knowledge to continue to improve education.

There has been a disturbing trend, in the past decade, for federal agencies that administer funds for the social sciences and education to specify the research to be conducted with the funds. Such a requirement is not unusual in *development*, where a definitive product like a science curriculum may be needed. However, when the judgment of bureaucrats is substituted for that of scientists on the most useful research to add to our knowledge, the strategy is not productive. A better responsibility for these agencies would be to concentrate their attention on conceptualizing the most effective mix of resources to further organized research, development, demonstration, and dissemination.

II. PERSONNEL PREPARATION

No program committed to continuous improvement can ignore the importance of an organized and well-staffed training program. One of the substantial contributions of federal funding to the field of special education was the early development of grants to universities and colleges, under P.L. 85-926, to train leadership personnel in mental retardation. Later, legislative amendments and extensions expanded those resources to include all areas of handicap.

A substantive result of this funding has been an increase in training capabilities. In 1957, then U.S. Commissioner of Education Derthick reported only 40 colleges and universities with course work in the fields of exceptional children. By 1976, more than 400 such personnel preparation programs were offered (Burke, 1976). The federal funds available for these training programs grew from about $1 million in 1960 to $40 million in 1976. A portion of these training funds are also allotted to state departments of education to distribute for continuing inservice training programs, an always-important aspect of a special education field that grew so fast that it lacked qualified personnel to staff its new programs.

With the emergence of P.L. 94-142, additional major training responsibilities and needs are evident. The strong emphasis on integrating a substantial proportion of mildly handicapped children with the regular educational stream has created urgent pressures for more special training of the regular educational personnel who must deal on a day-by-day basis with the exceptional children. Thus, training support may be reallocated from the more traditional special education training programs to meet the more immediate needs of regular education teachers. Both universities and educational service programs will be called upon to train special *and* regular educators for their new roles.

Periodically, one hears calls for the reduction of federal training funds on the grounds that such continued support may generate a future surplus of special educators. Such projections should be carefully examined. The demand from both legislatures and courts to provide full services for exceptional children implies a continued need for the training of personnel to match the expected program expansion. One of the major unsolved issues is how to maintain quality control and consistency over the more than 400 programs in existence in the field.

III. DEMONSTRATION

A popular component of an educational support system in the 1960s was the demonstration center. The initiative for these centers came from many sources, but the work of Brickell (1961) was particularly influential. In reviewing the influences for educational change in New York State, he identified as most important the direct observation of ongoing successful programs. Further, he showed that the more traditional devices, such as university courses, written reports, or convention presentations, exerted little influence in stimulating educational change.

A number of federal and state agencies provided funds for the establishment of demonstration centers that would show the best in exemplary practices and, it was hoped, encourage other school systems to adopt these practices. Through this osmotic process, it was thought that there would be created a continuing improvement of service programs.

In a classic evaluation study, House, Kerins, and Steele (1969) analyzed the effectiveness of a demonstration program for the education of gifted students in the state of Illinois. They concluded that the transplantation of ideas and practices was limited; in many cases, the visitors observing the exemplary programs could not identify the specific nature of the exemplary aspect of the program, and misinterpretations were not uncommon. Further, the investigators found that local factors within a given school system were much more influential in determining whether a program would be adopted than was the observation experience at the demonstration center site. As a result, the evaluators recommended that demonstration centers be modified to serve as regional support centers and that support center staff spend more time in local school systems where a change or the adoption of new program elements was under consideration.

Demonstration centers still appear to have great usefulness in education, but for a different objective than that for which they were originally designed. Now, instead of using a simple observation model for demonstration, they use careful evaluation and documentation of their programs to demonstrate how effective a program change can be. In short, the demonstration center now is expected to collect data and to review its own program in an intensive-enough fashion to provide documentation for *what* in the program is working under what set of environmental circumstances.

The documentation of environmental factors is very important in special education because it is clear that local conditions will be an important determinant of the success of mainstreaming programs. If we can identify the nature of these local conditions, we will have a better understanding of how well certain innovative programs can "travel."

IV. TECHNICAL ASSISTANCE

No matter how extensive the existing training progams, nor how effective, a different kind of support for individual programs is needed at a local level. This support, which consists of systematic consultation with and advice from professionals outside the program, has been labeled *technical assistance*. Gallagher (1975) defined technical assistance as follows:

> Technical assistance . . . [is] help from an outside agency designed to improve the competence of educational service delivery personnel by increasing their management, organizational or program skills, and/or their available information, relative to their multiple tasks of educational service delivery to students. (p.1)

Outside consultation has had a history of mixed success in local school systems or service delivery programs. The defects seem to result from the ad hoc nature of the relation, the failure to match expert skills with the needs of the school system, and the failure to reach a clear-cut agreement on what the nature of the help will be. A useful technical assistance program at a regional, state, or national level should be organized to meet these major objections.

Lillie and Black (1975) described a program of support to demonstration centers for preschool handicapped children called the Technical Assistance Development System (TADS), which provides some unique elements. Among them are the following:

> 1. A major talent bank through which diverse professional skills and judgments are available to meet the specific needs of the program requesting assistance.
>
> 2. The establishment of a written contract between the client and the deliverer of technical assistance which states in detail what help is to be delivered, under what circumstances, for how long a time, and when the assistance would be considered completed.

3. The use of a needs assessment program to focus attention on the specific felt needs of the client, instead of the judgments of the consultant, as to what needs help first.

The rapid delivery of new ideas and skills seems to be accomplished more effectively through the technical assistance process than such traditional devices as books, journals, and conferences. The dynamic nature of programs for the handicapped demand the continuing organization of support and resources to bring the newest in ideas and procedures on a regular basis to clients in the field.

Barriers to Systems Design

The process of devising a support system to undergird such a complex program is worth some attention. It involves complex political as well as educational issues. An interesting contrast is seen in the attitudes of the private and public sectors toward support services. In the fields of medicine and agriculture, in which research and development can be translated into profits, enthusiasm and support are expressed for the development of new methods and techniques.

In public education, the motivation for improvement often rests upon the desires of individual educators for excellence. Since collective decision making and concentrated power seem necessary for extensive action in education, such individual desires for excellence rarely reach the level of public policy. Indeed, much of the public actions of the educational establishment seem designed often to avoid controversy rather than to seek excellence.

ORGANIZATIONAL ISSUES

Educational research generally has focused its attention upon the learner and the teacher. Until recently, the complex organizational and decision-making processes within the system and between systems have been generally ignored. Iannaccone and Cistone (1974) raised the important questions that still are not anwered:

> The central question "Who governs?" is asked and answered enough to know that subsequent questions along these lines should be differently framed. The question, "Under what conditions, to what extent, and to what set of values do the organized school employee elites control most and least?" should command more attention in the future . . . we need to ask, "What choices should which people participate in, at what levels of educational operations, in which arenas of government, and with what degree of universality or specificity of outcome?" (p. 65)

The chronic nature of their organizational problems has persuaded educators to turn to management and planning experts, professionals who construct alternative futures and consequences in order to maximize potential gains and minimize potential losses in future actions. The direct application of such management tools has been very rare in special education but we should be able to adapt some of the ideas and concepts to some extent.

Argyris and Schon (1974) presented an interesting concept of *Theory-in-Use* — a system of ideas and assumptions that lie behind the observed behavior of a subject (individual or groups). For example, it is not necessary for a parent to be able to state a philosophy of child rearing. The behavior of that parent may be acting out a theory (e.g., children are little adults) although the parent may not be able to verbalize it. An individual or group's operative *Theory-in-Use* might be that any proposal disturbing the status quo is a threat to the person's or group's security; this attitude leads to certain predictable responses to suggested change, regardless of the nature of the change. We can be confident in our projection of the *Theory-in-Use* underlying our subject's responses to the extent that we are successful in predicting those responses: If we are consistently wrong in our predictions, our perceptions of the subject are wrong or incomplete.

Argyris (1973) commented that organizational openness and innovation require decentralization — a sharing of information and decision-making authority that, in turn, requires the effective integration of all parts of the organization. The importance of the local decision maker must be maintained in a complex educational system that also must take into account more comprehensive state, regional, and federal objectives. For complex organizations like the postal service or education, layers of decisions have to be made at each level but with substantial communication among the levels.

The political systems within which education operates display a number of characteristics that conspire against the full or easy implementation of comprehensive support systems. The allocation of resources for education at various levels of government rarely extends to program elements which are beyond the boundaries of the funding unit. In education, much of the existing power and resource expenditures are decentralized (although the trend is toward greater state and federal influence). Given the political control of funding, a local school system is unlikely to invest in a regional consultation effort, or a state to invest in a multistate program, unless there is a direct payoff to the specific system. The design of intermediate units in Texas, Iowa, and New York, for example, was, in some measure, an attempt to make better use of support system strategies for exceptional children. Harmon (1972) made the point that doing what comes naturally will not suffice. He identified the issue as fundamental for the future of society.

> It is the problem that the *microdecisions* of individuals, corporations, and other groups and institutions (e.g., to buy a certain product, to employ a man for a particular task, to apply a new tech-

nological advance) are not combining to yield satisfactory *macro-decisions* for the overall society (e.g., to preserve the physical environment, to provide citizens with suitably rewarding work opportunities, to foster high quality of life). (p. 22)

In other words, we cannot expect the individual decisions made in 16,000 separate school systems to aggregate into an effective state or national educational policy or an effective service delivery or support system. We need to think of organizational strategies that meet our educational macro-objectives.

Another reason that support system components and service programs rarely have been melded into a coherent interacting system is that legislative authority and funding are enacted separately for each specific program. Comprehensive and integrated long-range plans for funding have never emerged. However, the Bureau of Education for the Handicapped in USOE (Martin, 1976) comes closer to generating an overall support system plan because it administers research, development, demonstration training, and dissemination programs — all of the support elements — from one source. The Bureau is able to judge relative need and allocate funds to state, university, and local systems on a comparatively orderly and systematic basis.

PLANNED CHANGE

One of the serious deterrents to the development of a comprehensive support system has been the lack of a mechanism that could integrate its diverse components into a competent plan. The increasing popularity of planning at all levels of government, and the consequent increase in sophistication about devising long-range plans, provides an important missing link. Resources for the support system components must be allocated according to a systematic and rational long-range plan. That plan must be acceptable to educational leaders and given widespread visibility, with opportunities for comment from personnel at all levels of the special education community. Friedlander and Brown (1974) stressed the point that our current interest in organizational theory and operation has been stimulated by our burgeoning interest in planning.

> We are saying that current OD (organization development) theory and practice may be a small part of a rich, broad, far-reaching relevant field of planned change. As the wider field is legitimized and developed, and as broader technologies and theories are developed these will feed back into and enrich the field of OD. (p. 336)

If such a comprehensive support system were organized, it would become clear that the system could be of service to far more children in the local schools than just those who are eligible for special education services. Special educators, because of the unique problems with which they work, often have provided techniques and materials that were useful to a much broader constituency than exceptional children.

If the history of educational change offers a lesson, it is that instant change or the adoption of a support system across the entire education enterprise is an unlikely occurrence. If the program of support services described here were established through special education, it would be a demonstration vehicle that, by establishing its usefulness, could create a demand for the expansion of its capabilities to all of education. Until then, special educators should make a strong effort to include regular educators in various demonstration, training, and research activities to the mutual benefit of both groups.

How can the components of such a support system be coordinated to move ideas, materials, and services to consumers through the thicket of diverse educational enterprises? By overcoming such barriers as geography, tradition, concerns about professional status, and communication issues.

The Translation of Knowledge to Action

A major function of a comprehensive state or federal program focusing on the problems of handicapped children should be to facilitate the tranformation of research findings into practical application. This function can be organized through the appropriate choice of organizations and institutional settings that commit themselves to this purpose.

The complex problems of transforming basic scientific information more quickly into useful service programs rarely have been addressed successfully. It has been traditional to expect a 30-to 50-year lag (Levien, 1971). This pace is clearly unacceptable, given our current needs; therefore, specific strategies must be designed to speed the translation of new knowledge and skills into practice.

Knowledge, to be transformed properly, must move through several stages. Barriers to the movement from one stage to another may delay the entire process. The work of Skinner (1953) and Bandura (1971) in, respectively, behavior modification and social learning theory, exemplify two major areas of basic research which, despite their soundness and relevance, have yet to be adapted systematically for the full benefit of exceptional children. A lag of 25 years or more from knowledge to application can be noted for Skinner's work, although behaviorally oriented programs are increasingly being developed for handicapped children.

How can we reduce this lag between research and application? Table 2 lists the five stages through which basic research is translated into broad application.

Table 2

Stages of Applying Results from Basic Research to Programs for Handicapped Children

Stages	Characteristics
I. Discovery of Knowledge	The generation of new facts, ideas, and concepts about children or social systems or instructional strategies.
II. Knowledge Applied to Target Group	The knowledge available through Stage I must be applied to some groups of exceptional children and families by scientists interested in their special problems and familiar with the basic knowledge fields.
III. Generation of Systematic Programing for Exceptional Children	Knowledge gained in Stages I and II must be organized and specially designed to meet specific needs, problems, developmental levels, etc., of target groups of exceptional children. This material needs to be developed and applied in special environments where *control* is possible.
IV. Field Test of Programs	The merits of the special programs or procedures developed in III have to be proved in realistic situations. These trials demonstrate utility to local educators. Adequate evaluation is often missing from casual field testing and must be incorporated in effective programs.
V. General Applications to the Field	After sufficient field testing or trials of the procedures or programs have been conducted, there *is* general acceptance and adoption in the field. At this point, the new knowledge, now transformed completely, becomes known as "common sense," or normal operations.

Stage I, *Discovery of Knowledge*, is the conduct of basic research itself. Limitations in the funding of basic research projects provide a substantial brake to progress because one cannot transform knowledge that does not exist.

Stage II, *Knowledge Applied to Target Group*, is the application of research ideas and concepts to specific target groups. It is in this area that organizations like research and development centers, demonstration programs, and technical assistance programs can be most helpful. They can take many concepts derived from basic research and explore their applications to specific target groups of handicapped children.

Stage III, *Generation of Systematic Programing for Exceptional Children*, shows a major shift in the direction of applying knowledge. Past knowledge is synthesized and organized to provide more effective learning experiences for children. Often, however, educational materials or procedures originate not from the synthesis of research but from the accumulated experience of successful teachers. When the link between the research and practitioner is missing, the resulting product loses its conceptual base, although it may have some practitioner utility in a narrow sense.

Stage IV, *Field Test of Programs*, involves the application of newly developed procedures or materials to a more typical educational service delivery setting. While it is necessary to develop and evaluate new materials in special settings, their widespread use is possible only when they have proven to be successful in typical settings.

Stage V, *General Applications to the Field*, is the translation of new practices and ideas into materials and methods which can be used in the field. Unless there is some type of general adoption of the new ideas or products, the entire process has become an intellectual exercise with little immediate impact.

SPEEDING TRANSITION FROM KNOWLEDGE TO ACTION

Movement through the five stages is anything but systematic or automatic. Some of the barriers need explication so that systems improvements can be considered.

Role of the Special Education Practitioner

All the stages arrayed in Table 2 assume a receptivity in the ultimate consumer, the special education practitioner, to new ideas and products. Without the profit motive noted previously, and with the virtual assurance that new programs and materials will imply a need for retraining and increased effort, the assumption of receptivity and eager practitioner acceptance needs careful reevaluation. Often, the practitioner has been observed to stare owlishly at a new product or instructional kit that was designed and developed with great cost in resources, and then to remark, "Who asked for this?"

There are several ways for the consumer's ideas and judgment to be incorporated into the complex sequence discusssed earlier so that greater acceptance can be anticipated. In Stages I and II, comprehensive needs assessments of practitioners can reveal the major issues or concerns bothering them. Although such concerns (i.e., "I cannot control my hyperactive children") have to be translated into usable research language (i.e., "Teacher needs modeling techniques for reducing aggressive outbursts of behaviorally disturbed children"), communication between consumer and scientist can be fruitful. The consumers may not know how to frame the questions or design the experiments, but out of their experience they can surely identify the major and urgent educational issues that need attention.

In Stage III — Development — even more crucial sets of decisions that are important to the practitioner must be made. The investment of major resources in the generation of curriculum should not be considered without a careful analysis of the practitioner's own needs and suggestions, either by the developer or the agency planning the investment. In some areas, highly sophisticated technical work has generated white elephants of imposing proportions because there was little felt need for the results among practitioners.

In Stages IV and V, which deal with field test and adoption, there is an obvious role for the practitioner whose first-hand experience with the application of the new progam will determine feasibility as well as efficacy. There has been a rising trend to employ practitioners in all the roles discussed, but the central issue is that the lack of practitioner effort at the end of the five stages remains an impressive barrier to easy adoption.

A number of other barriers impeding movement through the stages deserve attention. One consistent strategy to overcome these barriers has been to design overlapping institutional entities. For example, the inclusion of curriculum specialists in research centers or researchers in field test or demonstration sites provides a mix of interdisciplinary talents that can facilitate transitional activities between stages.

BARRIERS BETWEEN STAGES

Stage I to Stage II: General Knowledge Applied to Exceptional Children

What is needed for managing this transition is a cadre of scientists schooled in the basic disciplines of psychology, education, medicine, and others who are interested in the problems of exceptional children and can attack these problems with the skills and concepts of their respective disciplines. Centers, institutes, and demonstration centers can provide interdisciplinary homes for such scientists.

Stage II to Stage III: Research to Program Development

Perhaps the most difficult transition to accomplish is between Stages II and III. Too often, program development emerges not from a systematic review of research but from the unevaluated experience of the individual teacher or clinician. Often, too, the researcher and practitioner are physically separated from one another — the researcher in the university, the teacher or clinician in a school or center. Whether the program is developed in a university center or a center in a major school system or institution, the staff should have a mix of practitioners and scientists who will devote significant time together to the synthesis and application of ideas.

Stage III to Stage IV: Program Development to Field Test

During the initial stage of development, it is important for developers and practitioners to have administrative control over the group of children to whom the new materials and procedures can be applied. Without such administrative control, the developer cannot actually test the needed variety of applications and formatively evaluate them under controlled conditions. Once developed, these innovative materials and procedures can be applied to other groups of exceptional children who are more representative of communities throughout the nation.

Stage IV to Stage V: Field Testing to Implementation

The full implementation of successfully field-tested materials depends on factors that are usually beyond the control of the development team. Sometimes, local political decisions are necessary; cost factors always play a major part in the decisions. There remains much to be learned about facilitating this last move in the sequence.

A Proposal

If we are correct about the usefulness of support systems to special education, then how can we design organizations and make decisions to insure their support? If our *Theory-in-Use* (Argyris's term) about public decision makers is that they will respond to rational arguments for support systems, even in the face of consumer demands for more direct service, we are liable to meet an unpleasant surprise. A far more likely *Theory-in-Use* is that the politician will make the decisions that will result in happy constituents (at least in the short run) and, consequently, will increase her/his prestige.

How can long-range goals be implemented in a society that is governed by decision makers with short-range goals? It is possible to so structure legislation and programs that the established needs of the decision makers are not interfered with. If the decision maker is forced to make a public choice on the allocation of scarce resources between research and direct service, the results are almost a foregone conclusion. Service will win every time. However, if the research is part of a formula written into the law, then the lawmaker need not make such a choice. He or she can relax and give some of the long-range objectives a chance to be implemented.

A number of years ago in the state of Illinois, for example, a law was in force by which the guardians of persons residing in mental health facilities were charged a nominal fee, which was placed in a Mental Health Research Fund. Because this provision was in the law, the politicians could afford to ignore complaints about it; and laws are notoriously hard to change. The lesson is clear: If we wish to have a comprehensive support system for special education with an adequate balance between service, on the one hand, and research, development, technical assistance, and training, on the other, then we must have such a balance specifically mandated.

A reasonable guess at what is being spent for special education each year in the United States is approximately $3 billion. If our rule of thumb for support services expenditures were about 15%-20% of that total, then we should be spending nationally about $450-$600 million on research, demonstration, development, and adoption. If we further agree that tradition and capability would place 75 per cent of the responsibility for supporting such an investment on the federal government, then we should identify between $340-$450 million for Congressional appropriations to support services. When one puts together the various existing federal programs to which funds of this dimension are allotted, the current sum for support systems can be seen to fall far short.

Such percentages might be used as a measure to judge appropriate requests for funds for support functions, but more specific actions should be taken also.

The implementation of P.L. 94-142 may well produce one of those painful paradoxes all too familiar to education: At the precise moment that there should be a major investment in the support mechanisms of development, demonstration, training, and technical assistance, these mechanisms may be shunted aside in favor of total preoccupation with service delivery. We need to initiate some steps to prevent this possibility, otherwise P.L. 94-142 will not be successfully implemented. One condition we might work for is to provide a bonus of 10 per cent over the regular P.L. 94-142 funds to each state that establishes support system components in accordance with an approved state plan. This bonus might be made available for the first three or five years only.

Increases in P.L. 94-142 funds could have an escalator clause for support services for the first five years. For example, every $100 million increase in service funds should automatically add $30 million to the support funds administered by that agency. In this way, the expansion of direct services would not outrun the support services, as it does in normal circumstances. Such a model would encourage states to set aside support money in their own funding. In most instances now, states rarely spend more than 1-2 per cent on support services, which is completely inadequate for program improvement.

The proposal for set-aside funds for needed but not popular program components is not without precedent. Challiner (1974) proposed a similar scheme in the biomedical field to avoid the ebb and flow of research dollars that are so damaging to long-range plans. He suggested a biomedical research trust fund tied to gross revenues of the health industry or to a percentage of health insurance premiums. A prestigious advisory commission would oversee the general research directions of the trust fund.

Summary

The proposition presented in this paper has been that quality special education services depend upon the development of a comprehensive support system, the dimensions of which are already familiar to us. Our manner of allocating resources for special education has not allowed us, so far, to carry through program designs which, professionals generally agree, are needed. Therefore, modifications of additions in the strategy of resource allocation must be explored vigorously so that this period of service expansion will not be accompanied by a deterioration in the quality of services and consequent disillusionment in this unique special educational enterprise.

References

Argyris, C. *On organizations of the future*. Beverly Hills: Sage, 1973.

Argyris, C., & Schon, D. *Theory in practice*. San Francisco: Jossey-Bass, 1974.

Bandura, A. *Principles of behavior modification*. New York: Holt, Rinehart, & Winston, 1971.

Brickell, H. M. *Organizing New York State for educational change*. Albany, N.Y.: State Education Department, 1961.

Burke, P. J. Personnel preparation: Historical perspective. *Exceptional Children*, 1976, **43**, 140-43.

Caldwell, B. The importance of beginning early. In M. Karnes (Ed.), *Not all little wagons are red*. Reston, Va.: Council for Exceptional Children, 1972.

Challiner, D. A policy for investment in biomedical research. *Science*, 1974, **186**, 27-30.

Dunn, L. M. Special education for the mildly retarded: Is much of it justifiable? *Exceptional Children*, 1968, **35**, 5-24.

Friedlander, F., & Brown, L. Organization development. In M. Rosenzwerg & L. Porter (Eds.), *Annual review of psychology*. Palo Alto, Calif.: Annual Reviews, 1974, 313-42.

Gallagher, J., Forsythe, T., Ringelheim, D., & Weintraub, F. Federal and state funding patterns for programs for the handicapped. In N. Hobbs and others (Eds.), *Issues in the classification of children: A sourcebook on categories, labels, and their consequences*. San Francisco: Jossey-Bass, 1975.

Gallagher, J. Technical assistance and the nonsystem of American education. In M. C. Reynolds (Ed.), *National technical assistance systems in special education*. Minneapolis, Minn.: Leadership Training Institute/Special Education, University of Minnesota, 1975, 1-11.

Garfunkel, F., & Blatt, B. *The educability of intelligence*. Reston, Va.: Council for Exceptional Children, 1968.

Gilhool, T. K. Education: An inalienable right. *Exceptional Children*, 1973, **39**, 597-610.

Goldstein, H., Moss, J., & Jordan, L. *The efficacy of special class training on the development of mentally retarded children.* Cooperative Research Project No. 619. Washingon, D.C.: U.S. Office of Education, 1965.

Harman, W. Long range societal futures. In M. Marien & W. Zeegler (Eds.), *The potential of educational futures.* Worthington, Ohio: Charles A. Jones, 1972.

Hensley, G., Jones, C., & Cain, N. *Questions and answers: The education of exceptional children.* Denver, Colo.: Education Commission of the States, 1975.

House, E., Kerins, T., & Steele, J. A test of the research and development model of change. *Educational Administration Quarterly*, 1972, **8**(1).

Iannaccone, L., & Cistone, P. *The politics of education.* Eugene, Ore.: ERIC Clearinghouse on Educational Management, 1974.

Karnes, M. B., & Teska, T. A. Children's response to intervention programs. In J. J. Gallagher (Ed.), *The application of child development research to exceptional children.* Reston, Va.: Council for Exceptional Children, 1975.

Kirk, S. *Educating exceptional children* (2nd ed.). Boston: Houghton-Mifflin, 1972.

Levien, R. *National Institute of Education: Preliminary plan for the proposed institute.* Santa Monica, Calif.: Rand Corp., 1971.

Lillie, D., & Black, T. TADS — a systematic support system. In M. C. Reynolds (Ed.), *National technical assistance systems in special education.* Minneapolis, Minn.: Leadership Training Institute/Special Education, University of Minnesota, 1975, 23-37.

Martin, E. A national commitment to the rights of the individual — 1776-1976. *Exceptional Children*, 1976, **43**(3), 132-34.

Skinner, B. *Science and human behavior.* New York: Macmillan, 1953.

President's Committee on Mental Retardation. *The six hour retarded child.* Washington, D. C.: U. S. Government Printing Office, 1970.

Some Economic Considerations in Educating Handicapped Children

Henry M. Levin[1]

*Stanford University
and
Center for Economic Studies*

Although many children with marginal physical, neurological, sensory, cognitive, and psychological impairments have been integrated systematically into traditional schools, and special provisions sometimes have been made for those with more severe conditions, substantial numbers of handicapped youngsters are not provided with appropriate educational alternatives. In fact, parents often have had only the choice of institutionalizing a child, if the family had adequate financial means, or keeping the child at home. States and local governments have varied considerably in their willingness to recognize the special educational needs of handicapped or, more euphemistically, exceptional children.

Recent court decisions and policy actions, however, have mandated drastic changes in the educational status of the exceptional child (Burt, 1975; Buss, Kirp, & Kuriloff, 1975; Gilhool, 1976; Kirp, Kuriloff, & Buss, 1975). (a) The courts have established the right of every child, including the most profoundly handicapped, to an appropriate education and provided legal recourse if any child is excluded from the educational system or is limited to inappropriate educational arrangements. (b) The stigma created by the unnecessary labeling and separation of handicapped students also has been attacked on both legal and educational grounds, and a major effort has been marshaled to place such children in the educational mainstream with regular students to as great a degree as possible (Birch, 1974; Reynolds, no date, 1975, 1976).

These changes raise a number of interesting questions for both educators and educational policy; and they also have important economic implications. For example, how much funding should be al-

---

[1]Professor of Economics, School of Education.

located to the education of exceptional children and how should it be provided? How should educational services for exceptional children be organized, and what are the resource implications of mainstreaming?

In this paper, I reflect on these questions in suggesting the economic considerations for addressing the emerging changes in the education of handicapped persons. I am noticeably at a disadvantage, however, because we lack a useful data base on such matters as the costs of different levels of educational results for particular types of exceptional children as well as clear models of instruction for them. Even the very diversity of educational needs that characterizes the population of exceptional children tends to argue against generalization. However, it is possible to discuss some principles of resource use and financing to establish an equitable and efficient policy for improving educational services for this often-neglected population.

Two major issues are addressed in the rest of this work: (a) What economic criteria might be used to set out requirements for financing educational services for exceptional children? (b) What are the resource and economic efficiency considerations of different modes of reorganizing educational services for this population?

Financing Educational Services for Exceptional Children

How much financing should be allocated to educational services for exceptional children? Before evaluating different approaches to answering this question, a brief discussion on the nature of the issue is in order. It is generally agreed that the handicapped population has special educational needs in excess of those of other children, but how much more funding is needed to support these special requirements? (This question is addressed for the economically disadvantaged population in Levin, 1973, 1975c.) At least one answer is provided typically by persons responsible for special education: "Whatever is required to do the job." Unfortunately, this answer lacks validity for the following several reasons:

1. General agreement is lacking on the specifics of what should be accomplished for any particular category of exceptional children, what is the best way to do it, and what are the resource requirements. That is, while it is generally acknowledged that some of the additional services for exceptional children must be highly specialized and provided by appropriately trained educators and health professionals, it is not clear precisely what is the relation between the use of additional resources and improved educational outcomes. That, generally, the relation is positive is certainly plausible, but the precise nature of that relation is not clear either theoretically or empirically without further specification of desirable outcomes and experimentation among different organizational and resource ap-

proaches. Accordingly, there is no easy method of judging "whatever is required to do the job"; such a judgment is highly subjective and differs with each evaluator.

2. Even if evaluators could agree on an answer, the judgment would ignore the fact that other needs are always in competition for public resources. Of course, this view of financing — "whatever is required to do the job" — tends to assume that among the competing claims for resources, few are as meritorious as special education for exceptional children. It does not take very much inquiry to find that advocates of housing programs for the poor, nutritional programs, preventative health programs, and programs for the aged, mentally ill, and orphans all have equally humanistic reasons for obtaining whatever is required to do the job in their domains. Each set of advocates does not recognize that from a social perspective the use of scarce resources must be balanced among a variety of meritorious programs; the satiation of all claims is not possible. In essence, a greater allocation to one need is necessarily a sacrifice of what might have been accomplished in the other domains with that allocation. (For a discussion of this dilemma in the area of health expenditures, see Fuchs, 1974.)

The difficulty of balancing competing claims for resources is seen in the following example: Persons who are faced with kidney failure must have their blood cleansed periodically through a process of renal dialysis. The cost for a typical patient ranges from about $5,000 a year for self-administered dialysis in the home on a weekly basis to over $20,000 a year for hospital-based dialysis of the same frequency. Even if we were to estimate the per patient annual cost at $10,000, the cost still would be rather prohibitive. Now, let us say that for every 100 children needing special educational services there is one patient needing renal dialysis; $10,000 would provide a life-sustaining service for one person with kidney failure or $100 in additional educational services for each of the 100 exceptional children, or $1000 more for each of 10 severely handicapped children. How can a choice be made between these two highly meritorious and competing claims?

To be sure, not all claims for public support are equally meritorious. For example, the highly controversial B-1 bomber is estimated to cost almost $100 million each, and the total budget for this weapon system is estimated at over $100 billion. Thus, the purchase of each B-1 bomber is equivalent to sacrificing $1,000 in educational services for each of 100,000 handicapped or exceptional youngsters or dialysis treatment for 10,000 chronic kidney patients. The problem is that without a political mechanism to earmark resources for handicapped children and kidney patients or other needy populations rather than questionable weapons programs, it is simply academic to argue for "whatever is required" without considering the choices that must be made among large numbers of deserving public programs.

Since not all programs can be satiated with resources, the economist attempts to apply a criterion whereby the last dollar spent on each public activity yields a contribution to the welfare of society that is equal to the last dollar allocated to any other public activity. Indeed, the purpose of so-called cost-benefit analysis is to ascertain which combination of activities yields the highest benefit-to-cost ratio. Needless to say, there are enormous information gaps in making these calculations; the political process does not necessarily take them seriously as the sole basis for allocating public funds, as is reflected in the relatively large expenditures for high-cost weapons that seem to be based more upon the political power of the Pentagon and the weapons' industries than upon any systematic public comparison or setting of priorities. However, some type of systematic framework does give a guideline for making claims on the public budget.

3. A final argument against the "whatever is required" approach is that the process of educating a given child over a given time period is likely to be characterized by decreasing marginal returns in relation to expenditures. That is, an additional $1,000 per child expenditure is likely to yield less of an improvement in educational outcomes for those children who already are supported at high levels than for children supported at lower levels. At some point the use of additional funds provides very little improvement in educational results; alternatively, when some reasonable level of expenditure is established, small gains in educational benefits become very costly.

The lack of agreement on the specifics of educating exceptional children and the absence of a concrete empirical base for the relation between program characteristics and particular educational results for different children tend to inhibit attempts to ascertain how much funds should be allocated for special educational programs. Also, the fact that these programs must compete for funds with all other public activities means that the criterion of "whatever is required" is not very useful because all claims for support must be balanced against social benefits in making allocations. Further, there is hardly unanimity from expert to expert on what is needed. Finally, the prospect of diminishing marginal returns for such investments suggests that so-called saturation levels of services are likely to be rather wasteful of resources. What criteria, then might be used to establish estimates for appropriate social investment in the education of exceptional children? At least three approaches are worth exploring: investment, exemplary progam, and separate component.

INVESTMENT APPROACH

One way of calculating the minimum investment that society ought to make in educating exceptional children is to estimate the social resources that will be spared ultimately if the competencies of this population in caring for its own needs are upgraded. That is, without appropriate education and training, many of the handicapped clearly would not be able to care for their own needs and, thus, would require continuing social resources over their lifetimes. In contrast, many exceptional children can be educated to care for all or some of their personal needs as well as to become partially or fully self-supporting through regular employment or in so-called sheltered workshops (provided by government and charities).

From a benefit-cost perspective, we should be willing to invest in the education of exceptional children at least the present value of the amount that would be "saved" in future social resources or earnings from productive employment by virtue of this investment. These benefits can be estimated by ascertaining to what degree a particular approach to special educational programing can develop among handicapped persons independence, reductions in institutional care, the ability to contribute to self-support or higher earnings, and the need for less medical care or other types of assistance.

What costs are associated with inadequate training and education of the handicapped? (a) There are the costs that are incurred for institutional or home care for persons who lack the necessary physical or mental requisites to take responsibility for their own daily needs. Whether this care is met through demands on public and private agencies or families, they represent a cost to society. (b) There is the loss of productive employment and earnings which might have been obtained by handicapped persons had the educational system assisted them in acquiring appropriate education and marketable skills. Clearly, for many exceptional children the possibility of productive employment depends crucially on the amount and quality of education and training that they will recieve. (For cost-benefit analyses of vocational rehabilitation programs for handicapped adults, see Bellante, 1972, and Conley, 1969.) (c) Educating handicapped youth may decrease future social costs by serving as an investment in preventative health and maintenance. For example, an exceptional child who is provided with training in handling his own needs may also become less prone to accidents and illnesses related to his handicap. That is, acclimation to the world through the educational process may reduce the contingencies that are suffered by persons without appropriate education and training. For this purpose, even the knowledge of one's limitations and capabilities acquired by exposure to the mainstream can be helpful. There may be other costs to society that are saved by providing appropriate instruction for the handicapped.

The amount of the investment in the early education and training of handicapped persons should be at least equivalent to the present value of the savings in future resource costs and additional earnings resulting from the instruction and care. A simplified illustration demonstrates this principle.

Let us suppose that appropriate education and training permit a handicapped person to care for himself in a community residential setting rather than to be cared for in an institution. Let us also assume that the value of the social resources that would be saved by reducing this person's need for institutional care is about $5,000 a year. This estimate is probably conservative; it is based on the view that some of the services that would have been provided in the institution still will be required in the home. We now can ask the question: How much should society invest in the education and training of this person to obtain a reduction in future social costs of $5,000 a year?

This question reduces to a normal investment problem in which we need only know the alternative productivities of investments to make the appropriate calculation. (See Becker, 1964, for greater detail on the methodology and its application.) These alternative productivities can be summarized in interest rates that represent the returns on different investments. Suppose that a reasonable rate of return on investment is 5%; that is, for every $100 of investment, we would expect a return of $5.00 a year. Clearly, then, an investment of $100,000 with an annual return of 5% would be required to yield $5,000 a year. Alternatively, at an interest rate of 5%, the savings to society of $5,000 a year would be worth an investment of $100,000. At an interest rate of 7%, such an annual savings would be worth an investment of somewhat less, or approximately $71,500.

This illustration certainly has been oversimplified but it indicates how society's minimum investment in the education and training of the handicapped can be calculated: Future cost savings associated with different amounts and types of special education are estimated and converted into investment values. This technique has been used to estimate some of the costs of inadequate education for various segments of the general population in order to ascertain whether additional public expenditure for compensatory education would be a worthwhile investment for society (Levin, 1972). Such estimates are important criteria for evaluating educational and training expenditures for the handicapped.

A number of important problems also should be kept in mind, however. First, the knowledge base required for assessing the future impacts of educating the handicapped is very tenuous. Although in certain cases it is possible to demonstrate the direct connection between appropriate training and reduced future costs of care or higher probabilities of employment, the precision of estimating savings is necessarily limited by the very diversity of the handicapped population, the associated diversity and complexity of instructional treatments, and the uncertainty about future developments. Further, even if such estimates could be made with great accuracy, they would not include many other benefits that might result from the education and training. For example, if good educational and training programs also were to increase the mobility of the handicapped and the variety of experiences that they could undertake, the increase in their welfare would not be reflected in the benefits calculated by this methodology. Likewise, the satisfaction of being able to care for one's own needs rather than depending upon professionals or family surely must be an important benefit to the handicapped which would not be accounted for. Thus, this approach only provides an approximate lower boundary rather than a rigid guideline for determining appropriate allocations.

EXEMPLARY PROGRAM APPROACH

A more traditional determination of the financing requirements for educating exceptional children is the exemplary program approach. (A prominent example can be found in Rossmiller, Hale, & Rohreich, 1970; see also Bernstein, Hartman, & Marshall, 1976.) The logic behind this method is that although there may be a lack of unanimity in the overall theory and concepts for educating particular types of exceptional children, there still may be exemplary programs that are characterized by a high degree of success in obtaining useful educational results. That is, exemplary programs might be identified as those providing a good environment and appropriate skills, attitudes, and proficiencies for their students. The task, then, would be to carry out rigorous analyses of the ingredients necessary for such programs, and the associated costs of the ingredients. (See Kakalik, Brewer, Dougharty, Fleischauer, & Genensky, 1973, for estimates of educational expenditures by type of handicap and source of funding.) If the total costs were within reasonable boundaries (i.e., those affordable within current budgetary limits) the exemplary programs would become the basis for making financial allocations. That is, the costs of those programs would provide the criteria for ascertaining how much to allocate to special educational programs. If the costs of such exemplary programs were too high to be met with present budgetary resources, a number of alternatives would present themselves.

1. An examination could be made of program ingredients and components in order to see which ones might be omitted or modified to lower expenses with the least harm to the program. For example, our studies of preschool programs suggest little evidence to support the view that there must be one adult for every five children, as some public programs require. Evaluations of similar programs with 10 children to each adult show no observable differ-

ences in what is happening to the children. In fact, at least some preschool centers with a ratio of one professional to each five children seem to provide less care for each child because of the greater tendency of the adults to interact socially with each other to the neglect of the children. Also, there is sometimes a problem of adults' getting in each other's way in such an intense environment. However, the difference between a 1:5 or a 1:10 professional to child ratio is the difference between a program costing about $1,000 per child and one costing $2,000 per child. (In programs for handicapped children, the average teacher:student ratio has been estimated as about 1:6; see Kakalik, Dougharty, Fleishauer, Genensky, & Wallen, 1974). That is, because the cost of personnel dominates the total budget, changes in the personnel requirements have profound effects on total costs. Other areas of cost reduction include the substitution of volunteers and parents for paid personnel and the substitution of paraprofessionals for professionals, where such modifications are feasible.

2. Programs can be maintained at the exemplary level by excluding some potential students from services. This choice does not seem desirable in the case of handicapped children, and it may be illegal now as well. In the case of public child-care programs, however, the practice of exclusion is precisely what has been followed. In general, the costs of such programs have been maintained at high levels with substantial personnel requirements in terms of both the ratios and qualifications of the employees. Accordingly, the existing public budgets for child care are adequate to provide services for only a small proportion of the eligible population, and large numbers of children have been excluded systematically.

3. Arguments can be made for larger allocations based upon the view that exemplary programs represent inviolable standards. Unless such a view is supported by strong evidence that it is impossible to modify program components or that very high investment returns will be found in the reduction of future social costs, it is not likely that such a strategy would be very effective. However, it is certainly an alternative that should be considered if social justice demands it.[2] I would caution against a doctrinaire use of this approach in an environment where the claims for program needs and effectiveness are difficult to document, and where there is often a tendency for professionals to confuse their own needs and desires with the rather independent issue of appropriate social policy. As I

---

[2]Rawls (1971) has referred to this claim as redress for "undeserved" inequalities: ". . . in order to treat all persons equally to provide genuine equality of opportunity, society must give more attention to those with fewer native assets and to those born into the less favorable social positions. The idea is to redress the bias of contingencies in the direction of equality" (pp. 100-101). Of course, the question of how much redress is at issue rather than the principle itself.

have noted in the case of compensatory education for the disadvantaged, increases in educational expenditures always have shown evidence of benefits to educational professionals in terms of smaller class sizes, greater employment prospects, and higher salaries. Unfortunately, the evidence on benefits for disadvantaged children has been considerably less substantial (Levin, 1974b).

A final thought on the exemplary program approach is its conservative nature. At a time when the methods of educating exceptional children are being revised and provisions must be made for persons previously excluded, it is not clear that an existing exemplary program is appropriate for the changes in the substance and organization of special education that seem to be in the offing. Accordingly, it might be useful to talk about a third approach to determining support requirements for educating the handicapped, the component approach.

PROGRAM COMPONENTS APPROACH

The advantage of the program components approach is that it enables the construction of cost estimates for alternative methods of educating handicapped children, in contrast with the exemplary program approach which is heavily biased toward the cost requirements of existing programs. There are two reasons for the concern with constructing cost estimates for future programs rather than focusing on exemplary approaches within the more traditional framework: (a) The emphasis on mainstreaming handicapped children to as great a degree as possible in regular schools and curricula requires some significant departures in designing education and training programs for the children. (b) The inclusion of handicapped youngsters who were previously outside the educational system clearly will have implications for program requirements and costs, particularly if this formerly excluded group is characterized by types and degrees of handicap that require considerably different instructional components than are required by the more traditional handicapped clientele.

There are many ways of constructing program requirements and then estimating their financial implications. In general, one would set out first the domains or objectives that are desired for particular classifications of the handicapped and the alternative program components to fulfill these goals. Then the program components would be analyzed for their resource ingredients: types and amounts of personnel, materials, facilities, and other elements (Levin, 1975a). Finally, the costs of these inputs would be estimated and aggregated into cost estimates for the different groups of children. Depending upon the numbers in each population to be served and the estimated costs of the "appropriate" type of education and training for each, one would be able to suggest financing requirements.

Of course, it is possible to divide program components in many ways. One categorization that may be useful is to think in terms of three sets of program components for each type of handicapped child or each child: (a) program components for meeting *standard* instructional objectives which other children of similar age and mental capability must satisfy; (b) program components for meeting special objectives that are specific to the nature of the handicap; and (c) program components for meeting learning-contingent requirements.

The standard program components are those that would provide the normally expected educational experiences, skills, and proficiencies that all children receive. To the degree that handicapped children are capable of benefiting from the program, the components can be thought of as standard instructional objectives. Moreover, they might be offered in the mainstream portion of the curriculum for exceptional children. That is, to a large degree it might be possible for these objectives to be achieved through the inclusion of many of the handicapped in conventional instructional settings.

The program components for special objectives include those that are necessary for meeting the other educational and training needs of the handicapped.[3] For example, they might include the specialized resources necessary to instruct handicapped children in the care of their personal needs, in motor skills or speech skills, or in physical mobility for the sight-impaired, and so on. These components represent education and training requirements that are normally in excess of those needed by nonhandicapped children and thus, they are necessarily added costs.

Finally, there may be a set of learning-contingent needs that normally are not found in instructional programs. They include specialized transportation, medical attention, prosthetic aids, and other ingredients that are necessary for the successful implementation of the standard and specialized program components. Although these particular components are not instructional in themselves, they are requisites to effective learning within the other two components.

The advantage of this partitioning of program components is that it enables a rather clear analysis of the basis for higher costs for educating exceptional children; each component can be explained on the basis of its usefulness in addressing the needs of the handicapped. The standard instructional aspects can be integrated into the mainstream program components. Thus, it would be possible not only to show why the costs must be greater for educating and

---

[3]Program components beyond those required for standard instruction are outside the regular costs of instruction and are "excess costs," according to Kakalik et al. (1973, 1974).

training the handicapped than students without exceptional needs but, also, to trace those cost patterns to particular program ingredients. Too, such a division of program categories is useful for examining cost differences among the educational offerings for different groups of handicapped persons and even for individuals with different levels of need within any particular exceptional category. Finally, the program components approach can be used in the formative period of program change when research and development and trial and error are necessary to construct alternative methods for providing educational services for the handicapped, and cost analysis can be a part of this evaluation of alternatives.

PAYING FOR EDUCATING THE EXCEPTIONAL CHILD

Who should pay for educating exceptional children, and how should the revenues be provided? In general, actual policy probably will be established by precedent as well as political and legal actions. There are some rather compelling reasons for requiring uniformity of policy within states, however. In many states, the courts have rejected disparities in support for education which are based upon differences in the wealth of local educational agencies. The argument is that the states are responsible for providing education for youth (according to their constitutions), and local wealth or income is not a reasonable basis for determining the allocation of funds for educating youngsters in different localities. Thus, differences in educational expenditures should not be a function of differences in local wealth in a state school system. (See Coons, Clune, & Sugarman, 1970, for one of the original arguments for this criterion.)

It would seem that this argument should apply with even greater force to the education of handicapped youth. That is, the resources that are provided for educating and training such youngsters should be a function of their particular needs and the means of the state as a whole rather than of the local wealth and willingness of local citizens to assist their handicapped populations. First, the handicapped always represent a relatively small portion of the total population, and it does not seem wise to leave the fulfillment of their needs to the vagaries of voters who may not set a high priority on special educational programs that do not affect their own children. The incentives to provide appropriate levels of support may be absent for reason of pure selfishness or because local voters are hardly concerned about educating the handicapped when the future investment returns to the larger society of such benefits are widely diffused among other governmental units and families.[4] That is, the

---

[4]Weisbrod (1964) made a similar but more general argument for the tendency of localities to underinvest in education.

future costs to society of neglecting the handicapped may not be perceived as affecting the present taxpayers in a given locality. Accordingly, there is reason to believe that local decisions are not socially optimal but are based largely upon the level of local resources and the ability of the small minority of families of handicapped children to convince their neighbors of the needs of adequate programs for such children.

Second, the existence of disparities among local educational agencies in the financial and program provisions for the handicapped probably result in the high mobility of families with exceptional children. That is, if one school district provides excellent educational programs for sight-impaired youngsters while another does not, there would be an incentive for families with such children to move from the latter district to the former. Over time, we would see a clustering of particular types of handicapped youngsters in the districts providing the best services for them, which would either raise the costs to the local taxpayers or lead to the dilution of services. The potential inundation effect also would reduce a particular district's incentive to offer exemplary programs for the handicapped because they would attract outsiders and, thus, educational costs would be increased for the entire district.

A good case can be made, therefore, for complete state and federal responsibility for financing the education of the handicapped and for uniform financial provisions within each state (Bernstein et al., 1972). States would not necessarily operate the programs; it is probably still most feasible for local school districts of adequate size to use state financing to maintain their own special education offerings according to state support and local needs. Of course, one might ask why the same logic of uniform financial support within the states does not apply among states. The answer is that the logic might apply, but there is no simple mechanism or strong precedent for initiating a federal policy to take complete responsibility for the handicapped. In contrast, the constitutions of the states do set such a precedent within their boundaries.

Thus, based upon the financial allocations that were discussed in the previous section, it would seem reasonable for the states to finance special educational programs for the handicapped on a uniform basis using federal funds as well as broadly derived state taxes. In essence, the state would set out diagnostic requirements for the classification of children for financing purposes. Local educational agencies would provide an accounting of the number of children in each category, and the state would provide financial aid according to the numbers of such youngsters and the amount of spending that was established for each type of handicap. Such an arrangement could distinguish among the degrees of handicap as well as making adjustments for multiple handicaps and their special requirements. Amounts also could be adjusted for the differences in resource costs in the various parts of the state, that is, where it is apparent that a given set of resources has a higher cost in some areas than in others. Such an approach is relatively simple if the classification and financing requirements for each type of child can be agreed upon. Obviously, these factors are crucially dependent upon how special educational services are provided and organized — the subject of the next section.

Provision of Educational Services for the Handicapped

How should educational services be organized for and provided to their clientele? This is another area in which economic analysis may provide some insights. Economists have a long tradition of studying how goods and services are produced and attempting to ascertain the most resource-efficient methods of production. Within the field of education, a rather large number of attempts has been made to explore the production of educational services with specific attention to the relative efficacies of alternative strategies and their costs. (See Levin, 1976, for a review of these efforts.)

It should be borne in mind that a general economic analysis is not a substitute for empirical research and concrete knowledge on the relations between the educational needs of the handicapped and methods of fulfilling those needs. Rather, economic analysis assists in setting out a conceptual framework for the collection and analysis of data on the production and organization of such services. In this context, four particular aspects are reviewed that reflect on the provision and organization of education and training for exceptional children and that may assist in constructing this research framework. They are (a) educational vouchers for the handicapped; (b) some implications of mainstreaming; (c) screening and diagnosis, educational needs, and implementation; and (d) effects of special education on school organization.

EDUCATIONAL VOUCHERS FOR THE HANDICAPPED

Since the middle 1960s, there has been much discussion about transforming the educational system from one that is operated and financed by the government to one that is financed through the use of tuition vouchers.[5] Under such a plan, parents would be given tuition vouchers for use at any school which was approved by the state to provide educational services. It is suggested that all kinds of new schools would arise to compete for the student vouchers, and

---

[5]The original voucher proposal, made by Milton Friedman (1955, 1962), was reinforced by the discussion of a government-sponsored experiment in the Center for the Study of Public Policy (1970). An early evaluation of that experiment is in Weiler et al. (1974). For a critical analysis of the voucher approach, see Levin (1975b).

the effects of such competition would be a healthy increase in the productivity and variety of experiences in American education. The federal government has attempted to foster experiments to assess these claims, but it has been found difficult to create an educational market for purposes of an experiment of only a few years' duration.

At first glance, educational vouchers appear to be an ideal alternative for providing services for the handicapped. Highly specialized services would be covered by tuition vouchers of a specified amount for any particular handicap and level of disability. Vouchers could be used by parents to purchase educational services from either private entities or public schools. Hence, parents would have alternatives, and the supplier of choice would have to attempt to satisfy the needs of the particular child in order to maintain enrollments. Accordingly, educational institutions that were competing for students would have incentives to provide highly individualized and attractive services, and probably, a very high degree of specialization in particular types of disabilities would emerge in the schools.

It is precisely this aspect of vouchers which is now deemed to have negative consequences for the handicapped, however. No matter how refined and productive the types of services offered within such specialized schools, it is likely that students will be categorized and segregated in environments with other students who have similar handicaps. Thus the very operation of a voucher type of arrangement with its attendant specialization will tend to create a very high level of stratification both among the handicapped and between handicapped and nonhandicapped students. In fact, the traditional arrangements for the handicapped have often furthered these children's disadvantages by labeling them and separating them from other children. (See Levin, 1975b, for a critique of vouchers in the more general educational setting.) Separation has tended to stigmatize handicapped children in their own eyes as well as in those of outsiders, and to create a situation of dependence on the specialized services that are provided. Thus, rather than providing preparation for increasing participation in the larger society, such segregation has tended to create permanent subcultures. Accordingly, recent movements in the education of the handicapped have started from the premise that it is probably more useful to think in terms of the maximum integration of the handicapped within the mainstream of education with supplemental services outside the mainstream provided as needed.

The use of educational vouchers for satisfying the educational and training needs of handicapped or exceptional children seems to be fraught with both positive and negative aspects. The positive aspects relate to the advantages of a market-type mechanism for maximizing the choices of parents and the incentives to providers to fulfill the needs of the handicapped students. But, the disadvantages are that the voucher mechanism is likely to segregate and label handicapped students in ways that are not likely to contribute to their integration in the larger society. It may be more useful to ask under what conditions educational vouchers might be used while integrating exceptional children into the mainstream of education.

SOME IMPLICATIONS OF MAINSTREAMING

The concept of mainstreaming refers to the maximal integration of handicapped children into regular school programs. It does not mean that for all handicapped children the standard school program is entirely suitable. What it does mean is that it is possible for a very large number of these children to benefit from at least some instruction in the standard school setting when other specialized needs are addressed by the provision of ancillary services. In some cases, regular classroom teachers can be provided with training and other information that will enable the handicapped child to take virtually all instruction in the conventional classroom. In other cases, the handicapped children might receive some educational services outside of the normal classroom either during or outside normal school hours, but the bulk of instruction will be in the regular setting. Only in the cases of greatest specialized need would an exceptional child be removed completely from the conventional classroom setting.

Mainstreaming requires a rather intricate mechanism for screening and diagnosing handicaps as well as prescribing and delivering the appropriate types of educational services. It also requires an elaborate set of alternative services in any school district, given the very large variance in type and severity of handicaps. In this context, it may be useful to consider the possibility of using "partial" vouchers when the organizational logistics and scale in a specific school district are inappropriate for providing high-quality services. For example, a particular type of handicap may be so rare in the population that the school district will not have adequate numbers of such children to justify even the minimum personnel and facilities requirements to serve them. By providing vouchers for such services, it may be possible to induce other public or private agencies to offer the services and to obtain economies of scale by drawing on several school districts for children with the specific handicaps. Another possibility would be to arrange for the state or county government to address those needs that cannot be met by local schools.

One of the most fascinating aspects of mainstreaming is the potential for using regular students to assist handicapped ones. While most school resources are fully employed, there is one that is heavily underutilized — the energies and talents of the student body itself. Students represent an enormous reservoir of resources which can be used to satisfy their own human needs to feel useful and serve others while providing additional capabilities for the schools to enhance their educational offerings. Although students have been used in a few programs to tutor other students, systematic attempts are rare to use their vast talents for helping each other (e.g., Melaragno & Newmark, 1971). As a part of the regular school program, nonhandicapped students could assist handicapped ones in both instructional tasks and other needs. By selecting such "assistants" on the basis of maturity, temperament, and other qualities, the schools could attach honor and prestige to such activities. In fact, each handicapped student could be assigned to a small group of students who would cooperate in providing the companionship and assistance that was required.

Not only would this arrangement enable the schools to provide more services for the handicapped child, but it would make other contributions as well: The exceptional child would become more fully integrated into the daily student life of the school rather than be in the organizational mainstream alone. Using older students as "big brothers or sisters" would encourage other students to interact with the exceptional children and help with their special needs. At the junior high school level and beyond, the student peers of the handicapped children could volunteer or be assigned to such activities. This arrangement could have great potential for enhancing the social integration of handicapped children into the regular school setting as well as creating an additional educational resource without increasing expenditures.

At least as important as this dimension is the educational effect on the regular students when they are encouraged to cooperate with and take partial responsibility for their handicapped schoolmates. To a very large degree, the schools tend to emphasize a narrow and narcissistic form of individualism and competition that detracts from the formation of awareness of social responsibility. As early as the turn of the century, John Dewey decried this emphasis in the school, especially since it also was reflected in the declining need for cooperation in the family as production shifted from the household to the impersonal environment of the factory (Dewey, 1899/1956). By mainstreaming handicapped children and involving fellow students in assisting them, the nonhandicapped students can obtain an invaluable and rare social experience that should enhance both their social sensitivity and their awareness of exceptional children. Mainstreaming can alleviate the underemployment of the "hidden" resource in an educationally and socially beneficial manner while reducing the costs of educational services provided for the handicapped.

SCREENING AND DIAGNOSIS, EDUCATIONAL NEEDS, AND IMPLEMENTATION

At the heart of the new educational approach exemplified by mainstreaming is the capability of schools to screen students for handicaps, diagnose their problems properly, and prescribe and offer educational experiences that are tailored to the particular needs of each student. Much of the screening and diagnosis actually will be done before children are of school age since many, if not most, handicaps are recognizable during infancy or early childhood. Yet, it is surprising how often various handicaps, sight and hearing impairments, for example, are not discovered during this period, especially among children from families that cannot afford regular medical care. Accordingly, many schools attempt to screen children routinely for hearing or sight deficiencies and to screen them for other handicaps when a problem seems evident.

Whether such screenings are adequate requires evaluation that is beyond the scope of this paper. It should be noted that multiphasic health-screening programs for the general population were considered to be the basis of a rational and efficient system of preventative medicine until quite recently. It was thought that such programs would provide early detection of problems that would reduce treatment costs as well as the problems presented by advanced maladies. Today, such programs are considered to be highly controversial in the sense that their costs are high and the benefits are not as evident as were expected.[6] Accordingly, the nature of educational screening programs for handicaps should be scrutinized carefully before substantial investments are made in comprehensive and multiphasic programs. It may be that screening for the major handicaps is still the most effective approach, with further screening and diagnosis reserved only for children who show indications of other difficulties.

Of course, screening and diagnosis are only the first step in organizing and producing educational services for the handicapped. Given a diagnosis of a specific type and severity of handicap, there must follow the specification of educational needs. Recent work on setting out educational domains for the handicapped represent an important step in this direction (Hively & Reynolds, 1975). This type of inquiry asks, in what areas should programs be constructed and what kinds of goals should be accomplished? Obviously, not only conventional school learning is involved in this exercise; the focus must be on the special instruction that the handicapped must have to understand and care for the unique needs that are related to their disabilities.

---

[6]See Flathman & Nestman (1976) and Collen (1969), for example. This subject fits directly into the economic analysis of information (Stigler, 1961). The more extensive and refined the screening program, the more likely it is that particular handicaps will be identified. However, the cost of identifying a latent handicap rises greatly when it is necessary to go beyond a few basic screening procedures, and the benefit of identification must be weighed against the benefits that would accrue if the same funds were devoted to treatment or instruction.

Once the appropriate domains for instruction as well as the goals within each domain are determined, it is necessary to plan the nature and implementation of programs that will address these areas.[7] The nature of these programs and their implementation will be the main factors determining costs. To understand this point, consider that the salary cost and fringe benefits of a full-time, experienced teacher are on the order of about $25,000 a year. Of course, this figure does not include the costs of other personnel, facilities, and materials. If the teacher is assigned to a class of 25 students, the cost per student is about $1,000 per year; but if only five students are in the class, the teacher cost rises to about $5,000 per pupil. Interestingly, by increasing the mainstreaming of handicapped students, the costs of regular instruction for each handicapped child can be reduced. It is these "savings" which can be used to improve the quality of other educational services that are needed by exceptional children. That is, it is conceivable that a sensitive use of the mainstreaming approach can also improve the productivity of expenditure for the handicapped by reducing the need for specialized resources for the conventional instructional components.

Of course, it should be recognized that this approach may be much more difficult to implement for many of the handicapped students who have been excluded from schools in the past. That is, it seems probable that the youngsters who have been excluded from instruction on the average will possess more serious handicaps than the group of handicapped students already in the schools. This probability suggests that the ability to place such new entrants into the mainstream for substantial amounts of instruction is likely to be limited severely. Rather, such students are likely to require a much higher concentration of highly individualized services than the handicapped students who have been served traditionally.

In sum, the overall effect of the combination of mainstreaming, on the one hand, and providing educational opportunities for all handicapped children, on the other, is likely to be a rise in both the average cost of educating each handicapped child and the total cost of providing special educational services. While the mainstreaming approach can reduce the use of expensive resources for the conventional instruction of many students and enable these "savings" to be reallocated to individualized needs, these "savings" will be offset by an increase in the cost of individualized services because of the higher incidences of severe handicaps among the prospective clientele that was formerly excluded. In addition, the rise in the numbers of handicapped children who are entitled to services will increase the total costs of the programs, unless there is a compen-

---

[7]See Snow (1976). Cost aspects are discusssed in the context of learner-differentiated instruction for mastery learning in Levin 1974a).

sating long-term decline in the demographic base from which exceptional children are drawn. The important point is that costs are likely to rise at a faster rate than the increase in the size of the population receiving special educational services, even if such programs are planned and administered in an efficient manner.

SPECIAL EDUCATION AND SCHOOL ORGANIZATION

A final aspect of the provision of services to the handicapped population is the degree to which a combination of mainstreaming and individualization will influence educational practices for nonhandicapped students. It has long been recognized that every student has individual strengths and weaknesses as well as different learning aptitudes which cannot be satisfied equally by a single instructional approach. Many attempts have been made to individualize instruction, but the efforts have left much to be desired. Is it possible that the successful combination of large-group instruction and individualized services for the handicapped would set a precedent for the expansion of this approach to all children? It would be remarkable if the implementation of this model for educating the handicapped became the prototype and stimulus for the initiation of individualized instruction for all students.

Summary

In this paper, I have attempted to suggest a number of economic considerations that are reflected by the two major trends in educating and training handicapped persons. The emergence of the legal right to an appropriate education for all the handicapped and the mainstreaming principle have implications for the financing, organization, and productivity of public investment in the schools. The lack of a concrete data base for the specification of actual alternatives and their consequences necessarily must limit this analysis to one of concepts and principles rather than specifics. But, within this framework are the elements of both policy alternatives and specific foci for initiating experimentation, evaluation, and further analysis to inform policy on the finance and organization of education for handicapped persons.

Addendum

Two topics arose at the conference that require some additional commentary, in my view: (a) the individualization of instruction and emphasis on individual differences in the education of both handicapped and nonhandicapped students; and (b) the nature of social change.

INDIVIDUAL DIFFERENCES AND THE HANDICAPPED

One of the more optimistic predictions voiced at the conference is derived from the implications of the new developments in educating the handicapped for the individualization of instruction and recognition of individual differences. In general, it was agreed that it would become increasingly necessary to evaluate each handicapped child as an individual in order to diagnose his or her learning needs and to construct an individualized program that would respond to those needs. It was also suggested that with the recognition of "aptitude-treatment-interactions" in instruction it might become increasingly possible to create individually prescribed and tailored instruction for all children, and that individual differences would become widely recognized and accepted.

It is important to note that the recognition of individual differences can have beneficial or pernicious consequences. I am reminded of Senator John McClellan's persistent plea for more funds for vocational education for those youngsters who do not have the ability to benefit from the academic curriculum. On its surface, such a statement is innocuous, and it is certainly within the spirit of the individualization of instruction. But, in fact, the Senator seemed to have in mind the view that this type of education was especially appropriate for blacks, if one took seriously his shining examples of "successful" vocational programs in his home state of Arkansas. The point is that differences in individuals in terms of learning style and personal need should be recognized in instruction. However, we should be very careful to see that "individualization" does not become a way of systematizing the expectation of lower or less-valued accomplishments in some children than in others.

Unfortunately, the rhetoric of individual differences suggests that variations among human beings and applications of human talents lie only on an horizontal plane; that is, there is a tacit assumption that differences among human attributes are of equal value to society rather than representing a hierarchy. It is obvious, however, that society does not value the capable office worker as much as the incapable professional, the capable nurse as much as an incapable physician, and so on. In our society, personality attributes and their translation into social and occupational roles have extremely unequal consequences in terms of power, prestige, income, and opportunities. To the degree that individualization and differentiation have been practiced in the past by the schools, it has been principally to provide differentiation, individualization, and certification of youngsters for very unequal social roles, often according to the initial social origins of the students.

Thus, it is important that we develop to a greater degree the concept of individualization of instruction and instructional objectives while we attempt to provide "equality" of educational opportunity and results. It is not clear that individualization of instruction always leads to happy consequences. To the extent that it has resulted in systematic social class biases in the treatment of youngsters and thereby reinforced initial disadvantages, its historical application has hardly been salubrious. Hence, the concept of individualization of instruction is not terribly useful without a clear presentation of its details and consequences.

EDUCATIONAL REFORM AND THE HANDICAPPED

One of the very encouraging signs of contact with reality at the conference was the recognition that educational reform is rarely a simple, linear process. In fact, where educational change has been successful, it has been characterized by considerable conflict among constituencies rather than passive acceptance of technocratic types of alterations. It is one thing to talk about models of education for the handicapped and quite another to determine how the models are implemented in the real world. Unfortunately, the mythology of education is characterized by a view that educational change is managed or planned in some rational way: (a) The objectives are set out; (b) the means of reaching the objectives are considered; (c) resources are obtained; and (d) the plan is implemented.

If conflict enters the model at all, it is in the competition for resources. But it is asssumed that other changes can be made in a rather planned and routinized way: that teachers can be retrained to change even their most basic attitudes about the handicapped; school organizations can be manipulated in a rational manner to assimilate organizational reforms on behalf of the handicapped; and professional organizations of educators will submit passively to the restructuring of curriculum and professional responsibilities. That a decade of compensatory education programs has not seemed to find this model of managed change valid has not altered the rhetoric of planned change. It is even common to hear of persons who are labeled "change agents," as if there were some evidence that it is only a matter of leadership or some other magic talent that is needed to reform education.

The participants in the conference seemed to accept the view that change is unlikely to take place in this planned manner in the future because it has failed to take place in this way in the past. Indeed, this view seemed to be one of the major challenges facing persons who wish to alter the traditional functioning of the schools on behalf of handicapped pupils. The emphasis on the theory of managed change has so dominated the thinking of educators that alternative approaches to change rarely have been explored. For example, to what degree can political conflict be used to enact change, rather than assuming that change is obtained by rational and purposive acts?

While it was encouraging to see so many participants from such different backgrounds reject the mythological approach to change, the dilemma is still present. How can we accomplish the important changes that have been advocated for the education of the handicapped? In recent years we have seen the limits of the courts in effecting such changes as well as the poverty of our previous conceptions about the change process. It is hoped that the problem will be cast in a more general framework rather than limiting it to the issue of how to improve the education of the handicapped. Certainly, this general area of education needs a great deal more research, analysis, and discussion before we can improve our understanding of institutional change. But it is interesting that our discussions on improving the education of the handicapped has forced this useful intellectual confrontation.

References

Becker, G. S. *Human capital.* New York: Columbia University Press, 1964.

Bellante, D. M. A multivariate analysis of a vocational rehabilitation program. *The Journal of Human Resources,* 1972, **7**(2), 226-241.

Bernstein, C., Hartman, W., & Marshall, R. Major policy issues in financing special education. *Journal of Education Finance,* 1976, **1**(3), 299-317.

Birch, J. W. *Mainstreaming: Educable mentally retarded children in regular classes.* Reston, VA: Council for Exceptional Children, 1974.

Burt, R. Judicial action to aid the retarded. In N. Hobbs (Ed.), *Issues in the classification of children.* San Francisco: Jossey-Bass, 1975, Ch. 25.

Buss, W., Kirp, D., & Kuriloff, P. Exploring procedural modes of special classification. In N. Hobbs (Ed.), *Issues in the classification of children.* San Francisco: Jossey-Bass, 1975, Ch. 27.

Center for the Study of Public Policy. *Education vouchers.* A report on financing elementary education by grants to parents. Cambridge, Mass.: Author, December 1970.

Collen, M. F. Cost analysis of a multiphasic screening program. *New England Journal of Medicine,* 1969, **280**(19), 1043-1045.

Conley, R. W. A benefit-cost analysis of the vocational rehabilitation program. *The Journal of Human Resources,* 1969, **4**(2), 226-252.

Coons, J. R., Clune III, W. H., & Sugarman, S. D. *Private wealth and public education.* Cambridge, Mass.: Harvard University Press, 1970.

Dewey, J. *The child and the curriculum and the school and society.* Chicago: The University of Chicago Press (Phoenix Books), 1956. (Originally published, 1899)

Flathman, K. B., & Nestman, L. The worth of a screening program: An application of a statistical decision model for the benefit evaluation of screening projects. *American Journal of Public Health,* 1976, **66**(2), 1-18.

Friedman, M. The role of government in education. In R. A. Solo (Ed.), *Economics and the public interest.* New Brunswick, N. J.: Rutgers University Press, 1955.

Friedman, M. *Capitalism and freedom*. Chicago: University of Chicago Press, 1962.

Fuchs, V. R. *Who shall live?* New York: Basic Books, 1974.

Gilhool, T. K. Changing public policies: Roots and forces. In M. C. Reynolds (Ed.), *Mainstreaming: Origins and implications*. Reston, VA: Council for Exceptional Children, 1976, 6-11.

Hively, W., & Reynolds, M. C. (Eds.). *Domain-referenced testing in special education*. Reston, VA: Council for Exceptional Children, 1975.

Kakalik, J. S., Brewer, G. D., Dougharty, L. A., Fleischauer, P. D., & Genensky S. M. *Services for handicapped youth: A program overview*. (Prepared for the Department of Health, Education, and Welfare, Office of the Assistant Secretary for Planning and Evaluation, R-1220-HEW.) Santa Monica: The Rand Corporation, May 1973.

Kakalik, J. S., Brewer, G. D., Dougharty, L. A., Fleischauer, P. D., Genensky, S. M., & Wallen, L. M. *Improving services to handicapped children*. (Prepared for the Department of Health, Education, and Welfare, Office of the Assistant Secretary for Planning and Evaluation, R-1420-HEW.) Santa Monica: The Rand Corporation, May 1974.

Kirp, D., Kuriloff, P., & Buss, W. Legal mandates and organizational change. In N. Hobbs (Ed.), *Issues in the classification of children*. San Francisco: Jossey-Bass, 1975, Ch. 26.

Levin, H. M. Concepts of economic efficiency and educational production. In D. Jamison, J. Froomkin, & R. Radner (Eds.), *Education as an industry*. Cambridge, Mass.: Ballinger, 1976, Ch. 2.

Levin, H. M. The costs to the nation of inadequate education. A report prepared for the Select Senate Committee on Equal Educational Opportunity. Washington, D. C.: U. S. Government Printing Office, 1972. (Summarized in Select Committee on Equal Educational Opportunity, U. S. Senate, *Toward equal educational opportunity*, 92nd Congress, 2nd Session, Report No. 92-000. Washington, D. C., 1972, Ch. 13.)

Levin, H. M. Cost-effectiveness analysis in evaluation research. In M. Guttentag & E. Struening, *Handbook of evaluation research* (Vol. 2). Beverly Hills: Sage, 1975, 89-121. (a)

Levin, H. M. The economic implications of mastery learning. In J. H. Block (Ed.), *Schools, society, and mastery learning*. New York: Holt, Rinehart, & Winston, 1974, 75-88. (a)

Levin, H. M. Educational vouchers and educational equality. In M. Carnoy (Ed.), *Schooling in a corporate society* (2nd ed.). New York: David McKay, 1975, 293-309. (b)

Levin, H. M. Effects of expenditure increases on educational resource allocation and effectiveness. In J. Pincus (Ed.), *School finance in transition*. Cambridge, Mass.: Ballinger, 1974, 177-198. (b)

Levin, H. M. Equal educational opportunity and the distribution of educational expenditures. *Education and Urban Society*, 1973, 5(2), 149-176.

Levin, H. M. Some methodological problems in economic policy research: Determining how much should be spent on compensatory education. *Education and Urban Society*, 1975, 7(3), 303-333. (c)

Melaragno, R. J., & Newmark, G. The tutorial community concept. In J. W. Guthrie & E. Wynne (Eds.), *New models for American education*. Englewood Cliffs, N. J.: Prentice Hall, 1971, 93-113.

Rawl, J. *A theory of justice.* Cambridge, Mass.: Belknap, 1971.

Reynolds, M. C. (Ed.). *Mainstreaming: Origins and implications.* Reston, VA: Council for Exceptional Children, 1976.

Reynolds, M. C. *Trends in education: Changing roles of special education personnel.* Columbus, Ohio: University Council for Educational Administration. (no date)

Reynolds, M. C. Trends in special education: Implications for measurement. In W. Hively & M. C. Reynolds (Eds.), *Domain-referenced testing in special education.* Reston, VA.: Council for Exceptional Children, 1975, 15-28.

Rossmiller, R. A., Hale, J. A., & Rohreich, L. E. *Educational programs for exceptional children:* Resource configurations and costs. National Educational Finance Project, Special Study No. 2. Madison, Wis.: Department of Educational Administration, 1970.

Snow, R. E. Consequences for instruction: The state of the art of individualizing. In M. C. Reynolds (Ed.), *Mainstreaming: Origins and implications.* Reston, VA.: Council for Exceptional Children, 1976, 23-31.

Stigler, G. J. The economics of information. *Journal of Political Economy,* June 1961.

Weiler, D., et al. *A public school voucher demonstration: The first year at Alum Rock.* Santa Monica: The Rand Corporation, June 1974.

Weisbrod, B. A. *External benefits of public education.* Princeton: Industrial Relations Section, Princeton University, 1964.

Three Years Past 1984

R. L. Schiefelbusch[1] and Robert K. Hoyt, Jr.[2]

University of Kansas

To place a 10-year forecast of special education in perspective, the authors examine the history of special education, consider the implications of recent research and development, and present an idealistic conceptualization of what it could all mean by 1987. The authors then define the developments that will be necessary in order to reach that idealistic plateau for special education. The ingredients that must be furnished by teachers, schools, and communities are considered from both positive and negative perspectives. The paper ends with an afterword that is both realistic and optimistic, one that makes no apology for the state of special education in 1977 and acknowledges fully that the next 10 years will be both rewarding and difficult. Educators are now challenged to meet the aspirations of society without a real and existing science of instruction. New ideas and different techniques will be needed to deal with all the problems that wait to be solved before all children with all degrees of handicap will have the equal education that too many have been denied too long.

In assessing the current scene of education for handicapped children, one could say, paraphrasing certain popular comedians, "There is good news and there is bad news." The good news is the national policy that recognizes education as the handicapped person's right. "Moreover, that right cannot be abridged, even on such grounds as that the necessary funds are not available" (NACH, 1967, p. 6). Our good news also includes the Education for All Handicapped Children Act — Public Law 94-142 — and related federal legislation. In his paper, Sarason characterizes this act and the advances mandated by the courts, which, increasingly, are being incorporated into state education statutes, as "the basic machinery for propelling the education of the handicapped into a new era. The

---

[1]Director, Bureau of Child Research, and Professor of Speech Pathology.
[2]Associate Director for Communications, Bureau of Child Research.

handicapped person's right to an education is now guaranteed and . . . there is now a firm foundation on which to build."

The bad news is the serious difference between the current educational practice and the requirements set out in state and federal legislative enactments. Desirable as the concepts of *equal rights to education, least restrictive environments,* and *mainstreaming* may be, we question whether the education community has the intent, resources, and know-how to put them into practice.

The primary purpose of this paper is to explore the current ability of educators to handle the major changes that are projected for our schools. These changes, which have resulted from the current advocacy movement, include the legal and ethical edicts for equal rights to education which are backed up by accountability provisions.

If we are to reach our goal of achieving full educational opportunities for all handicapped children by 1980, we must begin to train at least 200,000 new special education teachers (NACH, 1976). More significantly, however, we must train them in nontraditional ways, ways that depart from preparation to teach special classes in segregated education groupings. Maintaining special class traditions clearly is not in compliance with the concepts of least restrictive environment and, judging from the results, equal rights to education. A departure is required, then, from training and instructional practices that have been maintained for at least 30 years. To propose to accomplish so much in approximately three years is impractical, if not absurd. Furthermore, we have not yet agreed upon the changes that must be made or how the changes should come about.

If past experiences are any guide, the mainstreaming of handicapped children will be achieved by the administrative expedience of placing or retaining a high percentage of the children in regular classes and assigning the remainder to trial or experimental programs or, even, to programs that are merely projected. Administrators will take action when they must. For example, they will look for teachers who are able or willing to try to meet the challenge of teaching radically heterogeneous groupings of children. Nevertheless, a plethora of evasions prior to or in lieu of compliance with the new educational regulations can be expected.

Since the present authors are realists by preference and rational by design, we assume that a reasonable period for effecting the mandated changes is 10 years, not three, and so we have titled this exercise in education analysis, "Three Years Past 1984." Furthermore, we assume that at the current pace of educational change we are not labeling our chosen 10-year period as a *future* but as a *current* time frame. We concede, however, as a time-bound gesture, that this "1984 plus three" report is a projection toward the future.

We are talking about, in the parlance of Wall Street, a near-term, not a long-term analysis of our educational investment portfolio.

Before we talk about projection for the future, near or far, we should spend some time looking at the present (with a brief peek into the past). Our preoccupation in all time dimensions is with research and its effects. This preoccupation may not prove to be entirely practical. The facts are that research in any aspect of society is strongly influenced by political, legal, financial, and moral issues, not to mention social issues that ebb and flow, often in several directions at once.

The Special Education Scene

HISTORICAL PERSPECTIVES

Reynolds (n. d.), in presenting an historical perspective of the special education movement in this country, pointed out that fundamental changes came during the 1970s. These changes arise from a renegotiation of boundaries between regular and special education and between community-based and residential institutions.

> Perhaps the period can be summarized under the rubric "least restrictive alternatives" or "mainstreaming" . . . or "progressive inclusion". . . . Handicapped children have come, in a period less than two centuries, from total neglect, first into isolated residential schools — for just a few — then into isolated community settings — mostly in the form of special classes — and now into more integrated arrangements for many children. At this moment we are in the midst of . . . a remarkable reversal of a negative cascade by which handicapped children were sent off to isolated classes and centers. The agendas of local school boards all across the country . . . reflect the influx to the community of seriously handicapped children earlier sent off to hospitals and residential centers; and on the desks of virtually every school principal are difficult questions concerning accommodation of the more exceptional children in regular classrooms. (p. 8-9)

Obviously, we are now facing the challenge of teaching children with *all* degrees of handicap in school settings. This challenge may place great strain on our teaching formats, training strategies, and professsional credibility. In addition, economics may force the development of teaching systems that can be accommodated to the cost-feasibility studies of school districts. Thus, we may be forced to develop effective methodological procedures in arrangements that can be afforded. These issues are discussed later in this paper; now, let us take another perspective.

RESEARCH PERSPECTIVES

People who are not students of the history of American education may be surprised to learn that John Dewey maintained a laboratory school at the University of Chicago from 1896 to 1904 to work out practical development and demonstration techniques. In 1889, at the central point of his laboratory school effort, Dewey made a presidential address before the American Psychological Association in which he expressed concern about developing a linking science between psychological theory and practical work.

> Do we not lay a special linking science everywhere else between the theory and practical work? We have engineering between physics and the practical working men in the mills; we have a scientific medicine between the natural sciences and the physician. (Dewey, 1900, p. 110)

Unfortunately, his clear perception of the importance of a science of instruction did not match the practices in his laboratory school. For all of Dewey's pragmatism, it is not clear that he was seeking objective evidence of the strengths and weaknesses of new education proposals. In analyzing the history of Dewey's school, Tyler (1976) concluded that the school did not carry on disciplined inquiry or produce well-substantiated results. In fact, it seemed to presage the promotional emphasis that marked later laboratory schools. Dewey founded his school as an act of faith. His failure to develop a science of classroom experimentation is attributable to the success of his proposals. His ideas had wide appeal and, therefore, he was deprived of the stubborn and articulate opposition that might have pushed him to collect solid evidence.

In any event, Dewey and other educators of that time clearly perceived the importance of research on the process of teaching. Dewey's concern for a linking science has been noted and re-emphasized by Glaser (1976a), who suggested a Prescriptive Science of Instruction with the following four major components:

1. Description and analysis of competent performance.
2. Description and diagnosis of the initial state.
3. Conditions that foster learning and the acquisition of competence.
4. Effects of instructional implementation in the short- and long-run (Glaser, 1976a). (Glaser's major components are strikingly similar to those we have identified in an instructional system for teaching language to retarded children.)

Before Glaser's four components are examined we should look at his notions about the development of competence. He assumed that gross changes take place as an individual progresses from ignorance to increasing competence.

1. Variable, awkward, and crude performances change to performances that are consistent, relative, fast, and precise. Simple acts change into integrated complex responses and overall strategies.
2. Contexts of performance change from simple stimulus patterns with a great deal of clarity to complex patterns in which

relevant information must be abstracted from a context of events that are not all relevant.
3. Performance becomes increasingly symbolic and covert. The learner responds increasingly to internalized representations of an event, internalized standards, and internalized strategies for thinking and problem solving.
4. The behavior of the competent individual becomes increasingly self-sustaining in terms of his or her skillful employment of the rules, when they are applicable, and the subtle bending of the rules in appropriate situations. Increasing reliance is placed on one's own ability to generate the events by which one learns and the criteria by which one's performance is judged and valued.

Perhaps these general statements suggest the often-unstated objectives of education at all levels and with all kinds of students. The scientific rub, of course, is in designing the operations to accomplish these implied competency objectives. There follows a description of each of Glaser's components.

Description and Analysis of Competent Performance

Here the problem of task analysis is central. The analytical description of what is to be learned facilitates instruction by clearly defining what it is that an expert in a subject-matter domain has learned (e.g., what it is that distinguishes a skilled from an unskilled reader). When this analysis identifies classes of behavior whose properties as learned tasks are known or can be systematically studied, then inferences for optimal instructional processes can be formulated and tested.

Description and Diagnosis of the Initial State

There are two approaches to this component: immediate and long term. The immediate approach is to take seriously the fact that effective instruction requires careful assessment of the initial state of the learner. Glaser advocated an informal hierarchy of increasing competence in the instructional area to be pursued. These hierarchies take the form of structured maps on which a teacher can place a child and thereby direct attention to prerequisite skills that need to be learned, or to advanced skills that the child might explore alone. The hierarchical map is only a guide upon which both the teacher and the child can impose their individual judgments. Procedures for so assessing the current competence and talents of the learner that they provide a basis for instruction are generally not available in current educational methods at a level of detail necessary for the effective guidance of individual learners.

The long-term approach is used to decide upon instructional alternatives. Initial information does not tell how an individual should be instructed to improve his/her performance or how instruction can be designed to make the attainment of successsful performance more probable. The significant research in this area describes the initial state of learners in terms of the processes involved in achieving competent performance. This description allows us to influence learning in two ways: (a) to design instructional alternatives that adapt to the processes, and (b) to attempt to improve an individual's competence in the processes so that he/she is more likely to profit from the available instructional procedures.

Conditions that Foster Learning and the Acquisition of Competence

This third component refers to procedures by which one learns and to the nature of the environment in which learning occurs. There are at least two possible directions:

> The first is to recognize that we do know a little about learning. For example, we know some things about the effects of reinforcement — the contingencies consequent to performance; about the conditions under which discriminations, generalization, and concept formation take place; and about conditions of practice, interference with memory, the nature of attention, the effects of punishment, and how observational learning and modeling can influence new learning. We know these things in terms of descriptive science, but little investigation has been made from the point of view required for the utilization of this information for designing the conditions of instruction. Exceptions to this [are] the work on behavior modification and the work on optimization models described . . . by Atkinson (1976). However, neither of these enterprises has considered complex cognitive performance in any systematic way. (Glaser, 1976a, p. 309)

Glaser's second suggested direction would lead to research on learning cast into the mold of a design science that attempts to maximize the outcome of learning for different individuals. Glaser called for a new form of experimentation in which the tactic is not to develop models of learning and performance, but to test existing models by using them to maximize the effects of learning under various conditions. He also stated,

> We need a theory of the acquisition of competence. Such a theory would be concerned with how an individual acquires increasingly complex performances by assembling the present components of his repertoire and manipulating the surrounding conditions and events. (Glaser, 1976a, p. 310)

Effects of Instructional Implementation in the Short- and Long-Run

The fourth component of instructional design is concerned with the effects of instructional implementation in the short- and long-run: effects that occur immediately in the context of instruction and supply immediate feedback, and effects that persist (in terms of long-term transfer) in generalized patterns of behavior and ability for further learning. For effective instructional design, tests must be criterion referenced as well as norm referenced. They should assess performance attainments and capabilities in terms of available educational options, but in more detail than is possible with the current testing and assessment procedures.

It may seem inappropriate to talk about a science of instruction in our current context, given that a science evolves slowly and the dramatic scene which we face in the schools and society is in the here and now. This condition is acknowledged; but faced with problems of an immediate and difficult nature, we usually rationalize the need for expedient measures, even if the measures are inadequate for the task at hand. We simply derive moral satisfaction in doing the best we can with the procedures at hand. The political interval within which new policies must be implemented usually does not permit an adequate period for research and development. However, the only solution to some of our most pressing problems in education may be the development of a science of instruction that will deal with such problems as individualizing instruction; teaching reading and arithmetic; eliminating learning deficits; providing language instruction; and mapping a hierarchy of competency functions and the strategies for teaching them.

At this point we should consider a behavioral analysis approach to instructional design. A number of behavioral researchers provide us with an instructional system and an accompanying educational technology. For instance, Bijou's technology of teaching includes the following steps:

1. Specifying the goals of teaching and learning in observable terms.
2. Beginning teaching at the child's level of competence.
3. Arranging the teaching situation to facilitate learning (instructional procedures, materials, and setting factors and contingencies).
4. Monitoring learning progress and altering the situation to advance learning.
5. Following practices that generalize, elaborate, and maintain the behaviors acquired.

Applied behavior analysis researchers traditionally use behaviorally based, precise measures, and evaluation procedures, data-handling systems, and designed environmental arrangements (including positive reinforcement contingencies). These basic procedures are often adapted to fit preschool programmatic designs, that is, functional curricula for learning disabled children (Lovitt, 1976); designed direct instructional classroom procedures (Becker, in press; Haring & Gentry, 1976); and designed and maintained nationwide Follow Through classrooms (Bushell, 1976).

Some of the common components of behavior analysis classrooms are a motivation system, a specified, individualized curriculum with individualized instruction, a parent program, and team teaching. Hopkins and Conard (1976) demonstrated that a single teacher can use a simplified form of applied behavior analysis to achieve striking results over the course of a two-year period.

Progress in precise behavioral applications to teaching has been substantial, as noted by Glaser (1976a,b). However, he pointed out that behavior analysts have not designed an adequate approach to complex cognitive performance. Commendable efforts are underway in the areas of language intervention to create a rapprochement between cognitive and behavioral science (see Staats, 1974) and to work out effective designs that combine linguistic and other descriptive cognitive systems with behavioral tactics of instruction. Some remarkable efforts at designing a full language curriculum with accompanying instructions for teaching have been published (see Bricker, Ruder, & Vincent, 1976; Guess, Sailor, & Baer, 1978; Miller & Yoder, 1974). Nevertheless, these researchers reported difficulty in finding the cognitive codes and shortcuts required for teaching such complex curricula.

Developmental psycholinguistics and developmental cognitive psychology are exciting descriptive fields of inquiry but, as yet, neither field has mounted any noticeable effort to determine the variables that can be specified for acceleration or otherwise changing cognitive behaviors.

These observations emphasize that educational specialists cannot yet draw upon a linking science in designing their most difficult and complex educational programs. This realization must be acknowledged as we consider the remarkable technological strides that have been taken in educational research and development.

Educational Research and Development

There has been much confusion over the words *research* and *development* (R & D), according to Tyler (1976). The purpose of research is to gain greater understanding of a phenomenon; the purpose of development is to devise and perfect the means to accomplish specified instructional ends under certain conditions. Thus, research purposes lead to descriptions, theories, and basic information or reliable knowledge which can be drawn upon to serve many educational ends and means; on the other hand, development leads to "how-to-do-it" conclusions that may (should) be important in the practice of education.

Development often is an effort to design educational programs to facilitate learning. Development activities also may include designing a curriculum, producing instructional devices and materials, devising methods by which teachers and other persons can help students to learn, and performing evaluations. It seems probable that both Bijou (1975) and Glaser (1976a,b) conceptualized *instructional research* to encompass most of what is here defined as research and development. The implications of this issue are extensively developed in Bijou's writings.

One can establish targets for instruction or intervention research and design a strategy that extends across all operational steps to the final implementation of the targeted procedures. The term that appeals most to us is *experimental intervention research*. We would emphasize that all procedures are validated by a data system that is used experimentally to refine the functions. Nevertheless, we stick with the *research and development* terminology because it is the accepted concept in the education literature.

A common assumption in education circles today is that there should be a balance between research and development. This balance, however, is difficult to design, awkward to evaluate, and, perhaps, impossible to predict. The issue of prediction is especially acute because in times of rapid changes in educational practice development activities are numerous and varied. Since it takes less energy (and funding) to acquire knowledge than to develop and perfect the means by which something can be done with the knowledge, the crunch is likely to be at the application end of the R & D design.

In the past 10 years, there have been marked improvements in the hardware for both research and development. Nevertheless, obvious difficulties are experienced in each in direct relation to the issues that provide the urgency for their continuance and expansion.

Research in education must be conducted in the light of beliefs and practices that are implicit in cultures and societies. It is difficult to unravel the continuing designs and to examine them in the light of changing conditions. Nevertheless, the scientific enterprise must operate to produce and update dependable knowledge for the improvement of education, even when it may be difficult to agree on the improvements to be effected.

The difficulties in development stem, in part, from the same sources. How-to-do-it designs are only effective when we know what is to be designed. Even if the design begins with a needs analysis, the premises that lead to the development plan also probably suggest the class of needs that should be sought. After the design is selected, we narrow the alternatives to a specific, limited range of outcomes. All that research and development methods tell us is how to reliably and validly research what we have decided to study.

What is now described as educational technology is part of the R & D design. Much of the technology can be subsumed under six headings: (a) *systems and systems designing,* (b) *data-handling procedures and designs,* (c) *curriculum designing and programing,* (d) *measurement and evaluation,* (e) *management,* and (f) *environmental designing.* Much has been written about each.

We are not interested in describing the specific features of these technical areas or, at this point, delineating the progress made in each. We prefer to point out that available technology enables us to define issues and solve certain difficult agreed-upon problems, design interventions or instructional programs that can be initiated and refined through relevant data, construct and adjust functional learning in environments to fit children individually and collectively, manage groups of heterogeneous children to maintain individual designs for learning over time, and handle and disseminate information on any and all of these technically aided operations to give other educators access to designed and prescriptive successes. Use and replication are prominent concepts in current R & D efforts.

As an exercise in futurism, we have projected a view of the education scene that might exist beyond 1987 if we follow through on current R & D efforts and if infusions into the educational mainstream are used freely and actively. The view is idealistic, especially considering that it may have to come about without a fully evolved linking science of instruction. Beyond the time frame of our analysis and in consideration of a *science of the possible*, one can rationally say, "You ain't seen nuthin' yet."

The Future Glow

It did not happen. Our 1984[3] world was not dominated by Big Brother, nor did it become a world in which the individual and his/her problems and aspirations are suppressed and all information is controlled or revised to suit the interpretations and ambitions of the state. In fact, we have taken quite the opposite direction. Special education today, in 1987, is on the brink of realizing or fulfilling many of society's goals established for the handicapped when the normalization, deinstitutionalization, and mainstreaming concepts first became a part of the educational establishment. Many education programs that were beginning to emerge just then were the forebears of today's system.

Schools no longer consider it an objectional obligation to provide an appropriate education for each child; the obligation has been accepted as a part of the education process. Schools have increased their capacities or modified their operational procedures so that educational services are provided for all children, not just for those who are easiest to teach and quickest to learn. Parents receive a semi-annual set of instructional objectives for each child. These objectives are subject to the approval of the parents, and the parents

---

[3]The "1984" concept obviously refers to George Orwell's classic. Although Orwell did not address educational issues in his book, he strongly warned against the evils of technology, and his warning has apparent, if not actual, relevance for educators.

receive monthly reports that specify in measurable terms the progress of the child toward achieving the objectives set for him/her.

Referrals to special environments are now rare. The regular teachers, school psychologists, principals, and other school personnel all have received extensive training in procedures to help children with special needs to survive in mainstream settings. Elderly and retired persons substantially supplement the efforts of regular school personnel by putting their years of experience and career training to work in regular but part-time instruction in the mainstream organization. They are paid as part-time teachers and are accountable for the progress of their students in the same manner as regular teachers.

It is difficult to walk into any classroom today and to pick out the developmentally disabled children (except those with physical handicaps), and no teacher uses any artificial label to refer to any child. The only labels the children bear are the names their parents gave them. This situation has become possible, in part, because of the system of instructional objectives that are followed. Children are matched to programs according to their aptitudes. Each child has an individualized education program plan that covers a range of academic and life skills. And each child acquires these skills at his/her own rate, and no stigmatizing label is attached if the child does not progress at a certain predetermined pace.

This approach has required us to re-evaluate many of our old ideas about expectancy and capacity in relation to children's learning. We no longer demand of children that they do certain things at certain ages (within reason, of course). We place a greater emphasis on each child's capacity for acquiring skills and concepts, and we provide all the help any child needs to achieve an important capacity.

We soon will do away completely with all the grading and promoting systems that took so much time and caused so many problems in the past. A system of behavioral objectives permits parents and teachers to know how each child is progressing in the acquisition of both academic and social skills. With this system, we may one day do away with the graduations, diplomas, and other symbols that are meant to indicate that learning is complete.

We know now that learning is never complete, that it continues for as long as the person wants or as long as it takes the person to acquire some necessary or desired skill. Children stay in school now for as long as it takes them to learn what they need to know. Reinforcement and reinforcers are individually determined and are built into each child's program to motivate the child to learn as much as he/she is able to learn. Any time after children are 15 years old they can leave school and go to work for themselves or for someone else. But they still are free to take advantage of the educational system whenever they want and for whatever purpose. There are, of course, different settings for education. The universities are extensions of the high schools, and the high schools are extensions of the junior highs, and so forth. Students who want to pursue formal learning as a career eventually become part of the formal education establishment, developing specialized curricula, extending what they know into research to acquire and formalize academic paths for others who are following the same track.

The point is that isolated "special" education no longer exists. All education is special, and each student pursues whatever course of learning he/she desires for as long as he/she wants.

Thus, our educational support system is larger than the obvious educational system itself. The support system provides access to specialized knowledge from all over the world, and makes it possible for one specialist to share knowledge and skills with other professionals, who then provide direct services to students. Thus we have a completely different system for classifying and certifying educators. Although some specialists are an integral part of the educational system, others are not. Many specialists are immersed completely in other vocations; but they make their expertise a part of the common data base so that it is instantly available to any educational specialist who needs it anywhere in the world. Because such specialists may not be trained teachers, the educational system includes persons who are expert at simplifying complex information and packaging it for use by others. We still have credentials, of course, but the artificial degree system is out. Credentials are granted now on a continuing basis and as a result of proven competency (manifested by the utility of programs the specialists develop or the measurable progress of the children they teach), not according to an academic standard applied at some place remote from the educational environment.

A critical aspect of the educational system now is the participation of parents. Parents are teachers at home, and a significant portion of each child's education is dependent upon the guidance he/she receives there.

This system is much more dependent upon collaboration than were the old systems. Since education these days is a continuing process, there are direct ties between early education and what were formerly called institutions of higher education. In the old terms, we would probably say that the preschool is linked to the graduate school; now we recognize that they are just different points on the same continuum. Where a student chooses to get off is a matter of individual preference after, of course, some basic skills are mastered.

These developments have necessitated increasing federal support for all phases of education. Stronger intermediate and regional units, which are run by professionals, have been established to insure more comprehensive, integrated educational services; and leadership has been strengthened at all levels. The federal agencies and the intermediate and regional units also are operated and accredited according to measurable objectives. There is a system of real accountability all the way from the home to the federal funding agencies, but it is not a system of negative accountability. The system is designed to find weaknesses so that they can be overcome, not to attach blame or jeopardize careers.

The heart of the educational system is a computer-controlled, educational satellite technology that provides a dissemination and utilization system to bring coherence and direction to a very complex set of activities. Several technical advances during the past few years have made this system possible.

1. It is now possible to record both a video and audio image on a disc smaller than an old-time phonograph record. These audiovisual discs use a laser pick-up mechanism for both the audio and visual images, thus they never wear out and always provide excellent quality and fidelity. They are in wide use. Every home that has a television system has the capacity to use these discs. In the case of children with special needs, discs are available to parents for augmenting the child's home education and to children themselves for use in self-instruction. A system of disc libraries is established for parents who do not wish to purchase discs. However, the discs are not expensive; their cost is comparable to that of a phonograph record during the last decade.

The discs are used in the public schools, as well as in the homes. In the schools and outlying resource centers, however, the bulk of the media and materials come in via orbiting satellites. The National Educational Satellite Service Information Environment (NESSIE) Center is located near Wichita, Kansas, almost at the geographic center of the United States. NESSIE has a comprehensive and continuously updated repository of programed information on any subject and ranging from such basic skills as toilet training for developmentally disabled children to lectures by renowned world experts on current advances in the biological, physical, and behavioral sciences.

2. NESSIE has the capability to diagnose the learning needs of any child and, based on that diagnosis, to provide a sequenced series of instructional objectives to remediate diagnosed deficiencies in the child's academic, self-care, and social skills. The system processes information gathered by a diagnostic specialist and returns a fully programed curriculum in hard copy to be used by the child's mentor to provide an appropriate, individualized program. The system also produces diagnostic information for each child. It supports the treatment program by listing programs to follow and local experts to consult; it delivers hard-copy materials for use by the child's teachers and parents, and it provides programs that allow the child to interact with the system in self-directed education.

NESSIE is the educational clearing house and production center for information on anything that anyone knows anything about. It has become the major vehicle for the distribution of scientific information of all kinds, as well as of instructional materials. The information is so stored and indexed that anyone with a terminal can call up a catalog of information relating to any subject. Then, on request from the operator of the terminal, an audiovisual presentation can be scheduled and printed supplemental information can be requested. The system can even be used to provide ongoing instruction for such activities as baking cakes or replacing lightbulbs, and those instructions are provided in picture form for persons who have difficulty with written directions. The program offers an option to recycle to a more detailed instruction when the person encounters directions that are too complex to follow.

The whole system is based on a philosophy that education is something like a tour through a huge museum. Without individual guides and individual help, the child is stuck with the group. The group may be moving too quickly or too slowly under the direction of a single teacher. But given a private guide and his/her own interest to pursue, the child can advance as rapidly as is practical in any desired area. Some children, for example, are into anthropology in only a few months; others, applying the museum analogy again, still have difficulty finding the restroom. But it is no longer a matter of grouping children in an arbitrary fashion and then teaching toward the middle. That situation has been quite old-fashioned for some time. Each child, now, no matter what his/her ability or capacity, has an individual program with measurable objectives and a sequence of instructional steps designed specifically for him/her alone. Each child has all the help he/she needs from an education mentor. And NESSIE gives the child and the mentor and teachers instant access to the most knowledgeable expert in the world for help to overcome specific difficulties or to advance a particular area of interest.

Special education (as well as all other education) in fact has become special. The sky is the limit. And there are some people who say that our sky is not really a limit, that soon we will be learning through contact with other worlds that are now trying to communicate with our satellites.

A Summary (Optimistic)

Meanwhile, back at the ranch in 1977, vast improvements in educational programs for the handicapped are just around the corner. The primary ingredients of this improvement are landmark legal decisions; active constituent groups that insist upon equal education; technological improvements in planning, teaching, and evaluating progress; and resources for integrating the handicapped child into the life of the community.

A number of pilot programs featuring individualized instruction, designed learning environments, and cooperative educational arrangements have proved to be successful. Also, we are developing a technology for disseminating and replicating programs in remote areas. Then, too, we are improving our technology for teaching and training so that we have better preparation programs and training sequences to enable our teachers to become competent in all levels of childhood instruction. Finally, we are building our educational programs for handicapped persons upon a more enlightened policy of community involvement so that support programs aid the schools in developing open systems of education that extend beyond the physical confines of the school and use parents, citizen groups, and community agencies and settings. We seem, at last, to have a strong foundation for long-term growth in appropriate educational programs for handicapped citizens.

As a further extension of our optimistic view, we may assume that the needed changes largely can be effected by further investments in educational research and development. After some early confusion, we are now pooling and providing computerized access to successful program results on a nationwide basis. This access to the investments in better programing should enable any school district to draw upon program innovations for virtually any kind of handicapped child or for any arrangement in learning. We see all these developments in 1977 as potential heralds for our view from 1987.

The Current Scene

During our academic research for this manuscript, we became aware of a learning effect (our own) which is best expressed as an inverse of an old adage, "If we hadn't believed it we wouldn't have seen it." Our observations are not based on a sudden point of enlightenment but more on a steady, unspectacular realization. Two illustrative article titles that figured in our revelation were, "You can lead the public to educational technology but you can't . . ." (Gropper, 1976), and "What a great idea! Too bad it didn't work" (Walker, 1976).

If there is any doubt about our thesis, perhaps we should highlight it: *It may be easier to design technologically based innovations than it is to get them accepted and to make them work.* Sometimes there appear to be more innovators than there are innovatees. At any rate, the issue of *utilized* innovation is worth examining because it bears so heavily upon the established model of educational research and development. We assume that the end product of research and development is the successful dissemination, utilization, and replication of instructional products and educational programs.

We recall the story about the farmer who stopped his subscription to his favorite farm journal because "I don't farm as good as I know how to now." We are not flippant about educational change. We simply want to point out that change is resisted, and potentially valuable innovations are often delayed or extinguished by pragmatic forces within the educational community. *Educational community* may be a term virtually congruent with the broader concept of community.

Issues inherent in potential change are too numerous to approach in toto. Consequently, we are limiting our focal perspectives to three pragmatic themes: *the teacher, the school,* and *the community setting that supports the school.*

THE TEACHER

Guba and Clark (1975), in referring to educational knowledge, production, and utilization (KPU), recommended a closer link between researchers and practitioners. Each group can and should contribute to the activities of the other. To date, however, R & D activities are initiated and often completed without significant input from classroom teachers. Exceptions to this practice are the schools that have appointed coordinators to work with teachers in Title I programs. The coordinators help to identify the problems of learning encountered by particular disadvantaged children, and they assist teachers in devising a program to improve the learning of these children. In this sense, they are links in the KPU chain. The future of research and development will be influenced by the extent to which teachers can maintain a system for monitoring programs to identify emerging problems. Thus, teachers themselves will need to be involved in seeking and testing solutions and, in this effort, in drawing directly or through middlemen upon relevant knowledge to guide the development of possible solutions. In all probability, the involvement of more teaching personnel in R & D efforts will accelerate the impact of these activities upon the practice of education. In the absence of such involvement, the practice of research has a limited impact upon educational reform.

Since the role of teachers can be considered important to the effects of research, we should ask how the involvement of teachers can be increased. An obvious suggestion is to include more research emphases in teacher-training programs. Another way may be to define the roles of teachers to include the use and validation of educational research. Their work can be especially prominent in designing curricula, testing out classroom-management procedures, and individualizing instruction.

Realistically, if teachers are to be included more prominently in these modes of research, they will require differential pay scales and role recognition. Such developments require concomitant improvements in the design of schools.

THE SCHOOL

The school, together with its sponsoring district, is the accountable unit in the new designs for mainstreaming handicapped children. Their allocations of funds, space, teachers, and resource personnel to the designs of education should be carefully scrutinized. The administrators who are assigned the responsibility for planning for and managing the changes toward mainstreaming are especially vulnerable to possible charges from constituent groups. For instance, if they increase allocations to accommodate the handicapped, they may encounter charges from other groups whose allocations are cut. They are also caught between the attitudes and preferences of their boards and citizen groups and the demands of teachers and teacher unions.

Disagreements may often limit or slow down the accommodations to mainstreaming in the same manner that operational cost increases slow down other procedural changes in the schools. In addition, the mainstreaming of handicapped children, especially the severely handicapped, is likely to receive delayed action on several counts. As viewed by the parent groups who have pushed for the legal and legislative action leading to "progressive inclusion," the delays will be seen as a lack of good faith. Each explanation will be viewed as a rationalization. The rationalizations, it is hoped, will lead systematically to policy shifts and new instructional modes. Ideally, perhaps, the conservative actions of the administrators will be combined in a time sequence with demonstrations of instructional effectiveness from the R & D settings so that changes will be based upon good instructional designs. We hope that all the innovations will be happy ones.

THE COMMUNITY

The emphasis on mainstreaming commits the community as directly as the school. "Least restrictive" concepts refer to living arrangements and social recreational acceptance. It also means equal educational opportunities or, more directly, an education according to need. The community, then, must provide the ethical and economic support base for these new involvements. In all probability, these support requisites will be attained only at the expense of other alternatives. Otherwise, the tax base must be greatly enlarged and resources otherwise expanded to meet a burgeoning demand for educational and welfare services.

The collective conscience of the community will be tested as never before in reaching decisions that pit the wishes of individual citizens against their moral commitment to tenants of a mature, democratic society.

A Summary (Pessimistic)

All participants in the future educational scene have reason to feel inadequate. Feelings of inadequacy seem to stem from many sources: concern for lack of knowledge; frustration about the poorly trained and the poorly advised members of our child population; resentment born from our egocentrism in view of the large, complex, and confusing nature of public education; and guilt about our limited funds for programs that require inflated budgets. It seems that no matter how much we learn and how hard we try, we understand only a portion of federal and state legislation and regulations, educational technology, landmark research, and forces that may predict supported events in the educational community.

Furthermore, there is evidence that the greater unit costs and time constraints placed upon schools result in forced choices for educational programs. In the realities of public education, we must go slowly in developing programs that meet with school and community approval for tax supported long-term development.

Finally, teachers are constantly asked to work harder, develop additional competencies, and assume more and more responsibilities, even when the consequences for them are painful. In this regard, teachers are no longer passive members of the large educational establishment. They are insisting upon participating in the agreements about mainstreaming handicapped children. The outcomes of such negotiations are likely to be a more conservative but, also, a more shared and more predictable form of utilization of the many potential innovations stemming from educational R & D programs.

An Afterword

Educational technology has made impressive advances even though its designs are not supported by, or incorporated in, a science of instruction. Consequently, the advances in educational technology are characterized by improving techniques for collecting data and disseminating information, systems planning, information processing, and behavioral management. These aspects of educational research also support the development of useful products for educational applications. Nevertheless, the designs of instruction as applied to intricate higher functions of competence still expose our technology as gross and inadequate.

The optimistic view is that our gains are rapidly moving us into feasible designs for individualized instruction, programs for teaching language, computer-assisted instructional systems, home-based instructional packages, and a common technology for the use of all relevant educational team members. How far our current technological explosion will take us, however, may depend on extrinsic factors. The intent of society in support of the schools may be to delay rapid developments in the mainstreaming of handicapped children. The cost and exponential need of the schools for more programs in support of all children may produce an apparent conservatism that is objectionable to constituent support groups. The actual progress, then, may not be measured by the state of the science or the art, but by the willingness of society to invest in this feature of its ethical and moral commitment.

We believe that we are headed in the right direction. We see no need to apologize for the history of our educational system, and we have every reason to believe that most, if not all, of our grand aspirations for education can come to pass. The challenge is to produce a science of instruction that will make the best use of all our technology and intellectual resources for the good of all our children.

Our title is intended to emphasize an inescapable point. The negative utopia described by Orwell is a dire warning that man (through the applications of technology) contributes to his own dehumanization. Ultimately, then, technological progress contributes to moral and spiritual destruction. This premise, of course, counters the more traditional Western belief that human progress evolves from man's capacity to devise and create. In this tradition, education is the design for perfectibility. Perhaps it is this capacity to believe in progress that makes progress possible. So it may be in the education of the handicapped. To stop short of a full educational plan for all children and youth is unthinkable. To use less than all of our ingenuity and technical capability is obscene. We must believe that ways and means can and will be found "beyond 1984" to educate all our children optimally. To do so is our tradition and is in keeping with our national philosophy. Let us hope that it is also our destiny.

References

Atkinson, R. C. Adaptive instructional systems: Some attempts to optimize the learning process. In D. Klahr (Ed.), *Cognition and instruction.* Hillsdale, N. J.: Lawrence Erlbaum, 1976.

Becker, W. C. The direct instruction model. In R. Rhine (Ed.), *Encouraging change in America's schools: A decade of experimentation.* New York: Academic. (In press)

Bijou, S. W. Behavior analysis: Applications to the education of exceptional children. Address given at Northern Kentucky University, March 7, 1975.

Bricker, D., Ruder, K., & Vincent, L. An intervention strategy for language deficient children. In N. G. Haring & R. L. Schiefelbusch (Eds.), *Teaching special children.* New York: McGraw-Hill, 1976.

Bushell, D. *The behavior analysis approach to project Follow Through.* Report to Office of Education, U.S. Department of Health, Education, and Welfare, August 1976.

Dewey, J. Psychology and social practice. *The Psychological Review*, 1900, 7, 105-124.

Glaser, R. Cognitive psychology and instructional design. In D. Klahr (Ed.), *Cognition and instruction*. Hillsdale, N. J.: Lawrence Erlbaum, 1976. (a)

Glaser, R. Components of a psychology of instruction: Toward a science of design. *Review of Educational Research*, 1976, **46**, 1-24. (b)

Gropper, G. L. You can lead the public to educational technology but you can't. . . . *Educational Technology*, 1976, **16**, 40-45.

Guba, E. G, & Clark, D. L. The configurational perspective: A new view of educational knowledge production and utilization. *Educational Researcher*, April 1975, **4**.

Guess, D., Sailor, W., & Baer, D. Children with limited language. In R. L. Schiefelbusch (Ed.), *Language intervention strategies*. Baltimore: University Park Press, 1978.

Haring, N. G., & Gentry, N. D. Direct and individualized instructional procedures. In N. G. Haring & R. L. Schiefelbusch (Eds.), *Teaching special children*. New York: McGraw-Hill, 1976.

Hopkins, R. L., & Conard, R. J. Putting it all together: Super school. In N. G. Haring & R. L. Schiefelbusch (Eds.), *Teaching special children*. New York: McGraw-Hill, 1976.

Lovitt, T. C. Applied behavior analysis techniques and curriculum research: Implications for instruction. In N. G. Haring & R. L. Schiefelbusch (Eds.), *Teaching special children*. New York: McGraw-Hill, 1976.

Miller, J., & Yoder, D. An ontogenetic language teaching strategy for the mentally retarded. In R. L. Schiefelbusch & L. L. Lloyd (Eds.), *Language perspectives: Acquisition, retardation and intervention*. Baltimore: University Park Press, 1974.

National Advisory Committee on the Handicapped (NACH). *The unfinished revolution: Education for the handicapped*. Annual Report. Washington, D. C.: Advisory Committee on the Handicapped, Office of Education, U.S. Department of Health, Education, and Welfare, 1967.

Reynolds, M. C. *Trends in education: Changing roles of special education personnel*. Columbus, Ohio: University Council for Education Administration. (No date)

Staats, A. W. Behaviorism and cognitive theory in the study of language: A neopsycholinguistics. In R. L. Schiefelbusch & L. L. Lloyd (Eds.), *Language perspectives: Acquisition, retardation and intervention*. Baltimore: University Park Press, 1974.

Tyler, R. W. *Prospects for research and development in education*. Berkeley: McCutchan, 1976.

Walker, N. What a great idea! Too bad it didn't work. *Educational Technology*, 1976, **16**, 46-47.

Critics

A Critical Perspective of the Papers on "The Futures of Education"

Nicholas Hobbs[1]

Vanderbilt University

On Paper by Seymour Sarason

I am so much in accord with all that Sarason says and I appreciate so much the opportunity to learn from him that I have little to say about his paper except to urge that it be read and reread. However, I do have a few random observations that support or extend his arguments.

It is delightful to have a problem put in its historical context, especially by a psychologist. Social scientists in general and psychologists in particular have a truncated view of events. Except for the psychoanalysts and a few developmentalists, most psychologists treat their research subjects as though they had no history other than the events provided by the experimenter and a future that is best left to the astrologist. Sarason, on the other hand, has a sense of the significance of time — past and future — and this sense infuses his writing with an uncommon wisdom.

Sarason correctly links the last decade's attention to handicapped persons with the civil rights movement generally. It is an important perception because it provides what are at least good analogies in the resistance, for example, to the 1954 ruling of the Supreme Court that struck down the doctrine of separate but equal facilities in public education. It is useful, too, in making us aware that the process is not finished. Victories so substantial are never complete; reversals are to be expected. Although the movement as a whole will raise our society to a new level of effective concern for individuals, the plateau reached will be at a level considerably lower than the aspirations of advocates for equity and individualization. The genius of American revolutions (thus far, at least!) is that they all have ended up in more or less workable accommodations.

---

[1]Professor of Psychology and of Preventive Medicine

We have managed to avoid the excesses of the French, Russian, and Chinese revolutions, but always with a sacrifice of some ideological goals. And thus it will be with our concerns for the handicapped and with the remarkably advanced Public Law 94-142, The Education for All Handicapped Children Act.

There is one sentence in Sarason's paper that I would like to quote as a counterpoint to what seems to be a major deficiency in most of the conference papers and discussions, that is, an exclusive preoccupation with the individual child and the teacher-child relationship. "Problem behavior is not 'inside' a child, or characteristic of him/her, but a feature of a complex situation." Sarason then goes on to illustrate "the most dramatic and sustained change in behavior we have ever seen," when it became possible for them to change a child's classroom placement. The imperative in Sarason's position is that we always must think of children in settings, as members of unique, circumscribed social systems that are composed of the child himself (the defining member of the system) plus parents, siblings, friends, teachers, social workers, policemen, neighbors, nurses, and others. This mode of thought is not yet congenial to most special educators, but it is a critical perspective for dealing effectively with individual children or designing educational programs appropriate to the needs of all children, whether handicapped or not.

Sarason points out that all social organisms, such as schools, must have mechanisms for limiting disturbance — reducing "noise" in the system. Thus, most special classes for handicapped children have been used to remove from the system the children who are most disruptive, usually, those who misbehave or fail to conform to majority group expectations. Over the years, most handicapped children have been in the mainstream of education. The difficult children have been consigned to special education.

It is useful to note the role of classification in the maintenance of tranquility in regular classrooms and schools. The categories we use to classify children have little relevance to their instructional or other needs. The primary function of categories is to legitimize exclusion, to control deviance. From the standpoint of individual program planning for children, as opposed to controlling deviant behavior in the interest of organizational tranquility, what we need is some kind of ecologically oriented, service-based classification system. In such a system, there would be no place for the gallimaufry of categories we have inherited from medicine, psychology, education, social work, and corrections. Instead, the system would record (a) the specific service needs of a child, (b) who is responsible for seeing that the services are provided, (c) what the costs should be, (d) where the money is to come from, (e) by what date the service is to be provided, and (f) the criteria by which effectiveness will be judged. Such a simple and pragmatic scheme would have enormous advantages over our present classification system for both planning and management. It would make labeling all but impossible. And it would ease completely the nonfunctional boundaries between special and regular education. However, one can confidently predict great resistance to the idea because it would deprive schools of a tested mechanism for legitimizing the exclusion of unpleasant children and, in addition, it would expose the absurdity of the many bureaucracies, both private and public, that define their purposes in terms of outmoded concepts of how children should be classified. I surmise that the most vigorous opposition to the abandonment of categories in favor of a functional and accountable system emphasizing service delivery will come from special educators themselves, and especially from program managers at the federal, state, and local levels.

On Paper by R. P. McDermott & Jeffry Aron

This paper is brilliant: insightful, tightly reasoned, fresh, and beautifully written. It enriches enormously our understanding of the expectancy dimension of the teaching-learning situation. It further exemplifies how science adds to knowledge. Science advances by avoiding big questions like "what is life" or "how do we learn"; instead, it addresses limited problems with rigorous procedures and provides, cumulatively, a basis for speculation about overarching issues. But more on the method later.

I would like, first, to comment on the basic premise of the paper: that our educational system is "in reality an effort by those who have access to various political and economic resources to limit that access to themselves." The thesis is supported by the allegation that compensatory education programs and other efforts to equalize opportunity for advancement have failed. This allegation, levied against both those on the right who want to spend less money on children and those on the left who would revise the basic social order, is simply not supported by the evidence. Project Head-Start, for example, with over 1700 evaluation studies completed, shows impressive gains in the academic competence, self-confidence, and health of children, and in the effectiveness of parents. Some programs failed, of course, but many more succeeded; thus it is now possible to ask and get answers to the right question — "Under what circumstances do compensatory educational programs work?" As for the larger issue of schools as the instrument for preserving privilege, it is the familiar Marxist view. Capitalist societies, indeed, have difficulty in distributing opportunity equitably. The system is not without its advantages, however, and they should not be discounted. Schools always have reflected and always will reflect the structure and values of the larger society. From this perspective, the issue of educational reform must be seen first as social reform. If social reform is the agenda, then the context of the debate should be widened greatly.

To return to methodology: I am filled with admiration for what McDermott is doing. He and Aron report the results of two years of study of "two films of children in a classroom — one classroom, one day, one hour, one top group of readers, one bottom group of readers, around the same table." This rigorous, systematic, and sophisticated observation of children in natural settings is laudable. Bronfenbrenner has characterized most laboratory child development studies as emerging from strange people doing strange things to strange children in strange places, or something to that effect. The two years of McDermott's study must be considered an hypothesis-generating exercise, however. Confirmation with larger numbers is surely required. Intensity and frequency of observation in no way compensates for idiosyncratic situations, for the extreme case. It is instructive that in this paper the main variable assumed to be important is "time at task." In a companion and equally ingenious paper, "communication style" is presented as the main variable. The observational data are the same in both instances. How many more similar main effects can McDermott hypothesize? And what are their relative effects? Such questions can only be answered by investigation.

I resonate strongly to McDermott and Aron's emphasis on the importance of expectation in the behavior of children. Poor readers learn to be good at being poor readers, as the two authors point out. In the Classification Project, we came to recognize that every institution has its metaphorical imperative, demanding institution-appropriate behavior, just as in McDermott's classroom.

I think McDermott's thesis puts too heavy a burden of responsibility on one teacher, or on the child-teacher relationship. There is no compelling reason to believe that spending twice as much time with the slow group would make any difference. Segregated classrooms are designed to make it possible for teachers to spend more time with children with particular problems, but they generate a pervasive expectancy of inadequacy. It is altogether possible that if the teacher did spend more time with the slow-reading students, they might read even worse, if McDermott's expectancy hypothesis holds true.

One of the problems with McDermott and Aron's paper (and in others as well) is what seems to me an overemphasis on teacher-child relationships in the classroom. Schools tend to work best with children who are already prepared to do what schools expect and who are sustained outside the school by parents, siblings, and friends. Emphasis on teacher strategies is okay for nice kids but not for children who are in trouble. In Project Re-Ed, dealing with children who were rejected by families, schools, and communities, we found it necessary to couch the troubled child's problem in ecological terms. As Sarason points out in his paper, the "problem is not in the child." The goal must be to make the ecological system — the small social system defined by the being of the child — work. The teacher simply cannot do it alone. The research evidence is now overwhelming that instructional programs for children with special problems work best when parents are intimately involved. And it seems likely that parents of children who are progressing well are, in fact, quite involved in the process, although their contribution to the progress of the child is seldom observed.

Let me point out, finally, that the Pirandello parallel requires a different conclusion from McDermott's intimation that improved instruction might result in improved performance. In Pirandello, only one last act is possible; by the time the actors arrive, the most skillful director could make no difference in how things worked out. One is reminded of Mia Kellmer Pringle's survey of British children in the aptly titled report, "Born to Fail." By the time the children get to school, many are destined to failure. Gallagher's work is important here. He starts with children quite early in life and emphasizes not just cognitive development but the acquisition through experience of the belief that the world can be managed, that the child can make a difference in what happens to him. Investments in the improvement of reading cannot be confined to an elementary school classroom but must start early and must extend into many aspects of the child's life.

The great thing about McDermott and Aron's paper for such a conference as ours is that it raises provocative questions ranging from details of research methodology to the need for revolution in the social order.

On Paper by Reginald L. Jones

Reginald Jones's disciplined and graceful paper is of great value in thinking about the future of special education. I admire especially his attentiveness to research literature and his restrained evaluation of such highly lauded ideas as diagnostic and prescriptive teaching.

Jones underscores what several of the papers allude to, that is, the difficulty of bringing about planned change and the inadequacy of our understanding of the process. It is interesting that the social engineer perceives others as resistant to change but exempts himself from such an allegation. We might all be more effective in bringing about change if we eschewed a "we-they" dichotomy and recognized our community with all others who cherish the status quo.

I was much impressed by Jones's four recommendations, all of which suggest the need for a new kind of scholarship and new federal and state funding practices to encourage synthesizing studies, the involvement of new disciplines, the improvement of research and graduate training in special education, and the deliberate avoidance of intellectual provincialism. These notions, all appealing to me, run counter to much of the current research effort in education, and they suggest new directions in the pursuit of enlightenment in the future of special education.

On Paper by A. W. Chickering & J. N. Chickering

The Chickerings' excellent paper on life-long learning by handicapped persons reveals their extensive knowledge of promising developments in higher education and in life-long learning. It also reveals their abundant optimism that the gains in education for handicapped children attendant upon the passage of P.L. 94-142 somehow will be extended throughout the life-span. Indeed, in an opening statement designed to capture attention, which it does successfully, they go through the exercise of substituting the word "persons" for the words "handicapped children" in the Education for All Handicapped Children Act. The result is a fresh and challenging statement of what education should be like for all people of all ages at all times.

The Chickerings rightly identify the spirit and intent of the Education for All Handicapped Children Act with other movements of the past two decades that were designed to increase equity and to open up our society to the participation of groups previously excluded or limited by custom or law. This heightened commitment to equity has been pressed in the interest of blacks and other minorities, women, prisoners, juvenile delinquents, mental patients, institutionalized mentally retarded people, participants in scientific experiments, parents who want access to their children's school records, persons charged with criminal acts, and others, as well as handicapped children. We all have been privileged to witness a remarkable transformation of a society in the service of individual rights. I think the Chickerings are correct in asserting that these changes are not reversible and that, indeed, they will continue to open up opportunities for self-enhancement, including opportunities for life-long education for handicapped people.

The Chickerings cite a number of developments in higher education that, if extended, could facilitate life-long learning for the handicapped. They describe the British Open University, the programs of colleges and universities (e.g., Antioch College) that extend the campus to where people live and work and study, the satellite learning centers developed by many universities, the provision of work-study opportunities beyond the collegiate years (e.g., at Goddard College), the weekend college, the development of new methods for the individualization of instruction based on computer and television technology, the development of contract learning, the remarkable proliferation of self-instructional materials, the development of a concept of experiential learning, the flourishing of competency based on educational concepts, and so on. I do not repeat their whole catalog of carefully described educational developments. Certainly, a lot is going on in education, and the Chickerings do us all a great service by assembling in one place and describing lucidly some of the developments that can enhance life-long learning opportunities for the handicapped.

I wish I could share the Chickerings' fine optimism for the future, but I cannot. Normally, I am buoyantly optimistic and dismiss almost too readily the rumble of the distant drum, but I am forced by what seems to be a heavy freight of evidence to be cautious about the future growth of higher education. Colleges and universities are cutting the kinds of programs the Chickerings describe. Retrenchment is the watchword of the time and austerity the promise of the future, or so it seems. The great advances made in programs for handicapped children during the 1960s were part of a growing economy; we did not have to face the question that surely will be with us for years ahead: *What is it that we are now doing that we are willing to stop doing in order to start doing something new?*

The disposition, in some quarters, is to regard the stringent times we are in as transient, as nothing more than a period of regrouping prior to a new surge of economic (and educational) growth. This reading of our situation seems to me erroneous. Barring some remarkable discovery not now forecast, we are moving into a steady-state future in which choices among finite options will be pressed upon us. If life-long education for the handicapped flourishes, something else will languish. Success in providing life-long education programs will mean that we cherish education and value the handicapped, and that we want more for the handicapped and less for others, that we are willing to give up some attractive things in life, including security, health, and various forms of self-gratification. It will be interesting to see how it all comes out, when the chips are down. Actually, the future is not without its attractive features. Problems we have solved (splendidly, I think) with compassion, hard work, and money, we now have to solve with compassion, hard work, and wisdom.

On Paper by James J. Gallagher

This paper is extraordinarily knowledgeable and instructive. It should be useful not only to people concerned with the future of special education but, also, to those concerned with the future of all education. Much in Gallagher's paper implies that the "we-they" dichotomy may not be useful for the future. We might, then, consider his description of organizational needs as applicable to education in general, including special education.

James Gallagher has rare if not unique qualifications for describing the organizational needs for quality education. He has worked as a scientist on basic problems of teaching and learning, an engineer in designing model demonstration programs, a scholar in synthesizing and interpreting the work of others, an administrator of a major child development research organization, and a leader and statesman in his past roles as President of the Council for Exceptional Children and Director of the Bureau of Education for the Handicapped. Thus he speaks with special authority at each level of knowledge generation and transfer in his model for systems design and change.

The concept of a broad-based support system for special education and general education wil be tested in the crucial years immediately ahead. The question will be whether educational policy makers can successfully advocate the long-term advantages of a comprehensive support system, which will require a substantial investment in the future, over short-term gains, which may produce apparent economies. Gallagher comments on the remarkable 300 per cent increase in state funds for special education between 1966-1972, a growth preceded by federal investments as early as 1961. It is important to recognize that the expanded resources required for the handicapped came from marginal funds and a growing economy. The nation *did* have to decide to spend the money on special education rather than on something else; however, it *did not* have to face the tougher question, "What is it we are now doing that we are willing to give up in order to help handicapped children?" As competition for scarce resources increases, we shall have all the more need for a rational support system for special education and education, but it will take wise and inspired leadership to bring it about.

I have two suggestions about the comprehensive support system described in Gallagher's paper: (a) The model omits evaluation as an essential component of the process, and (b) in my judgment, it gives too little attention to the issue of knowledge diffusion and implementation.

Although evaluation seldom is done well, it is, nonetheless, a crucial component in the knowledge development and transfer process. As I am sure Gallagher would agree, there is no way to distinguish programs deserving augmented support from programs deserving a *coup de grace* other than by carefully designed and meticulously executed evaluation studies. Most human services programs are guided by convention, habit, professional preferences, and, as Gallagher notes, by the desire "to avoid controversy, rather than seek excellence." Evaluation is an essential but not sufficient measure against mediocrity.

Gallagher raises but does not treat adequately the difficult issue of knowledge diffusion and utilization. The final step in the knowledge-transfer operation is often "the missing link" (to use the title of Erwin Hargrove's monograph on the subject) in the process. The neglect stems, in part, from the lack of verified knowledge about the process itself and, especially, about the optimum alignments of scientists, professional groups, advocacy groups, policy makers, and program people. A convergence of effort among all these groups seems to be required to overcome the myriad resistances that cumulatively defeat change. That the process is not altogether rational does nothing to simplify it.

Should one be disposed to audit the contributions of special education to all of education, surely one of the major items to be recorded would be the concept of a comprehensive support system for improving teaching and learning in the classroom. James Gallagher was a principal architect and, in this splendid paper, is a persuasive advocate of such comprehenisve support systems.

On Paper by Henry M. Levin

I almost feel that I should disqualify myself from commenting on Levin's paper because of a growing disaffection with the tautologies of economic analyses in addressing human development problems. I may simply extend my general disgruntlement to Levin's amiable and well-written paper, and expose my own limitations as well.

The one great lesson economists teach, a lesson appropriately reinforced by Levin, is that resources are finite; choosing to expend funds for one purpose diminishes by precisely the same amount the funds available for other perhaps equally worthwhile purposes. The lesson needs to be dinned into all of us, and especially into non-economists in the human development professions who tend to believe that people are so important that governments should spend whatever is required to assure the fullest development of their individual potentials. Levin correctly points out that such expenditures will never happen as long as there are competing requirements, as there always will be.

Levin applies traditional economic concepts to the question of what resources should be allocated to finance educational services for exceptional children. His analyses, ingenius as they are, seem to be almost wholly unrelated to what actually happens when congressmen or state legislators vote on special education legislation. I would wager that not one vote is likely to be influenced by the outcome of the analyses.

I found Levin's argument about who should pay for special services for the handicapped to be more persuasive, but the argument seems to me more political or philosophical than economic. Or we might call it an argument in political economy, to use a neglected term. Equity and local options are the goods to be maximized. Both can hardly be achieved by placing decisions at the school district level, where equity considerations may easily fade from view. Equity might be well achieved by federal intervention, but then the benefits of local decision making would be lost. Levin suggests the state as the unit of government that is best equipped to achieve equity and resource allocation and to display sensitivity to the local exercise of informed options.

I share Levin's restrained enthusiasm for vouchers and I applaud him for pointing out the limitations of this instrument, which is sometimes cited as the harbinger of the millennium in education.

Levin sees in mainstreaming an opportunity to use regular students to assist handicapped ones. I like the idea but I would chide him a bit for forgetting the economic maxim that resources are finite: If a student invests two hours in instructing other students in mathematics, does he or she not give up the opportunity to learn additional mathematics himself? A parallel notion, but one that Levin neglects, is that families are the major source of support for handicapped children and, therefore, resources could be enhanced considerably by the prudent investment of public funds in the family rather than in agencies and institutions external to the family. The economist may point out rightly that there is not economic gain if mothers, fathers, and siblings must be paid the minimum wage for caring for handicapped children, but they are not so paid and not likely to be. This argument should not stop a strategy of optimizing the investment of resources in families.

Levin is appropriately wary of the economy of screening to identify children in need of special assistance. Experience with the Early and Periodic Screening, Diagnois, and Treatment Program attests to the soundness of his position. But there are alternate means for identifying the resource needs of children; they need much further exploration than is currently being supported. Our current classification system essentially precludes, in my judgment, a rational and economic allocation of resources in the service of handicapped children.

On Paper by R. L. Schiefelbusch & R. K. Hoyt, Jr.

It is a bit difficult to know at what level to pitch a reply to this interesting paper by Schiefelbusch and Hoyt. Their brave new world, modestly discounted by a pessimistic paragraph or two, presents a ringing challenge to each of us. It also carries with it a chilling responsibility. If we, the members of this conference, could will into being their vision of the future, would we do it? Should we do it?

When I was a lad, I believed in the perfectability of man. As a matter of fact, reflecting on the burden I must have placed upon my parents and teachers, I surmise that occasionally I may have acted as though I had discovered the idea or, at least, that I was the only one who had ever really believed in it. I also had the charming notion that the best instrument for perfecting man rested on the banks of the Potomac River, a notion not altogether puerile since my hourly wage as a hired hand in an ice cream factory was raised overnight from 9 cents an hour to 35 cents an hour by order of Franklin Delano Roosevelt. But, alas, in the wisdom or weariness of age, I have embraced the concept of original sin. Perhaps I should add that I have not embraced the panoply of invention that goes with it, but I have come to accept the notion of original sin as a metaphorical representation of one of the profound truths about man.

There is a wistful sentence in our colleagues' paper: "We hope that all the innovations will be happy ones." Here we see the decent doubt of two fine human beings. One man's median is another man's Poisson. What our friends would delight to see as central tendencies, our enemies would rejoice to see as random distributions. And this is probably the way it should be.

Every major reform has within it, at the outset, the seeds of its own undoing. Thus there is a kind of continuing rectification in the affairs of man that results from an ongoing redefinition of the good. While, generally, I support the vision of the future painted by Schiefelbusch and Hoyt, I suspect that the concept of the good will be radically restated by 1984 + 3.

Theories and Their Applications

Michael Timpane[1]

National Institute of Education

Reactions To Levin's Paper

Special education is not, to say the least, an area with a long tradition of economic analysis. Benefit-cost studies and comprehensive public finance planning have had low priority in this field that struggled to achieve a minimal recognition of its clientele's needs in legislatures and courts, and to develop effective treatments for the stubborn, complex, and diverse educational problems of handicapped children. Now and in the future, however, the nation's schools may finally provide minimum adequate educational treatment for each child who needs it. Constitutional requirements being satisfied, special education then will be in more or less even competition with other educational and public services for the taxpayers' dollars. In such a context, the rudiments of benefit-cost analysis will be a necessary tool for special educators, for it will have become fair enough, even from their point of view, to ask the question, where should the next available tax dollar(s) be spent — upon special education's most pressing unfunded priority or upon the most pressing unfunded priority of, say, secondary education or local mental health services, or upon a moderate-income housing subsidy?

Levin's paper is an excellent primer for this necessary learning. Its special virtue is that it provides some workable economic notions and sensible advice for budget and policy planning, without suggesting that economic reasoning should become anyone's excuse for failing to provide adequate educational services for the handicapped. He is right that "whatever is required" will not be an adequate rule for the future of special education finance; and his helpful alternative suggestions are meritorious and persuasive strategies for obtaining and using resources that will be (let us hope) generous but not unlimited.

---

[1] Assistant Deputy Director. Formerly at the Rand Corporation, Center for Educational Finance and Government.

Nevertheless, in setting forth these inevitable economic considerations, Levin's paper illuminates a critical shortcoming in the state of the art: Special education cannot, for the most part, satisfy his assumptions that there exist special education programs "out there" (in development or in classrooms) that will provide generally predictable educational outcome, in various locations, at reasonably consistent costs. No refrain is more prominent in the special education finance literature than that similar programs (even similar exemplary programs) in special education have inexplicably wide variations in expenditure and presumably in cost (e.g., Bernstein et al., 1976).

Not for a minute is this to say that there are not many effective special education activities in operation throughout the country or in development in university laboratories and institutes. There are many such; more than a few have been carefully studied and, in some scientific sense, have "proven" their effectiveness. Experts and advocates in special education can say, in truth, "Yes, we know how to overcome at least some of the educational barriers represented by many handicapping conditions," and school programs should be assumed and expected to do so.

But these activities merely sharpen my point about the dangers and opportunities of our present situation. We are at the stage, in federal and state legislative development especially, where we may reasonably hope to create some nationally recognized (as distinguished from federally enforced) criteria for determining what is and is not a "free and appropriate" education for handicapped children, and for laying in place a new federal-state financing system that will deliver such services in a manner that is both fair and fiscally prudent. But we are missing the essential building block of the "program" — the configuration of resources (teachers, curricula, support services, and materials in an appropriate local organizational structure) — that are, at once, the educator's tools for instruction and the financier's unit for collecting and allocating dollars. For the most part, the elements for effective programs already exist. What is lacking is not so much knowledge as an effort to apply what we know in the creation of classroom- or school-level programs of instruction, to make sure that they work in real classrooms or schools, and then to encourage their adoption. Here, it seems to me, is a top federal program priority: to stimulate for all handicapped children what it has begun to provide, through its early childhood demonstrations for the very young — an array of definable, predictable, and financially supportable programs of service. Experience in both regular and special education indicates that the development of such programs is both slow and expensive, but not so expensive as the possible wasted dollars and missed educational opportunities.

The need for such programs seems to be especially pressing, and their absence especially dangerous, in the burgeoning context of mainstreaming. Let me illustrate with a simplified example.

In average district A, average school Aa has 500 "regular" children in 25-child classrooms, at an average cost of $1,000 per child, plus 50 special education children (all "mainstreamable" to some extent) in four classrooms, at an average cost of $2,000 per child. Total budget: $600,000, of which $100,000 is devoted to special classes. The order comes down: Mainstream all special education children with existing resources. The school thus has $100,000 to reallocate for a new type of special education services. What should be done?

First, at least $30,000 will go to provide two extra classroom teachers, to keep class size in the 550-child school at 25:1. That leaves $70,000, at most, with several alternative uses, each of which will have advocates. For example, $70,000 might provide,

- 10-12 full-time (or 20-25 half-time) aides to help out in the regular 25-child classrooms; or
- 4-5 classroom teachers, to reduce regular class size by one, for each special education student, to a school average of about 22:1; or
- one resource room, with two special education teachers and two aides, plus 3-4 full-time aides for the regular classrooms; or
- the same resource room, plus slightly smaller regular classes (say 24:1).

This simple case raises at least two fundamental questions:

1. Which of these equal-cost "programs" will be more effective? Some answer seems essential since political forces (parents, regular classsroom teachers, special education teachers, community-based aides, etc.) will develop behind each alternative. The arrival of additional resources for special education would provide a somewhat more pleasant variant: Which program should best be added: smaller regular classes? more aides? more intensively staffed resource room?

2. In the absence of well-developed programs with predictable effects, is there not, in mainstreaming, a cost-cutting threat? A temptation, in our example, to devote less than $70,000 to new special education activities? From Massachusetts, with its path-breaking mainstreaming law, the evidence is disturbing: School districts that have the lowest levels of extra expenditure per handicapped child also have the highest proportions of special education children in the "mainstream," and these low-expenditure districts are also the less affluent, less educationally ambitious communities (Wilken & Porter, 1973). Maybe "mainstreaming" is simply a more productive way to provide better special education services at lower

per-pupil costs; but it also could be an excuse for some communities simply to cut costs. In the context of special classes, a plea for "programs" may be intended to forestall inefficient expenditures by the well-meaning; but in the context of mainstreaming, good "programs" (i.e., some worked-out ideas of what an adequate mainstreamed education amounts to in a classroom or school) may be seen, instead, by the politically alert as a necessary defense against false economies.

Until we have invented the necessary special education programs, the full application of each of Levin's suggested financial strategies remains beyond our reach. His "Investment Approach" will be most useful in developing the rhetoric of program justifications; but once we are beyond the easy case of deciding that we prefer the marginal benefits of special education to those of the B-1 bomber, we will be in heavier analytical traffic. The honest marshaling of what evidence we have on these program trade-offs is perfectly legitimate (Rivlin, 1973) in the competition among public interests; but we may not, even so, wish to press too sharply any slender analytical advantage over the regular educational programs or other social services, upon whose greater effectiveness the education of our clientele may increasingly depend.

The "Exemplary Program Approach" suffers not only from the conservative bias that Levin detected (the assumption that last year's best is next year's best, too), but also from a certain overambition (the assumption that most schools can successfully implement exemplary programs in an exemplary fashion).

Only the "Program Components Approach" recommends itself for short-term use. It may be immediately useful in local budget building and it needs only the "programs," whose development I have urged, to have wider applicability in state-level financial planning, in particular.

Levin's comments on financial and organizational provisions for special education are very abbreviated and should mostly call our attention to important areas for additional analysis: (a) the relation of state special education finance systems to state general aid reforms; (b) the articulation of special education programs with the also-expanding federal and state programs for compensatory education of disadvantaged children; (c) the revision of tuition-grant policies in the context of mainstreaming; and (d) the development of effective local implementation strategies for special education programs.

I cannot resist saying, finally, that as a former school board member, I am distinctly less worried than Levin about the potential political weakness of special education's minority status. Never have so many listened so often to so much presented so well by so few!

Reactions To the Conference

In my comments on Henry Levin's paper, I adopted, as had he, the convenient assumption that an important part of the future of special education could be described and analyzed as a process of linear change. Under this assumption, we could display the relevance of the economic conceit that consumer preferences, production possibilities, costs, and prices (budgets) interact in some predictable way to produce various systematic outcomes. One need not deny the utility of economic analysis to admit that such assumptions of linear change, and of readily applicable paradigmatic explanations, did not dominate the conference. To the contrary, there were several presentiments of a more turbulent future.

The recent advances in the status of special education — through court decisions, state legislative and appropriations actions, the creation of a federal civil rights charter and financial commitment, Section 504 of the Rehabilitation Act of 1973, and the Education for All Handicapped Children Act of 1975 (P.L. 94-142) — are nothing less than a quantum leap forward. On that we agreed. But there seemed to be some considerable chance that the subsequent policy development and implementation processes could easily get out of control. Many conferees remembered well the long years of hard-won progress in gaining special attention (usually special classes) for handicapped children, and they wondered aloud at where the new campaign veritably to "desegregate" special education in the United States would lead. Several deep cross-currents seemed to be running.

1. The equalitarian and democratic values embodied in the move to mainstreaming are, as Sarason suggests, manifest and proper; but they may yet be an insufficient value basis for special education policy. The more subtle demands of individual liberty, in terms of the recognition of each person's ever-present, ever-changing needs, also must be embodied in policy. Individualized education plans (IEPs) were not necessarily the answer, either; the entire human development system must be keyed somehow to what Madjid called the "wholeness of life."

2. Even the equal opportunity objective of mainstreaming cannot be taken for granted. Various actors in the education system could have different motives for adopting it: Some may be devoted egalitarians; some may be simply devoted professionals trying to make the most productive or extensive use of limited resources; and some may be mere cost cutters, using mainstreaming for little or no positive educational purpose. Even more unsettling, to me at least, is McDermott's further insight that, in the political economy of the "sort-'em, teach-'em, test-'em" classroom our social system currently seems to promote and fortify, the less able or more-difficult-to-teach students may have little chance for equal educational

opportunity by the basic and practical measure of time-on-task, even when the teacher is trying to spread his/her attention fairly.

3. Political support for the expansion of services for the handicapped has been and is high. The civil rights of the handicapped are being widely affirmed. Billions of new dollars, mostly from state and federal sources, have been and will be added to special education's resources. And yet, the bandwagon can be pushed too far. There is some public confusion about the reasons for the sudden switch to mainstreaming after years of promoting special classes. There is also the potential, at least, for backlash from the general education public, from the representatives of other minority interests, and from the teaching profession, if the gains of special education come to be perceived as their loss.

4. Special education may be moving into a new and relatively untested partnership with general education. The very distinction between the two may begin to blur. The institutional configurations that formerly had excluded or neglected the handicapped were not, by some miracle, to serve them well. There seems to be high hopes that the insights of special education practice have much to contribute to the improvement of *everyone's* education, but only medium conviction that general education is ready for the challenge of educating all children, handicapped and not, together.

5. The regular classroom teacher was a particular focus of concern. Both outside observers and their own spokesmen are worried about the capacity (and to a lesser extent, the desire) of the typical classroom teacher to recognize and educate children with unusual learning problems. Among the teachers, this fear is tinged with considerable cynicism about the intentions of school authorities to provide the resources needed for the task. The problem occurs, moreover, at a time when the structure of teacher training is in disarray. Schools of education are trying to adjust to precipitous declines in the enrollment of students, combined with hefty increases in the relative demand for special education training. Local structures and resources for providing inservice instruction to the teachers now in the classroom (who are more and more likely to remain there in times of declining enrollments) range from the inadequate to the nonexistent. The organized teachers are responding to this mess by proposing to establish their own self-training system (*vide* the federal Teacher Center legislation whose passage they have recently secured); but they have, so far in this process, paid little attention to the skill requirements that mainstreaming will place upon them.

6. The institutional structure of schooling is such that significant changes are difficult to accomplish, especially when they are imposed from above. Each actor has an interest in the system as is; expeditious changes of the scope represented by mainstreaming rarely have been observed. Sarason observed "relatively sincere

tokenism" when he studied the implementation of mainstreaming. No obvious techniques were mentioned for surpassing that outcome.

7. The blessings of higher level (state and federal) funding for special education are likely to be accompanied by the curse of very specific forms of higher level control. Federal judicial and regulatory actions to secure students' rights may bring procedural requirements, programmatic constraints, and a predictably awkward federal enforcement system. Moreover, state governments are likely to tie to their increased funding some inappropriate accountability standards — inappropriate, in general, as measures of educational effectiveness and inappropriate, in particular, for gauging the success of rapidly changing local provisions for the education of the handicapped.

All in all, the conference conveyed to me a sense of building momentum greatly complicated by a sharp and difficult turning onto a rather uncharted new heading. I end up with two pieces of advice for special education policymakers, one micro and one macro:

1. Concentrate on the programing requirement for an array of definable, predictable, and financially supportable programs of services, especially, programs that will represent acceptable expressions of "mainstreamed" education. These programs must be accompanied, however, by implementation strategies that can help school systems and teachers to adapt them to local conditions and to operate them successfully.

2. Conduct the "renegotiation" — Reynold's characterization of the unique political process in which special education is now entered — with caution and concern for the new educational system (not just special education services) which the renegotiation will be helping to create and upon whose vigor and effectiveness special education will more than ever depend.

The motto for the renegotiation could well be taken from the advice of one experienced educational policymaker whom I know. After months of advising her state on plans for implementing the new dispensation in special education, she concluded that the present opportunity is unique; it will not recur. Her succinct advice was, "Whatever you do, do it right!"

References

Bernstein, C. D., et al. Major policy issues in financing special education. *Journal of Education Finance*, 1976, **1**(3), 300-305.

Rivlin, A. Forensic social science. *Harvard Educational Review*, 1973, **43**(1), 61 et seq.

Wilken, W. H., & Porter, D. O. *State aid for special education: Who benefits?* Washington, D. C.: National Foundation for the Improvement of Education, 1976, Ch. III.

Issues Relating to the Future of Special Education

Geraldine Joncich Clifford[1]

University of California, Berkeley

Among the myriad possible case studies of attempted educational change which the historian of education could use to profit, the contemporary push for mainstreaming can hardly be surpassed. The coming together of interest groups around a redefinition of individual and group rights has had its many counterparts in our educational past. The recourse to a broadened, more humane definition of the educational responsibilities of society, through schooling, illustrates powerful elements that have been marshaled before in our history in the effort to evoke educational and social reform. In this discussion, however, I concentrate, first, upon indicating how advocates of mainstreaming may be repeating the errors of past proponents of educational change by perpetuating an unsophisticated view of change; and second, through looking again at how persisting social and cultural bias reappears in the mainstreaming movement, we can be clearer what it is that we are asking of schools — their students, teachers, administrators, and sponsors.

In his pre-conference paper, Schiefelbusch wrote, "Desirable as the concepts of equal rights to education, least restrictive environment, and mainstreaming may be, there is a question of whether the education community has the intent, the resources, and the know-how to put them into practice." Of the three — intent, resources, and know-how — the nub, I am convinced, is intent, this despite the long-established habit of educators to blame failure on insufficient resources and inadequate research. My reasoning is based on sociological more than historical grounds. Let us, then, turn first to intent, which is also the subject of Sarason's paper.

A number of the conference papers cite or quote John Dewey. He wrote, in 1897, "Next to deadness and dullness, formalism and

---

[1]Professor of Education and Associate Dean, School of Education. President, History of Education Society.

routine, our education is threatened by no greater evil than sentimentalism" (p. 15). Sentimentalism is with us still. Draped about mainstreaming, as about other educational reforms, are hopes, dreams, and a romantic faith in human possibilities. Like Sarason, however, my research cautions me to be sympathetic toward but hard-headed about the public and professional commitment to and the structural capacity for change in public education, change of the kind that our sentiments may impatiently demand. It is laudable to see in mainstreaming, for example, the possibility that Levin sees in it: regular students helping and taking some responsibility for their handicapped classmates, an antidote to the "narrow and narcissistic form of individualism and competition which detracts from the formation of an awareness of social responsibility" — a goal for which Dewey also devotedly wished. It is true, of course, that heretofore we have promoted more competition than cooperation in our schools. Hence we have little hard evidence on how children react when they are asked to be generous and tolerant. According to a recent news magazine account, the students in Cheremoya Elementary School in Los Angeles rose to the challenge of mainstreaming in one instance by electing a cerebral-palsied child as school president. But in Alexandria, Virginia, the schoolmates of Bobby Gorman did not respond kindly to his hyperactivity and may have unwittingly encouraged his suicide (*Time* Magazine, 1976). The evidence on student interaction in racially desegregated schools is similarly mixed and highly complex, too complex for romantics to abide.

Change and the Obstacles to Change

Despite the fact that many — perhaps most — exceptional children historically have been found *de facto* in ordinary classes, mainstreaming as *public policy* for education demands change. It is about change that we should generate some discussion. As space permits, the following issues concerning educational change are raised here briefly: (a) assumptions and expectations about change, especially the presumption that change is linear and progressive; (b) the role of economic factors in change; (c) differential responses to change, which lead us to postulate a theory of positive correlation; and (d) most especially, structural and psychological resistance to change.

ASSUMPTIONS AND EXPECTATIONS ABOUT CHANGE

Sarason cautions us against assuming that even a powerful coalition of social forces and special interests, which is needed for the successful achievement of a moral and legalistic mandate for change, will insure either a synchronous compliance or outcomes consonant with our expectations. He encourages us to understand resistance, especially the resistance that is structural and not simplistically attitudinal. McDermott and Aron advance the same understanding through a different approach. All three authors also remind us that good intentions can provide unanticipated and unintended consequences, mixed and perhaps damaging outcomes. After this society's experience with the reactions to busing and other efforts to bring about the racial integration of schools, perhaps we should build "backlash" into our sets of assumptions. Indeed, small signs of backlash already have been evident around mainstreaming.

The reason that we do not assume such negative responses lies, I think, with the progressivist and optimistic drift of this culture's assumptions about change. We also assume that supporters of change will continue to support it. Once we stop for better consideration of the possible consequences, however, it becomes entirely conceivable that parents of exceptional children would reverse their pressures for mainstreaming should they perceive — or think they perceive — that the integration of special students into regular classes fails to realize their often high hopes. Morton and Hull (1976), parents of exceptional children, even argued that "selling mainstreaming to minority parents may be difficult" (p. 41), given parents' apprehensions about the loss of the special class shelter, their first-hand knowledge of how cruel people (including children) can be to those who are different, and the fact that "the mainstream does not generally enjoy a happy reputation even for normal children" (Morton & Hull, 1976, p. 37).

Optimism about the possibility of change and its benign consequences characterizes the history of American social and educational thought. It is particularly evident in the Chickerings' paper. They predict that the signs of greater institutional accommodations to diversity, now visible in some aspects of college and university life, will mark future higher education. Yet, as was pointed out in discussions at the conference, main-line institutions have beeen remarkably successful in conducting business as usual. A case in point is the University of California where a University committee recently recommended to the president that the needs of the part-time student receive more consideration. Without denying the claims to services of such students, the president nonetheless asserted that the state's entire system of public higher education already provides such services, and he reaffirmed that we in the University "must concentrate our energies on those activities we perform best: principal among them is full-time education" (Academic Senate, 1977, p. iii). To this small event we can add recent other signs of resurgent academic conservatism in California — the tightening up on nongraded courses and the "incomplete" mark; reinstatement of high-school requirements that were relaxed a decade ago; Governor Brown's ridicule of providing tax-supported instruction in "macrame-type" courses in the community colleges; the consolidation and centralization of services in response to budgetary restrictions; and the Legislature's persisting unwillingness to finance the "Extended University" plan — and it becomes difficult indeed to be confident about the Chickerings' contention that (for California, at least) ideas about individuation "are becoming basic tenets for many institutions supporting major developments that will *permanently* expand the range of alternatives for higher education" (emphasis added). There are few grounds in the history of education for assuming that reform movements bring permanent change or that they are unaccompanied by events that provoke counter movements.

A final example of what regrettably strikes me as an historically doubtful progressivist assumption about change in education is Jones's implication that urban cultural diversity will, *this time*, bring forth the respect for and accommodation to the "styles and preferences of diverse groups" that have been singularly lacking in the history of American education. As an institution for the promotion of cultural integration, public education understandably tries to effect assimilation. It is true that, in the face of highly diverse populations in the late nineteenth and early twentieth centuries, schools sometimes bent to pressures for the preservation of cultural difference. The incorporation of German language instruction in the schools of St. Louis is an example of flexibility that is the exception proving the rule: that the dominant pattern is one of cultural imposition. Even in St. Louis the schools were able to "wait out" the German-speaking population, which became steadily more enculturated, and eventually, lost interest in this issue which had so agitated the first generations of German-Americans in that city (Troen, 1975).

At an earlier conference on mainstreaming I remember feeling obligated to lend an historical perspective, to call into consciousness and question the pervasive progressivist expectations that underlie our theories of change. I said,

> One of the tendencies among educators is simply to assume that change is linear. Historians of education, of course, have contributed to this assumption by writing the history of American education as the history of more and more children going to school for longer and longer periods of time, studying a richer and richer curriculum under better and better trained teachers, with the public contributing more and more money to the process. It is a progressive story, as it has been written but it does not accord with the facts as we begin to know them better. (Clifford, 1976, p. 12)

The example I used was that of assuming continued judicial activism:

> In the discussions of the role of the courts, which have become much more focused in recent years, we see the assumption that the courts will continue to play a more and more aggressive role in edu-

cational policy making and that the direction of court decisions will be more or less uniform. We want to watch that assumption. . . . (Clifford, 1976, p. 12).

In the deliberations of this conference, and despite claims to the contrary, presumptions about the linearity of educational change continued to exercise a grip on our thinking.

The analogy that Sarson draws between mainstreaming and the push in the 1950s and 1960s for racially integrated schools urges us to be cautious in assuming that historical facts inevitably promote historical "progress." Segregation to desegregation to resegregation, for example, is a phenomenon of this and the previous century. Another example, for an earlier period in this century, is of the feminists who assumed that a progressive inclusion of women in education, already begun, would continue and would bring them into the economic, occupational, and political mainstream. Instead, women were a smaller proportion of the college class in 1960 than in 1900, and a smaller proportion of college faculty in 1970 than in 1870. Although I do not equate mainstreaming with racial integration or gender equality in the challenge it poses to social norms, careful historical examination undoubtedly will reveal many patterns in educational history that do not conform to a progressivist model. Ought we, then, to assume that mainstreaming will, even eventually, mean that more and more special education students will be found in regular classes, offered more and more individualized instruction, under better and better trained teachers, with more and more parental involvement of a steadily more meaningful kind, with less and less bias, sexism, and racism implicated in their assessment and placement, and with progressively better outcomes in learning and satisfaction? Clearly, such an assumption is dangerous. Holding it will, perhaps, only further widen the gap between what is expected of schools and that which will and can be delivered by them.

THE ROLE OF ECONOMIC FACTORS IN CHANGE

The many problems in devising economic criteria for the financing of schooling and education-related services for handicapped students emerge in Levin's paper. Even the cautious historian would probably agree with the people who predict that, despite the appeal of mainstreaming to the cost-conscious, expenditures for the schooling of exceptional children will increase even without an increase in the numbers of such students. This situation has occurred with other educational innovations which were believed to have the potential of improving education and, at the same time, promoting efficiency and economy. The school consolidation and unification movements are examples from the past that may be useful historical analogs.

At this point I would invoke the past to underscore the fact that there has been a powerful tradition of cost saving in the history of public and nonpublic education. Advocates of new or altered educational programs may speak of "savings" and "good investments" without revealing their real and nonpecuniary motivations; conversely, appeals to fairness, relevance, enduring education values, or other "goods" may mask primarily economic interests.

To illustrate the variety of ways by which cost saving has influenced educational development and its operations, consider the following four examples: (a) It was the humble professor who subsidized the great proliferation of colleges in the nineteenth century, at a time in our history when neither social need, sufficient personal demand, nor available student tuition income could rationally justify such institutional expansion; very low salaries and the actual withholding of wages in times of frequent financial crises were the means employed throughout the period to pick the professors' pockets (Rudolph, 1965). (b) The economy of hiring women as teachers was of central importance in the spread of universal primary education in the same century, and expansion for which there *was* social demand; the economic changes that lured men to other occupations and opened mill work to women facilitated the conversion of public opinion to the novel view that women were uniquely fitted to "keep school." (c) Cost-saving continues to figure in the operation of the education profession through the process that Lortie calls "eased entry" into teaching; to recruit and partially compensate prospective teachers for the low salaries and extremely limited opportunities for promotion in teaching careers, the government had made available for a century and more "low-cost, dispersed, non-elitist training institutions" (Lortie). Until very recently, eased entry also has promoted the great turnover of persons in the teaching profession. (d) Cost has been a persisting factor in conserving a more traditional curriculum in financially strapped church schools and liberal arts colleges, usually accompanied by an elaborate philosophy; taxpayer resistance, when not overcome has also effected curricular conservation in public schools.

The interplay of financial incentives certainly will be important in the future of mainstreaming. Consider only the elements that could enter into future equations: the past appeal and power of federal and state subsidies for segregated special education (Sarason); the, at least, initial attraction for administrators of integrating special education pupils in regular classrooms, where it promises to enlarge class size by increasing the districtwide ratio of students to teachers and to reduce the claims for special services like busing; the probability of costly structural changes to existing school buildings; and the viability of current limitations on where federal aid can be spent to further mainstreaming — structures in the law aimed, first, at ending exclusion and, second, at giving priority to the most severely handicapped pupils. These and other considerations will be played out, in the near future at least, in the context of a "small-government, less-is-better" ideology and with considerable public and political skepticism about the formula of "throwing money" at social problems.

DIFFERENTIAL RESPONSES TO CHANGE

In discussing the probable consequences of P.L. 94-142, Sarason predicts that outcomes will vary with both size of the school district and "factors highly correlated with size: racial and ethnic composition, average achievement levels, serious problems of management and discipline, class size, frequency of moving of families within a school district, teacher morale, and level of conflict between school personnel and the community." With this list of community and school attributes I would suggest considering two others. One is implicated in Sarason's list: socio-economic status of the school-community. The other is the level of schooling in which mainstreaming is sought.

While the issue of race or ethnicity runs through these and other recent discussions of the policies and practices of special education, whether in special or mainstream classrooms, social class factors are also implicated in their histories, as they are in all the history of education. Recall the differing reported class backgrounds (a) of the parents who pushed hardest for special education provisions for the handicapped, and for the extension of such services to more children: people like the Kennedys of Texas, recently featured on the television series about six American families; (b) of such "children's rights" interest groups as the Children's Defense Fund of the Washington Research Project; (c) of the litigants or their supporters; (d) of the children who are overrepresented among those labeled "requiring special education"; (e) of the skeptics of both "restrictive" and "least restrictive" environments; and (f) of the public school teachers and administrators charged with implementing change. One does not have to subscribe to a deterministic theory of class conflict in order to anticipate that cultural differences associated with socio-economic status will eventually place great strains upon coalitions and affect the transactions of class with class.

We know that social-class status was implicated in the acceptance of some other movements in innovative education in America. Successively, the high school, progressive education, and alternative schools were apparently most favored by and were creatures of the upper-middle class in the United States. It has been remarked frequently that while the British perform their pedagogical experiments on the lower classes and provide a conservative education for the social elite, the Americans tend to do the reverse.

In some instances, educational novelty has been attacked on the grounds of its being, or having the potential to be, "class ridden."

Examples over the past century include the reactions of the white working class against vocational education and the junior high school movement; both were interpreted as representing threats to the upward social mobility through education of youngsters from blue-collar backgrounds. Although any generalization positing an historical parallel must be tentative, the suspicion about special education today does not appear to represent a qualitatively different phenomenon.

Among the examples already given, the results of the attempts at educational change have varied. The junior and senior high schools took hold, despite opposition to the former and much initial apathy toward the latter. Neither vocational education nor progressive pedagogy, however, made the inroads for which their supporters had hoped. And, of mainstreaming, what can one anticipate with respect to the responses in schools and systems that differ by social class? Reluctantly, I would be forced to the cynical observation that the principle of "correlation," not "compensation," is more likely to operate; that is, mainstreaming will go better in middle-class schools where schooling generally is conducted more smoothly.

If mainstreaming receives the treatment accorded certain other contemporary innovations, one can predict that implementation will encounter more difficulties in secondary than in elementary schools (Berman et al, 1974-1975). The explanations are several. They include the greater identification of high-school teachers with subject matter than with students, the teachers' lower tolerance for "remedial" activities and students, and the lower levels of job satisfaction among teachers in secondary education (Clifford, 1975b). Although the rate of growth in college attendance may slow or stop entirely, competition for places in higher education will not abate precipitously. Hence, the high schools do not promise to "loosen up" in the near future. More than once before, social pressures have stayed the momentum toward change in secondary education. And what the meaning of the trend toward high-school equivalency examinations may be for special education pupils is still too obscure even to guess at.

RESISTANCE TO CHANGE

A degree of conservatism is built into the teaching profession through an interlocking and mutually reinforcing set of structural characteristics. Lortie (1975) very insightfully untangled and gave meaning to these elements. Until his book, no major analysis of the place of the teacher in the structure of teaching, as distinct from "*learning*" or "*instruction*," had been undertaken since 1932 when Willard Waller's *The Sociology of Teaching* appeared; even that classic was neglected and long has been out of print. This neglect is not accidental; researchers, including historians of education, resemble policy makers in their relative disinterest in "women's work," as teaching below the college level long ago became (Clifford, 1975a).

Along with the conscious feelings of teachers that they are unprepared for mainstreaming (Sarason) and their justified cynicism about getting the "support system" promised them to ease the difficulties of mainstreaming, one must consider the whole psychic structure of the uncertain business that is teaching. This structure puts a premium on psychic or affective rewards in the absence of clear or reachable goals and sure knowledge of results that plagues most of schooling. Psychic rewards seem especially important in the culture of the elementary school, but in all of schooling it operates to a degree; and it may help to explain why "emotionally disturbed" students destroy many teachers' remaining self-confidence.

Unconscious constellations of motivations and interpersonal needs hold powerful implications for mainstreaming. Lortie (1975) wrote, for example,

> Unlike other major middle-class occupations involving children, such as pediatric nursing and some kinds of social work, teaching provides an opportunity to work with children who are neither ill nor especially disadvantaged. Those who want such contact can visualize it taking place under "normal" conditions which do not include sickness, poverty, or emotional disturbance. (p. 27)

The longer that students who are "special" in some such way stay in school and appear in the classrooms of more teachers, the fewer the teachers who can realistically continue to expect to work under "normal" conditions. That they should be fearful, resentful, or resistant should occasion no surprise. If such feelings are understood and ventilated, *can* they then be overcome? Indeed, can the "normality" of exceptional children acquire the saliency which has beeen so much called for in the literature on mainstreaming? Not easily, I would guess.

A number of these papers refer, more or less directly, to the teacher's concern with management; McDermott's essay gives it the most attention, but the imperative to sort students is far from the whole story. One of the dimensions of management is discipline, and discipline consistently has been a core element in this society's charge to the schools, from their beginnings in the colonial period to the present. This charge is amply recorded in official and personal documents, as well as in public opinion polls in more recent times. Moreover, "management" is a central construct in most teachers' ordering of their work reality. Teachers *are* managers, but without the power and independence required for effective management. Sarason writes of researchers, "We can enjoy the luxury of being in the classroom without the responsibility of the teacher for managing and thinking about 25 or more unique personalities." We might, then, recall the discrepancy between teachers' stubborn perceptions that classroom size *does* make a difference and the failure of educational research to prove the case. The contradiction may stem from the inability of the researcher to consider, or consider as "important," teachers' management functions when the researcher's preoccupation rests with what he defines as "learning" or "instruction." While the difference between 25 and 30 students may not regularly show on test scores, it is a difference of more than half a reading group, and it *is* noticed by the teacher.

In the eyes of teachers, if Lortie's (1975) analysis is correct, "all but teacher and students are outsiders" (p. 169). Administrators, school psychologists, counselors, specialist teachers, and supervisors are regarded more as intervenors and interrupters than as colleagues of positive value. Is there good reason to believe that "resources" in the form of special education professionals will be regarded differently? If the teacher's management needs are not properly understood and respected, the specialists assigned to assist teachers in mainstreaming will probably fall far short of their potential and may further heighten teacher frustration levels. It would be useful for the historian of education to rethink the failures of progressive education in light of teachers' management needs.

This discussion of management must lead us to the issue of how pupil behavior influences the labeling of a student as mentally retarded, educationally handicapped, or emotionally disturbed. The observation that disruptive behavior provokes often-biased and incorrect referrals to special classes properly calls our attention to how nonobjective factors operate. But where there is no ability to empathize with teachers, can there be the grounds to assist them? There has been too much scapegoating of teachers. What is needed is a more adequate understanding of resistance to change, including the need and capacity of the teachers and of the educational system to "domesticate" change — to shape it in ways that better suit the institution's characteristics and traditions. There is no reason to believe that mainstreaming will be able to resist some degree of such domestication.

Labeling and Placing: Historical Perspectives on Bias in Education

The issues surrounding classification and labeling are fascinating for the social historian or, indeed, for any reader of Hobb's (1975) *The Futures of Children*. Classification, which he considers positively, and labeling, which he considers negatively, may provide the special services and resources which a target population badly needs, or which well-meaning people believe satisfies those needs. But the process of singling children out for extra help may also stigmatize them and, at the same time, severely limit their real opportunities.

In a variety of ways, classification or labeling and a consequent placement or delivery system have profound social meanings. For one thing they assure the "normal" members of the social group that their anxieties about or compassion for those who are different are being satisfied. This probably universal "pacification-need" has contributed, in the United States and industrialized Europe, over the past century and a half, to the creation or great growth of institutions: hospitals, asylums, prisons, and schools. Aided greatly by a cultural faith in science and its powers of diagnosis and remediation, institutional "solutions" for the problems of deviancy have monopolized public-policy deliberations. Such institutional aggrandizement has, of course, spawned its own countermovement, best expressed in the educational area by Ivan Illich's *Deschooling Society* (1970). To the extent that parents are involved more meaningfully in the schools' identification and treatment of "handicapped" students, however, one sees a degree of deprofessionalization rather than de-institutionalization.

Schools are not microcosms of society nor perfect social mirrors. As well as being social institutions, they are also *social systems* pursuing their own goals and vested interests, and they capture within their walls a nonrepresentative sample of the entire population. Nonetheless, they must appear to be legitimate as they conserve and perpetuate the values and aspirations of the sponsoring social group. The society is not fair, and some or much of that unfairness is found in schools. The society does not esteem all personal traits equally highly, and the educational system is prone to reflect some or much of that inequality. Thus, even within the circumscribed universe of special education, certain labels appear to be more demeaning than others. Sarason worries that pupils who are labeled mentally retarded will suffer relative neglect under mainstreaming because "intellectual deficit" lowers the child's "social-educational-productive worth" more than do other labels. There is a great need for more attention to be given to understanding the social factors surrounding different types of exceptionality.

The history of American public education provides two good examples of how social norms and the prejudices of the majority are reproduced in school arrangements for dealing with exceptionality. The first is an example of some continuity over time; the second illustrates change brought about through the substitution of groups. We turn, then, to a brief elaboration through the perspective of history.

GENDER AND LABELING/PLACEMENT

Little or no attention is given in these conference papers to the fact that boys are in the majority of children who are identified as mentally retarded, emotionally disturbed, and educationally handicapped. Sarason cites Milofsky on the overrepresentation of boys among children labeled emotionally disturbed in Springfield, Massachusetts, and presents the case history of an emotionally disturbed boy. McDermott does not attend to sex difference in his study of population; he is concerned with behavioral patternings that, presumably, are unrelated to gender. In these papers, and perhaps in the mainstreaming and special education literature generally, it is much more common for investigators to note racial, ethnic, and class factors than to call attention to discrimination associated with gender.

In the linking of labeling and placement with the disruptive behavior of some students, however, implicit recognition of gender is probably widespread; it is undoubtedly well known that boys are greatly overrepresented in incidents of behavior problems, from the keeping-in at recess to suspension from school. (A gender-specific form of suspension, however, affects pregnant girls [Cottle, 1976].) Some authors relate greater male boisterousness and aggressiveness to race or ethnicity; Dent (1976) observed that "it is not coincidental that the typical student in an EMR class is an aggressive black or other minority male. Boys outnumber girls in EMR classes as many as four or five to one in some programs" (p. 79). In the same volume, Abeson (1976) wrote,

> In some school systems, minority group status and discrimination is present for handicapped children on the basis of sex. It is recognized that more boys than girls appear in elementary special education programs and particularly those for the mentally retarded and emotionally disturbed. One explanation for this phenomenon is that boys tend to be more aggressive and less neat than girls, thus leading the female-dominated elementary schools to find alternative nonregular class programs for the males. (p. 16)

Modern social science, however, raises some doubt that the presence of the female teacher is the critical explanatory factor for the predominant identification of boys as behavior problems. Although Lee (1973) reported on the basis of research that male teachers promote rougher play, assign boys more leadership roles, and relate to male sex-typed activities, he also concluded that schools socialize teachers, "irrespective of sex, to place a high premium on pupil control" (p. 87); the attributes of neatness, quietness, conservatism, and inaction issue partly from the nature of school tasks and social expectations of schools, provoking both male and female teachers to try to get pupil compliance (Lee, 1973). Tending toward the same observation is Ziegler's (1967) finding that male teachers are more likely than their female counterparts to be agitated by disciplinary issues. If true, generally, it is plausible that some of the heightened sense that discipline problems in schools have reached crisis levels is probably due to the greater presence of males in teaching, currently.

Insofar as history speaks to the question of a differential response to male students, the record suggests that boys always have contributed disproportionately to the pupils who are identified as troublesome to teachers, and largely regardless of the sex of the teachers. Since girls were not educated in schools with boys in large numbers before the nineteenth century, the same period that women teachers became commonplace in the United States, it is not possible to draw on large numbers of diaries, recorded observations, or other documents before that time. What documentation does exist, however, supports the conclusion; extant illustrations and engravings of classroom scenes tell the same story: Miscreants (males) are shown suspended from ceilings in baskets, displayed on the fool's stool, or being paddled.

The long history of formal education worldwide clearly shows the male sex to be dominant among the literate and the schooled, and probably among the labeled, the placed, and the disciplined, as well. Aside from differential sex-role socialization, which places a premium on male activism and aggression while discouraging the same traits in females, social expectations about adult roles also figure in the relative attention given to deviancy in males as compared to females. A prevailing assumption has been that males will be wage-earners and heads of households; hence, conditions that will impinge on their abilities to perform these roles will have greater social consequences. Conversely, deficient females have been expected to find domestic shelter, except where their deviancy is extreme. Such assumptions undoubtedly lie behind Abesons's (1976) report that "handicapped girls at the secondary level are often deprived of equal access to the vocational opportunities available to boys" (p. 16).

Earlier reports on placements of the mentally retarded, which lead to the same conclusion about the differential social meanings attached to some handicaps in the two sexes, were included in Hollingworth (1922); her data were referred to in the very brief (less than one page) discussion of gender in the differential responses to deviancy in Hobbs (1975). Hollingworth summarized two surveys that helped to contribute to the erroneous inference that feeble-mindedness is more common among males than females; the survey reports are shown in Table 1.

Hollingworth properly observed that "Institutional statistics may be merely an index on the degree to which it is easier for one sex to survive outside of institutions, than it is for the other" (p. 10). Reporting on research at New York City's Clearing House for Mental Defectives in 1913, Hollingworth noted that among the 1,000 individuals (586 males, 432 females) brought in for diagnosis, (a) males outnumbered females (490 to 273) among those identified and referred before age 16; (b) females outnumbered males (159 to 78) among those identified between ages 16 and 30; and (c) of individuals over age 30, there were three times more females than males. The figure illustrating these differences was entitled, "Distribution by age of 1,000 mental defectives, 568 males and 432 females, pre-

Table 1

Summary of Two Surveys of
Males and Females in
Institutions for the Feeble Minded

	Number	Per Cent
1. 1915 Questionnaire, Returns from Seven States		
Males	4,046	53.5
Females	3,518	46.5
2. U.S. Report for 1910		
Males	11,015	53.8
Females	9,716	46.2

Source: L. S. Hollingworth, *The psychology of subnormal children*. New York: Macmillan, 1922, p. 9

sented consecutively for diagnosis: showing inequality of social and economic pressure upon the two sexes" (p. 11). Hollingworth's research also demonstrated that

> ... the males brought to this clinic for diagnoses and commitment were of distinctly higher mental status, age for age, than were the females. The figures proved, for instance, that a girl or woman with a mental age of six years survives outside of institutions about as well as does a boy or man with a mental age of ten or eleven years.
>
> The reason for this state of affairs is not far to seek. To interpret the facts we have but to reflect on our social organization. Women and girls as a class do not follow competitive careers. The work of the majority is in the house, domestic service and child-bearing, performed in isolation, and not in competition with others for a wage.... The boy who cannot compete becomes an object of concern, is brought to the clinic, and is directed toward an appropriate institution. The girl who cannot compete is not so often recognized as defective.... Social and economic pressure bears very unequally upon the sexes in the matter of commitment to institutions for the feeble-minded (Hollingworth, 1922, pp. 11-12).

The greater competence and independence expected of boys, and the consequent higher probability that more boys will be considered to have failed to meet those expectations, were noted long ago by a supervisor of the ungraded classes in the Bronx schools.

> The fact that more boys [258] than girls [103] are found in these ungraded classes permits of explanation other than that of greater [mental] variability in males. One of these is based on the fact that boys have greater freedom, are less restrained than girls. Because of this, they come into conflict with their school environment. This maladjustment makes it imperative that some motive be given to them and some explanation sought (Hollingworth, 1922, p. 13).

These extended quotes are reproduced here to remind us how

much some things have stayed the same, even as other things have changed, such as the proportions of married women in the competitive labor force, which grew from 4.5% in 1890 to 21.6% in 1950 to over 32% in 1962, and is still climbing. In the schools' responses to the current legal and moral mandates to effect mainstreaming, special educators should be alert to evidence that gender may bias the responses in the future as it has in the past.

ETHNICITY AND LABELING/PLACEMENT

A very active current line of historical inquiry is aimed at proving that the educational system systematically discriminates against certain groups. Such discrimination is not accidental under this theory, but it is designed to serve the interests of a social and economic structure that, in modern times, puts the schools in the business of sorting students for places in a stratified society. The emphasis upon the sorting function is central to McDermott's paper; he briefly introduces the theme by contrasting the liberal or progressive view of American education with a negative, revisionist interpretation of our educational history. Books that lay out such a negative critique of our educational past and present include Clarence Karier et al., *Roots of Crisis* (1973); Colin Greer, *The Great School Legend* (1972); and Joel Spring, *The Sorting Machine* (1945).

Of particular relevance to special education is the revisionist interpretation of the enthusiastic acceptance of the testing movement by the public schools. Katz (1975), for example, wrote, "Science enabled schoolpeople to label groups of children inferior; often those groupings reflected ethnic origin or race. Testing legitimized segregation within American education" (p. 171). This historical interpretation clearly supports those people, especially "New Left" social critics and some minority spokesmen, who, today, are attacking the use of educational and other tests.

Although Katz emphasized social-class interests that operate in the testing movement, vocational education, bureaucratization, and other "reform" thrusts, especially in urban education, he noted that sometimes social class and ethnicity coincide, and when they do this analysis easily leads to the charge that schools have been consistently biased along lines of race and ethnicity. His examples of such coincidences include the Irish in the mid-nineteenth century, the Italians around the turn of the twentieth century, and blacks for longer periods.

Given the frequency of contemporary statistics indicating that the children of the poor are more frequently labeled as requiring special education, and more frequently placed in segregated school groupings, it is inevitable that historians will have sought to discover any parallels with the past. In his fine history of American urban school-system development, Tyack (1974) reported the conclusions of a 1909 study by the United States Immigration Commission, "Children of Immigrants in Schools" (1911). In this study of 12 eastern and midwestern American urban school systems (excluding New York City), "retardation" was defined as characterizing pupils who were two or more years "over age" for the classrooms in which they were placed. The following tabulation identifies the percentages labeled retarded, according to the national origins of their fathers:

National Origin	Per Cent Retarded
Native-born	30.3
Foreign-born, total	40.4
English-speaking	27.3
Non-English-speaking	43.4
German	32.8
Russian Jew	41.8
South Italian	63.6
Polish	58.1
Swedish	15.5

Earlier in this century, the children of immigrants from southern Italy and Sicily were particularly likely to be identified as troublesome, unable to learn, and culturally or genetically unendowed for success at school. This judgment was voiced by both public-school educators in many cities and officials in the Irish-run Catholic parochial school systems. In the latter, manifest discrimination combined with modest tuition fees to cause Italian-American parents to reject the parochial schools even more than they evaded public education whenever possible. High retardation, truancy, and drop-out statistics stigmatized the Italian-American student and community. So, too, did the standardized intelligence test, adopted quickly by the larger school systems immediately following World War I. It was reported that the *average* IQ score for the Italian school child was 85. In the San Francisco schools in the same period, the Italian boy was the typical student assigned to the district's "opportunity room."

Recently, the Children's Defense Fund reported that the chances of being enrolled in special classes for the emotionally disturbed and mentally retarded are five times greater for black pupils than white pupils in any one of 505 Southern school districts (Cottle, 1976). It is the existence of such groups of political and legal activists as the Children's Defense Fund, the NAACP, the American Civil Liberties Union, and the like, that makes ours an historically different era than that of the earlier years of this century when school and society also faced the existence of great variability in the student population.

References

Abeson, A. Legal forces and pressures. In R. L. Jones (Ed.), *Mainstreaming and the minority child*. Reston, VA: Council for Exceptional Children, 1976, 15-36.

Academic Senate, University of California. Address by the President. *Record of the Assembly*, March 3, 1977.

Berman, P., et al. *Federal programs supporting educational change* (5 vols.). Santa Monica: The Rand Corporation, 1974-1975.

Clifford, G. J. Discussant. In M. C. Reynolds (Ed.), *Mainstreaming: Origins and implications*. Reston, VA: Council for Exceptional Children, 1976.

Clifford, G. J. Saints, sinners, and people: A position paper on the historiography of American education. *History of Education Quarterly*, Fall 1975, 257-272. (a)

Clifford, G. J., *The shape of American education*. Englewood Cliffs, N. J.: Prentice-Hall, 1975. (b)

Cottle, T. J. *Barred from school: Two million children*. Washington, D.C.: New Republic Book, 1976.

Dent, H. E. Assessing black children for mainstream placement. In R. L. Jones (Ed.), *Mainstreaming and the minority child*. Reston, VA: Council for Exceptional Children, 1976, 77-92.

Dewey, J. *My pedagogic creed*. New York: E. L. Kellogg, 1897.

Greer, C. *The great school legend*. New York: Basic Books, 1972.

Hobbs, N. *The futures of children: Categories, labels, and their consequences*. San Francisco: Jossey-Bass, 1975.

Hollingworth, L. S. *The psychology of subnormal children*, New York: Macmillan, 1922.

Illich, I. *Deschooling society*. New York: Harper & Row, 1970.

Jones, R. L. (Ed.). *Mainstreaming and the minority child*. Reston, VA.: Council for Exceptional Children, 1976.

Karier, C., et al. *Roots of crisis*. Chicago: Rand McNally, 1973.

Katz, M. B. *Class, bureaucracy, and schools: The illusion of educational change in America* (rev. ed.). New York: Praeger, 1975.

Lee, P. C. Male and female teachers in elementary schools: An ecological analysis. *Teachers College Record*, September 1973, 79-98.

Lortie, D. C. *Schoolteacher, a sociological study*. Chicago: University of Chicago Press, 1975.

Morton, K., & Hull, K. Parents and the mainstream. In R. L. Jones (Ed.), *Mainstreaming and the minority child*. Reston, VA: Council for Exceptional Children, 1976, 37-52.

Rudolph, F. *The American college and university, a history*. New York: Vintage Books, 1965.

Spring, J. *The sorting machine*. New York: David McKay, 1945.

Time Magazine, Into the Mainstream, November 15, 1976, 90.

Troen, S. K. *The public and the schools: Shaping the St. Louis System*, 1838-1920. Columbia: University of Missouri Press, 1975.

Tyack, D. *The one best system: A history of American urban education*. Cambridge, Mass.: Harvard University Press, 1974.

U. S. Immigration Commission. *Children of immigrants in schools* (Vol. 1). Washington, D. C.: U. S. Government Printing Office, 1911, 4-5, 31.

Zeigler, H. *The political life of American teachers*. Englewood Cliffs, N.J.: Prentice-Hall, 1976.

Some Reflections on Renegotiation

Dan C. Lortie[1]

University of Chicago

Relations between special education and education-at-large will change as P.L. 94-142 takes hold. What can we do to make the resulting renegotiation as effective as possible? This question arose at the conference because impending events pose serious issues for both the mission of special educators and the vitality of public schools. The answer is difficult to forecast when we must generalize to a "system" in which decisions will be made in dozens of states, hundreds of regional units, and thousands of school districts. Federal laws probably will not produce national uniformity as state and local bodies interpret and fulfill their obligations in diverse ways. At best, we can make some estimates full of "mights" and "maybes." Nevertheless, in my view, some intellectual preparation, no matter how tentative, is superior to thoughtless muddling through.

Legislation and the allocation of funds end one phase in the reorganization that is now taking place; new complexities loom, however, with the shift to implementing programs throughout the nation. Experience with other national undertakings should help us to realize that problems occurring during implementation all too readily can frustrate the original intentions. If the hopes of the people who fought so hard to ensure that the schools will serve all children are to be achieved, the contingencies that could frustrate reaching that goal should be identified now. Potential contingencies can serve as "watch-points" for serious, expanding inquiry that monitors events as they occur; such inquiry can add new problems as they arise and discard those that prove to be inconsequential. Without such systematic observation, however, unintended consequences may once more swamp high purpose in a sea of irrelevancies.

---

[1]Professor, Department of Education

My discussion here is organized around two major topics. (a) What can serve to bind persons in special and regular education together as they work out new relationships: What is the point of *common* interest? (b) There are identified a few specific risks that could endanger successful negotiations; they are stated as hypotheses, so to speak, to be tested and refined by subsequent observers. On the assumption that most readers will be special educators, my comments are addressed primarily to them and to the problems that they are probably best equipped to attack. My orientation is that of a sociologist deeply interested in organizational processes in education, and although I claim no special knowledge of special education, I do not consider myself a partisan for any particular segment of our complex system of schooling. I hope planners and decision makers in special education find it useful to encounter an approach that stems from somewhat different assumptions and preoccupations than their own.

The Common Interest — Viable Public Schools

Mainstreaming is important to the relationships between special and regular educators, so important, in fact, that it can serve as the foundation for working out new organizational structures. People who have special concern for handicapped children now share a vital bond with school personnel; the proper education of children who were previously segregated demands that public schools become effective organizations. If schools are weak, thousands upon thousands of handicapped children will suffer along with their more fortunate peers; if schools are strong, all will benefit. Schools with insufficient resources (broadly defined) will be more likely to adopt the token compliance outlined in Sarason's paper; viable schools will have more of the energy and other resources it takes to undergo serious reorganization.

The historical segregation of special and regular educators has taken its toll in the relations between them; shared viewpoints and mutual understanding, it appears, are not the rule. Educators outside special education are often perceived as either indifferent to, or even prejudiced against, the needs of children with handicaps. Special educators, on the other hand, sometimes project the attitudes of an embattled group with its "them vs. us" mentality. It would not be surprising if some special educators, armed with novel legal and financial resources, asserted their new status without too fine a regard for the organizational consequences of such behavior.

Assertive behavior by special educators might be tough enough for other educators to accept at any time; the success of others is not always an occasion for unmitigated joy. Given current realities, evidence of hubris could provoke strong, dark reactions — other educators are undergoing a difficult period that, in all too many instances, produces anxiety, depression, and a sense of hopelessness. The (relative) euphoria and flexibility induced by the expansions of the 1950s and 1960s have given way to tensions associated with contraction as inflation and declining enrollment reduce funds and force painful and unpopular decisions. Internal relationships are showing the strains of collective bargaining and the accountability backlash, and they are put under further stress by large-scale firing and staff dislocation. Some school districts are disoriented by equalization laws while the spread of legalism increases the vulnerability (never that low) of school administrators. Reduced hiring coupled with staff cuts, which are based on seniority, threaten schools of education and result in an older teaching force; the shift to inservice education now taking place intensifies the conflict among teacher associations, central offices, and universities. Hope for continuing innovation founders as outside attacks shift to the "back-to-basics" theme and shake the political support base of the research and development sector. I do not cite these tensions to provide excuses for those who would drag their feet on complying with P.L. 94-142, but to describe something of the context within which it will be worked out. The depressants present in public education today should be taken into account as efforts are made to renegotiate relationships.

The special tensions of the late 1970s add to the customary sentiments and behaviors, which are so ably detailed in Sarason's paper. What are the implications for persons in special education? As I see it, it is extremely important that special educators avoid either the stance or the appearance of being "just another pressure group." School board members, superintendents, principals, teachers, and counselors, for example, are already inclined to feel that they are being overloaded; unless persons in special education exercise care, they could be seen as the final straw.

Tactics suited to winning legislative support may prove ineffective if they are carried over into this new stage of rebuilding school organizations and working out the myriad details of everyday operations. Single-minded pleading for special needs will prove less useful than finding out how to reorganize to meet both the needs of handicapped children and the total capacity of schools. Although crusades and massed voters can sway lawmakers and influence officials, they can also stiffen opposition within organizations. Moreover, organizational opposition can take covert forms that defy identification and effective counteraction. The loosely coupled nature of schools and school districts means that the motivations of all participants (custodians, teacher aides, parents, teachers, assistant principals, etc.) must be mobilized to bring about large-scale change: compliance by higher echelon figures is not enough. Patient persuasion and systematic cultivation of support must replace earlier models of action; what works in the drama of legislation may fall flat in the workaday world of school affairs. Persistence, attention to detail, and understanding of the exchanges that underlie give-and-take — these are the kinds of tactics that make up effective organizational action. In short, a different kind of sophistication is now needed.

Jones's paper is remarkable, as I view it, in capturing these new necessities. His emphasis on overcoming parochialism in thought and action, his call for more sensitive paradigms for research, and, in particular, his focus on pluralism are apt as special education moves into the mainstream. Special educators have many natural allies within the ranks of education-at-large and they should pay particular attention to the opportunities that result. School persons who place high value on fostering individual differences and cultural diversity share the interest of special educators in broadening the definition of what is acceptable among young persons. Like special educators, they press the limits outward, challenging persons whose image of human nature is a tall, narrow "normal curve" that excludes many children as deviant and unfit. The cause of special educators is advanced by those who question the right of school authorities to insist on "one best way" and those who work for options available to children and families. As a case in point, more choice for (regular) individual children reduces the special burdens associated with the new law. In short, "special" students will fare better to the extent that the educational "mainstream" is seen as the many-branched Mississippi rather than the Old Mill Stream.

Reform instituted through judicial decree and legislative enactment carries its particular complications. An obvious one is overreliance on bureaucratic rules at the expense of judgments made by individuals close to the scene and directly concerned with the outcome. Renegotiation will call for thoughtful decisions based on the sensitivity, experience, and knowledge of thousands of persons acting in and around schools. Where knowledge is lacking, it should be generated; unlike Gallagher, I would not place my confidence entirely in center-periphery models of research. Regrouping students into units that encompass greater variety and work well is not a simple task; this and other tasks flowing from the new law will require acute intelligence as well as good intentions. Local characteristics will influence outcomes. It is not likely that formulas developed in remote centers of research will always help particular principals, teachers, families, and students to work out their problems. What kinds of heterogeneity, class size, and teacher assignment patterns should we try here in East Simpson? Given our resources, how can we give a fair shake to all? If we make the work of some staff members more demanding, what can we do to reward their effort? Data and analysis will best supplement human judgment if they deal with immediacies in a cool yet committed atmosphere; some persons with unique abilities in analyzing concrete situations and providing insights should be close to decision making and confronted with its complexity and consequences. Research funds should, in some quantity, be spent to support local decision making. So buttressed, moreover, local school people will be more likely to resist unwarranted centralization induced by state and other bureaucracies.

Some Specific Dilemmas

If we define organizational perfection as the simultaneous realization of all desirable outcomes, it is clear why it does not occur; it is also evident that "trade-offs" are unavoidable as dilemmas of choice occur. Every structure sacrifices something desirable for something that is also good; the full achievement of all positive values is the stuff of Utopia, not of organizational life as we know it. Large-scale change provokes additional dilemmas as it shifts the balance, quite apart from the merits of the proposed reform. If statesmanship is the ability to cope with dilemmas of this type while avoiding excessive costs to the overall welfare, it appears that statesmanship will be called for as we move to schools that accommodate the needs of more children. I wish to identify some of these dilemmas and the risks they pose as special and regular education confront the difficulties that are inevitable if change is to be genuine.

1. The large-scale distribution of public resources to previously undersupported persons is, on the face of it, the righting of wrong and evidence that justice is finally being done. Specifically, who can justify the exclusion of handicapped children from the same education assured others? It is right and proper that if many millions of dollars are needed to rectify this situation, they be spent.

Yet even this rose has thorns. It seems to be a characteristic of categorical assistance that the correction of one injustice leads, without anyone so intending, to new feelings of inequity and calls for redress. This may be the case particularly when others are undergoing the reduction of resources, as in the case cited by George Young, Superintendent of the St. Paul Public Schools. He told of the high-school student whose teacher was laid off because of budget reductions and who complained about unfairness: kids in special education were not losing *their* teacher. The anecdote illustrates a key principle in American conceptions of equity: sacrifice should be equally distributed. Why, indeed, should one student suffer while another does not? Is this question not the very basis on which the rights of handicapped children were fought for?

The administrators of funds under P.L. 94-142 will experience dilemmas of the kind found in Young's account. If close attention is not paid to principles of equity, envy will lead to conflict which could, if sufficiently strong, prevent the cooperative relationships that are needed to renegotiate and, even, weaken the fabric of public schooling as a whole. It is difficult to foresee particulars in a problem of this kind and to specify the antidotes that are indicated. The general point is, I suppose, that the efficacy of the new law will call for great sensitivity to situations in which special education may appear to be claiming excessive resources at the expense of other educators. Some restraint seems essential.

2. Providing necessary facilities for children who are not mainstreamed will, at least in some states, further the development of regional units of school administration. Several school districts would be included in each unit. Such units are, of course, a rational way to deal with problems which cannot be dealt with effectively by local school systems. We should recall, however, that local school districts, over the last two decades or so, have lost functions to the federal government and the states; some people fear that the schools are already too far eroded. If the funding and support of "superdistricts" lead to futher erosion, the local school district may become an empty form. One need not be convinced (as I am) that tendencies toward centralizing school decisions should be resisted to agree that there is considerable danger in the *indirect* revision of our school governance. It is one thing to hold open debate and settle on the desirable size and shape of school government; it is quite another, and clearly undesirable, to revise it as an unintended consequence of serving part of the population.

The difficulty is that the issue of governance may come up in ways that mislead us into missing the key issues. One might, for example, see conflicts between local and regional boards over specifics in special education which, in turn, might be resolved by state officials entirely in terms of the manifest content of the disputes and without attention to latent trends in school governance. I would caution against such single-minded support for regional units, and I would urge special education administrators to examine the effects of such units on local school districts. Opportunistic support for larger units of governance could, at a later time, prove extremely costly if it turned out that such bodies, given their remoteness, proved to be unresponsive to public sentiment.

3. Categories of thought that are appropriate to building and sustaining coalitions to mobilize political support may prove to be harmful when they are carried over to the planning and conduct of instructional programs. The power of large numbers makes it entirely rational for people who are seeking redress to band together and, in the course of winning support, to minimize the differences in their concerns. There is danger, however, that the reinforcment so obtained ("nothing succeeds like success") may overpower thinking about the instructionally relevant differences among children with diverse handicaps. It would be ironic if the people who have sought the rights of the "different" themselves were to overgeneralize about handicapped students!

It is difficult to estimate the extent of this danger. I noted during the conference, however, that all of us were forced, in combining all disabilities under one rubric, to make some doubtful generalizations. The special insights brought by Phyllis Stearner and Hadi Madjid illuminated the problems and strengths of physically and visually handicapped persons. Some papers dealt with issues involved in the education of retarded children. But as one moves to questions of organizing instruction, the strong hypothesis emerges that differences among the handicapped suggest different programs, and that different handicaps provide schools with diverse challenges. If specialists of the calibre of those who participated in the conference find it hard to avoid overgeneralization, will it not also be difficult for policy makers and administrators in the years ahead?

Specialists in the field of special education face a serious dilemma as new kinds of education are institutionalized for handicapped children. Political realism, on the one hand, may prescribe keeping one's coalitions in good repair; who knows when hard-won gains may be threatened? Progammatic considerations, on the other, suggest that more refined subdivision and instructionally relevant categories should now dominate thought and discusssion. One can hope, of course, that increased enlightenment in the general population will reduce the need for political intervention, but one could easily hope for too much too soon. In the meantime, special educators, working with others, might concentrate on developing new and action relevant categories that inform planning and implementation while "keeping their powder dry"; perhaps the trick is to make a clearer distinction between the rhetoric and symbols of politics and the concepts and practices of schooling. This distinction may prove, in fact, to be one of the salient points for clear-sighted research in the years ahead.

4. The process of mobilizing support for large federal programs and the subsequent enactment of new laws and funding normally raise public expectations that problems will be solved; all too often it also happens that hopes exceed possibilities, and a gap opens between public expectations and reality. As we witnessed during the 1960s, this gap can produce cynicism and resistance to further action; it could happen as many millions are spent on the education of the disabled. Some disappointment is probably inevitable — we may as well resign ourselves to it — and some attacks. There are two risks, however, which might be reduced if intelligent steps are taken to prevent them.

a. Administrators of new programs may project excessive hope in mobilizing support for their implementation; if resistance occurs, it will be tempting to motivate action through visions of a far fairer day. Such stimulants, however, should be administered in small doses, given that unfulfilled promises breed contempt. Other motivators should be sought out lest excitation turn into disillusionment with the mission of special education and the utility of all education.

b. We must beware of how persons respond to attack when it occurs; the urge is all too common to find someone or something, preferably far from one's self, to blame. Regular educators may find it handy to impugn the motives and capacities of specialists while the latter, in turn, mutter about the sheer thickheadedness of nonspecialists. Such mutual mud-slinging, although bringing temporary relief to the nervous system, does nothing for education as a whole; in fact, it invites the public-at-large to swear a plague on both houses.

One worrisome tendency showed up at the conference. Much was said about the need to educate (or "change the attitudes of") regular educators toward special education and handicapped children: a valid point. But subtle depreciation can underlie such statements, or, at least, be read in by the educators who are thought to need teaching. Is it, for example, asserted that any and all disagreement voiced by regular educators is "resistance" to the greater wisdom of specialists? Is it implied that when regular educators act in ways unacceptable to special educators that it is primarily because of "prejudice" against handicapped children?

Jones's careful review of the literature indicates that the knowledge base of special education, as is true in education-at-large, leaves much to be desired. My research on teachers indicates that they find much of what is asked of them (even in "regular" classes) very hard to achieve, and that teaching outcomes are uncertain, fragile, and often disappointing; people who teach do not see pedagogy as a well-developed craft, much less a scientifically rooted profession. The exciting paper given by McDermott dramatizes the inability of a highly rated teacher to insure anything like equal time-on-task among her students and, given the constraints and values of the larger system, how difficult it would be for her to remove that inequality. There are, in short, limitations imposed by both the incompleteness of educational knowledge and technique, and societal and organizational arrangements.

It is not easy to distinguish between failures rooted in the inadequacies of people and the limitations imposed by "external" qualities of knowledge and the social system. But intelligent action requires that the distinction be made and the appropriate remedies found; simplistic formulations will not work. It is currently fashionable (as in accountability discussions) to assume that educational problems stem primarily from the lack of effort or improper attitudes held by teachers and other educators who work directly with children in the schools. All would be well, this view holds, "if only they would try harder." Now it is clear that trying helps and lack of effort does not, but it does not follow from these truths that all deficiencies in our schools are personal inadequacies. All of us must stand ready to admit our ignorance and to determine to reduce it; if we do, we may be able to win public support for the imaginative thought, hard inquiry, and thoughtful practice that will make educational results more predictable for all kinds of children.

The Present State of Teacher Education and Needed Reforms[1]

Dean Corrigan[2]

University of Maryland

The tragedy is that most people do not recognize the life and death nature of teaching, critical decisions of motivation, reinforcement, reward, ego enhancement, and goal direction. Proper professional decisions enhance learning and life; improper decisions send the learner towards incremental death in openness to experience and in ability to learn and contribute. Doctors and lawyers probably have neither more nor less to do with life, death, and freedom than do teachers. To deny the child the skills and qualities of the fully professional teacher exacerbates the assaults on freedom which much of mass education renders inevitable, and leaves to chance, the kinds of interventions by teachers that open minds and enhance self images. Therefore, the teaching profession must continue its negotiations with society in behalf of more perfect education for its children. Teaching is definitely a matter of life and death. *It should be entrusted only to the most thoroughly prepared professionals*. (Howsam, Corrigan, Denemark, & Nash, *Educating a Profession*, 1976, p. 15.

As I read the papers and participated in the conference discussions, I was struck by the high expectations that were expressed for teachers and teacher-preparation programs. However, I could not reconcile these expectations with the reality of teacher education as I know it today.

The conference participants seemed to spend an inordinate amount of time suggesting reforms in school environments and changes in education policy that would permit the implementation of P.L. 94-142, but they gave little attention to the specific changes in pre-service and inservice teacher education that would produce the kind of teachers who can implement the proposed reforms. For

---

[1]For this paper, I have drawn heavily on the work of the Bicentennial Commission of Education for the Profession of Teaching and its publication, *Educating a Profession*, by R. B. Howsam (Chairman), D. C. Corrigan, G. W. Denemark, and R. J. Nash (1976).

[2]Dean, College of Education. Formerly, Dean, College of Education and Social Services, University of Vermont.

example, Sarason closed his paper by stating that the major deficiency of P.L. 94-142 is that no major changes are called for in our college and university training centers. However, he did not go on to suggest the specific reforms needed in training institutions to produce the kind of teacher he so beautifully described in his scenarios.

Most of the other conferees were quick to point out that teacher education had low status on their campuses and elsewhere; but they did not appear to be very eager to analyze the causes for this low esteem or to propose measures to change the image of teacher education in America. Because the reform of teacher education should be a major consideration in our continuing dialogue on the future of special education, there are considered here, albeit briefly, the following questions:

1. What is the present status of teacher education on university campuses?
2. What are some of the major reforms needed in pre-service and inservice teacher education if we are to prepare teachers who are qualified to implement the ideas in the papers presented in this report and in P.L. 94-142?

Present Status of Teacher Education

THE UNIVERSITY SETTING

Teacher education long has been concerned with its status on the university campus. It has not been able to shed the image of marginal academic respectability, a carry-over from its normal-school past, or to convince the academic community that it is or could be a genuine profession (i.e., possessing a common base of principles and repertoire of unique skills) to which all teachers belong. Consequently, teacher education has existed in a "no-man's land": between the needs of teachers on the one hand and the attributes of academic disciplines on the other. Teacher educators are asked to make their professional knowledge more practical, that is, more relevant to the solution of problems that teachers face in the schools, but, at the same time, they are pressed by the university to make the knowledge they deal with more "scholarly" and to direct their professional pursuits toward publication in scholarly publications, especially if they expect to be recommended for reappointment, promotion, or tenure by university committees. While the university has coveted the presence of teacher education on the campus, it has not valued the purposes of teacher education; indeed, many faculty members in other disciplines express open disdain for these purposes.

The reasons for the continuing low status of teacher education on the campus can only be speculated, although they appear to be many and varied, as the following examples suggest:

1. The conscious or unconscious realization that to accept teaching as a legitimate field of study and colleges of education as co-equal professional faculties would require professors (a) to admit the inadequacy of their own training and (b) to endorse the necessity of professional preparation for their teaching role. (If one can teach without preparation and teaching is an act that cannot be improved, then it is the only career activity in which these conditions prevail.)

2. To the academic community, teaching appears to be less professional than other activities and, therefore, teacher education is lower on the academic totem pole than other disciplines or professional schools. Neither the university nor the general public recognizes that teaching is as much a matter of life and death as doctoring.

3. The competition for the course time of students in teacher education reflects the negative attitude toward courses in teacher preparation.

4. The question of whether teaching is an art or a science is answered differently by different faculties.

5. University faculties differ over the importance of the application of knowledge and whether it is a high-priority purpose for universities. On most campuses, lower status is given to the applied sciences; discovering knowledge of how to *use* knowledge to improve the quality of other people's lives is considered to be less important than expanding the fields of knowledge — "searching for the truth." The university does not view itself as an instrument for carrying out educational and social reforms like those implied in P.L. 94-142.

6. Teacher education has failed to assert its uniqueness and to develop a distinctive presence on campus and in the public eye.

7. No outside force is sufficiently concerned about teacher education to come to its aid politically or institutionally. Even the professional teacher organizations, which, logically, would be expected to do so, have not yet made the reform of teacher education on university campuses a high priority.

Teacher preparation has not always been a function of universities; only in this century have they taken over the responsibility. The improvements in teacher education and the teaching profession expected from the university relation have not occurred, however. The idea of locating teacher education in a university where it could draw upon the resources of different academic disciplines was great in theory. But just try to get those resources to make a commitment to the goal of improving the practice of teaching in elementary and secondary schools and see how far you get! I cannot blame the arts and sciences professors for refusing to spend their talent, time, and energy on this goal because very few university systems and academic professional societies provide commensurate recognition and rewards for such activities.

Teacher education units on most campuses do not have a chance. They find themselves between the proverbial "rock and hard place." The faculties of university disciplines comprise the larger proportion — at least one-half — of the total staff. Teacher educators are much fewer in number. Thus, when votes are called for, education often loses. It is this situation that causes some educators to believe that teacher education will never be anything more than an academic major. Who has decided? Certainly not teacher education; it has the institutional and professional responsibility for the professional component of teacher education.

Both the organization and programs of teacher education have been misplaced under the control and domination of the academic disciplines that have too little understanding of or sympathy for the purposes of teacher training. Organizationally, teacher education programs operate best when they are established in a professional school or college on the campus, or, when other forms of organization are used, they are treated in the same way as other professional programs on the campus. Teacher education is seldom healthy under any other conditions.

CONFLICT IN PURPOSES

The problem is fundamentally one of conflict of purposes. Professors of education are professional educators who were prepared by graduate programs for continuing professional service. They expect to be involved in a lifetime of teaching, educational development, and professional leadership. They do not come to higher education to adopt the life-styles of academicians in other disciplines. The other disciplines exist for the purpose of contributing to the pool of valid knowledge upon which the professions depend for existence. Professions and professional schools exist for a different purpose: to develop and disseminate a professional body of knowledge and skills which are suited to the needs of practitioners who, thereby, will be able to make more intelligent decisions in their professional roles.

ALTERNATIVES

Unless universities can learn to accommodate the multiple purposes of both colleges of education, which function as the training arm of their profession, and disciplines in which the primary route to the highest rewards is publication in the referreed journals of a particular discipline, problems will continue to exist.

Universities could resolve the problem internally but they are unlikely to do so on their own initiative. What remains then is to resort to state agencies for the requirements for program accreditation and the certification of graduates. However, even accreditation and certification are subject to influence from the academic community. A third alternative is to shift the control of programs to professionally oriented bodies which are willing to fight for professional gains. Teacher centers, jointly developed as collaborative governance structures by the faculties of colleges of education and the organized teaching profession, may well be the wedge that is needed by colleges of education to change the institutions in which they now flounder with little power.

One thing is sure: If colleges of education are to be the training and development arm of the education profession, professional practices will be the proving ground of colleges of education. Now that the romantic illusions have faded, colleges of education either will increasingly meet the needs of their professional constituencies or will become obsolete.

At the present time, however, teacher education not only does not operate in a governance structure that allows it to control its own program development and reward system but it lacks also the "life space" that is necessary to prepare teachers. Teacher education is funded at the lowest level of any professional training program in the United States (Olson, 1975). It attempts to do too much with too little.

Status of Pre-Service Teacher Education Programs and Needed Reforms

LIFE SPACE

If teacher educators are to provide the essential knowledge and skill to pre-service students, then they will need the "life space" to do so. The term "life space" is used to refer to the resources which often are in short supply in many teacher education programs — time, facilities, personnel, instructional and research materials, access to quality instruction in academic units, and the like.

Across the country, today's teachers with only a minimum of professional preparation are certified and placed in service. The number of hours allotted to the professional component for secondary education majors is about 18 hours of a 128-hour program (9 of which are student teaching). For elementary education majors, the total is a little more. The professional education sequence, which, on the national average, comprises only 13 per cent of an undergraduate program, is completely inadequate. What is needed in the professional education of teachers is a protracted program similar to that in other professions: extending the training period from four to five years and adding a sixth-year internship under the supervision of a mentor and/or local review board of professional peers. The internship could be a critical part of teacher preparation in a school or teaching center that is operated collaboratively by the college of education and the organized teaching profession. Licensing should be awarded only after this period of demonstrated competence (internship). In New York and Ohio, State Commissions already have submitted proposals for five-year programs (Teacher Education Conference Board, 1977; Ryan, Kleine, & Krasno, 1972). Also, many other state units of the American Association of Colleges for Teacher Education are studying five- and six-year patterns of preparation.

KNOWLEDGE BASE

Once the "life space" is provided, teacher education can identify and teach the valid knowledge base that is needed by teachers to insure that prior to entry into the teaching profession they are competent to take on the complex task of teaching.

Teaching is an *applied science*. The difference between an educated person and a professional teacher is *pedagogy*, the science of teaching. Teacher education is a process that transforms educated persons from lay citizens to professional educators; there is the assumption that the role performance of the teachers in training will be defined and given substance during the preparation process.

The complexities of teaching require rigorous pre-service preparation. Teachers need to be well-educated in liberal arts or general studies because *all* school teachers are teachers of general education. They must also be well-versed in the disciplines connected to their teaching fields. Teachers also require intensive preparation to develop diagnostic and planning skills, and a broad repertoire of teaching behaviors to meet the individual needs of students. Teacher education must incorporate both theoretical and experiential components.

To assist pre-service students in understanding the relevance of generic skills and theoretical components to the needs of specific community and school settings preparation programs should provide elective options for every student to enable the study in depth of at least one local, regional, or national subculture. Such study should be linked to a broad framework of sensitization to individual and cultural differences and the implications of these differences for teaching and learning. All of these program components are essential to the preparation of a teacher. Each contributes to the shared systematic, and scientific knowlege base for pedagogical decisions.

There follows a sample list of some of the specific subject matter and skill areas which should be completed by every teacher in training to prepare them to work with children with special needs. (Gruber, no date). Keep in mind that this list is merely illustrative, not exhaustive. Abbreviated as this list may be, could the essential knowledge it comprises conceivably be taught to anyone in 9 to 18 credit hours of study? especially if teacher educators were to use the kind of teaching strategies that are powerful enough to insure that teachers in training internalize the knowledge and skills and make them part of their behavior?

1. *Legislation and Court Cases*
    a. historical
    b. parent rights
    c. child rights
    d. school-based implementation: viewpoint
        1. parent
        2. teacher
        3. administrator
        4. taxpayer
        5. businessman

2. *Philosophical Considerations*
    a. purposes of public education
    b. individual and group processes
    c. moral issues facing teachers

3. *Human Relations*
    a. individual differences
    b. strategies for classroom use
    c. labeling issues

4. *Delivery of Services*
    a. description of program types
    b. supportive services within school
    c. parent support/involvement in program
    d. auxiliary services — community

5. *Intellectual-Personal Uniqueness of Human Beings*
    a. unique learning patterns
    b. behavior patterns requiring intervention
    c. academic patterns which are unique

6. *Observation*
    a. presentation, analysis and application of four methods of observation
    b. techniques for recording and graphing

7. *Informal Inventories*
    a. academic
    b. social

8. *Diagnostic Teaching*

9. *Referral Procedures and Multidisciplinary Team Process*
    a. determine when referral to MDT appropriate — through case studies
    b. describe referral process used by local systems
    c. awareness of formal assessment instruments used by MDT members
    d. M-Team staffing
    e. parent conferencing

Programing for Individual Differences

11. *Environmental Control Strategies*
    a. time-space arrangements in the classroom
    b. structuring classroom instruction to meet individual academic, social and emotional needs
12. *Reading*
    a. skills development
    b. selecting and adapting materials
    c. teaching strategies to meet varying needs
13. *Mathematics*
    a. skills development
    b. selecting and adapting materials
    c. teaching strategies to meet varying needs
14. *Spoken and Written Language*
15. *Application of Strategies to other Curricular Areas*
16. *Teaching/Learning Strategies* (individual focus)
    a. describe and explain behavior
    b. describe terminology and basic concepts of operant conditioning applied to behavior management
    c. describe terminology and basic concepts of counseling techniques applied to behavior management (Gruber, no date, pp. 1-3)

In addition to the professional component and specialization in a discipline, all prospective teachers must have a solid background in the so-called "undergirding disciplines" of education (psychology, sociology, anthropology, and philosophy) in the same way that medical and legal students are required to take pre-med or pre-law courses. However, a series of changes must be made in the formats and conceptual frameworks of the undergirding disciplines, too. As in the professional component, the emphasis should be placed on "theory in use," not merely memorization and regurgitation. Also, general education requirements must be revamped to include the interdisciplinary study of the nature and implications of knowledge which, I hope, would be taught by an interdisciplinary team from the social-behavioral sciences and include at least one professor from education. Throughout all aspects of the program, there should be an interlocking relation between practice and theory. Prospective teachers should be trained to operate from a sound professional base of principles rather than as functional technicians.

We also need to ask whether the knowledge being offered to prospective teachers is appropriate to the communities they will be entering, and whether those communities are humane in orientation. If not, then the trainees should be taught the skills and understanding which must accompany the desire to change things. This means that prospective teachers will have to be educated to be tough-minded on occasion, capable of dealing with the unexpected, and skilled in the politics of school and community change. If teachers are to become advocates for the handicapped, they must learn to clarify their own values and stand up and affirm them in their actions. (See Sarason's paper for the relevant discussion.)

To prepare teachers to work with clients aged 3-21, as prescribed by P.L. 94-142, the knowledge base will have to be applicable to teacher roles outside of schools as we now know them. In the future, teachers and other educational personnel will operate out of community-school centers to perform a broad range of human services. They may act as street workers; they may teach both children and their parents in home or community settings; they will relate to social services personnel in corrections, mental health, and rehabilitation agencies; and they will be part of teams whose goal is to create healthy human communities. Indeed, the range of education in the reformed programs will probably be as broad as the needs of the communities the trainees will serve.

The professional teacher educators of the future will be much less deferential to arbitrary authority, less specialized (in terms of specific knowledge or particular tasks), and more assertive, flexible, advocative, and political. Because they will be competent to provide a variety of services in a variety of situations, they will move easily and productively in and out of classrooms, counseling sites, storefront schools, social agencies, correction centers, senior citizen centers, and so on — however their services are needed. Training programs will stress practical skills and techniques and the multidisciplinary knowledge that is needed to understand the dynamics of people relating to people in a variety of social and educational situations. Trainees will view themselves as "human service educators," not solely as classroom teachers. Understanding that a teaching/learning component is at the heart of all human service work, they will be able to function flexibly and effectively in a variety of educational situations and settings.

DIRECT EXPERIENCE

Teacher education is most effective when it is campus based and field oriented. But teacher preparation programs today, partly because of time and resource limitations on the programs, too often are lecture oriented, a format with teaching strategies that are similar to those in other areas of university study. The fundamental problem with this approach is that it grossly underestimates the complexity of preparing a person for effective teaching. Teacher-training graduates do not feel that they are particularly competent as a result of exposure to such programs. In fact, they are not. Teacher education programs have insufficient impact on prospective teachers when the content has little transfer to educational practice; and, there is much that cannot be taught or taught well because of the place in which teacher education is conducted. One does not adequately learn to teach merely by learning *about* teaching. It is also necessary to have experience in the roles of the teachers as a professional beyond the classroom. One semester or part of a semester of student teaching near the end of the college work is not adequate for this purpose.

Quality teacher education must include programs and facilities for extensive *laboratory* and *field-based* experiences as well as the more traditional methods. Most of the institutions that prepare teachers do not have program time, resources, or facilities for making such experiences adequately available.

The fact that many educators quote what is in the book and deny what is in the learner may be directly attributable to the sequence of events in the "shoe box" approach which is the core of many present and past approaches to teacher education. We have been suffering from a "hardening of the categories." There is no reason why we cannot organize education programs vertically rather than horizontally so that students can study professional education and a specific discipline or disciplines as they acquire direct experiences. Each dimension adds meaning to the others when they are integrated into the professional growth of the prospective teacher.

Knowledge about the educative process, that is, the nature of children and youth, subject matter, the educational setting and school and society, the process of learning, teaching, instructional materials and media, one's self, the professions, and evaluation, cannot be taught meaningfully if any part is isolated from the complex problems to which it will be applicable later. All dimensions of teacher education — liberal arts, specialization in a discipline or broad fields, professional studies, and personal study of self — can be integrated if they are offered throughout the careers of teachers as part of the study and practice of new methods of teaching.

Engagement with the real work of teaching should begin as soon as a person thinks he/she wants to teach. The ideal form of preparation is to divide useful work into goals that can be achieved by the most inexperienced students and then into increasingly difficult goals. There should be choices, many choices, to recognize the imperative need of young persons, at whatever age they are ready, to *engage* in the real affairs of schools and communities and *participate* actively in the real world of teaching, in order that they may be enabled to find out what they need to learn and, equally important, what they can contribute to the lives of others through their chosen profession.

We need something like a system that, without exploiting prospective teachers, would permit them to move in and out of direct interactions with and involvement in the profession. First-hand experience in schools and communities would enable prospective teachers to *inquire* into the conduct of human affairs as they worked and studied and to acquire practical skills along with professional ideals. The value of these first-hand experiences would accrue not merely to the students by hastening their maturity and professionalism, not merely to the university by enlarging its knowledge and acceptance of students' life styles, but to the community also, as it demonstrates for the trainees the realities of life and challenges them to reform and improve those realities through participation.

Central to this new design is recognition of the fact that teacher education, schools and other community educational agencies, and colleges and universities are interrelated and interacting components of *one* system. Schools and the communities they serve and colleges currently are unnecessarily isolated from one another to the detriment of each. We must replace the present isolation with a new interlocking process of educational improvement and training that connects all levels of the educational spectrum.

Status of Inservice Education and Needed Reforms

Even though a professional culture for educators has developed rapidly during the last decade, we should not underestimate the enormous task ahead: to continue to construct valid, generalizable teaching and learning principles and to disseminate them meaningfully to the two million teachers in the schools and the thousands of other trainers in human service agencies.

At present, there is no significant effort to provide a continuing education program for teachers during their professional service. Other professions (e.g., medicine, law) recognize the needs, especially in times of change, to provide for the re-education of their practitioners. Yet, few school districts expend as much as one per cent of their budgets on inservice and the continuing education of teachers. Sabbatical leaves are not funded for teachers. Teachers are expected to take further college work after initial certification but at their own expense and in night schools or during summer vacations. Teacher salaries do not permit adequate expenditures on books and journals, going to conferences, taking formal education toward advanced degrees, participating in cultural events, traveling in other cultures, taking development leaves, and so on.

There is a great dearth of support for research, experimentation, innovation, and dissemination in education. The magnitude, intensity, and direction of the efforts needed for continuing education reach far beyond present resources. Teacher education needs a level of support that approaches the research, development, and training base in other professions. Eastman Kodak, for example, puts 10% of its gross profits into the continuing re-education of its employees.

Much has been learned during the last 10 years about the delivery of inservice education, if the resources can be found to put them into practice. The most notable contributions to education have come from the experiences and the concepts which were developed in such nontraditional programs as those described by the Chickerings in their paper. They remind us again that knowledge about adult learning and development must be one of the bases for designing programs and delivery systems for experienced teachers (Chickering, Chickering, & Durchholz, 1976). Within the teacher education community, the National Teacher Corps has been most helpful in providing opportunities for field-tested practices and programs for inservice education. A list of these concepts may be useful here as guidelines for developing effective inservice teacher education for the future.

1. Inservice education must be easily accessible, job-embedded if possible, and evaluated by its impact on the school, not just on the individual teacher.

2. Inservice education must be based on a knowledge of *adult learning theory* and the *work situation* of the teacher. The schools will not improve by just giving teachers more knowledge, skills, and values. The conditions in the work situation must change to permit them to use this training. Teachers are already overtrained for some of the situations in which they are expected to work.

3. In the making of a teacher, it is highly probable that inservice education is infinitely more important than pre-service education. However, the two should not be viewed as separate entities. They should be viewed as interlocking phases of a *career-long* preparation program.

4. The first two or three years of a teacher's experience are the most critical, and the supportive environment provided by the principal is a key to the teacher's success.

5. Practicing teachers who are good adult educators as well as good teachers of children are often the best possible trainers of other teachers in the work situation: They have credibility. Also, broadening the definition of expert to include the local teacher decreases the probability of discounting the expert and keeps the responsibility for achieving goals with the individuals in the local setting — scapegoating is lessened. The emerging role of the university teacher-educator is as a trainer of on-site trainers. This multiplier model extends the impact of the colleges and provides back-up support for the on-site trainers.

6. Changing the behavior of a group often is easier than changing the behavior of an individual. The school — the work setting — should be the focus of reform and everyone in it should be a participant, either as an *innovator* or, at least, agreeing not to be a *blocker*.

7. Any school, if it wishes, can arrange for the professional growth of its faculty and administrators as a regular part of the work load.

8. Inservice education is virtually useless if the objectives of training programs are not valued and rewarded by the power structure of the school system.

9. There is a vast range of difference between good and poor teachers. We should build our training models on the skills, knowledge, and values possessed and demonstrated by the *good* teachers.

10. Professional growth, particularly when it requires the exchange of old habits for new, breeds considerable insecurity. However, it may well be that we have greatly overestimated the psychological resistance of teachers to change.

11. If we fail to attend to the teacher's emotions as well as his/her mind, we will again blunder. Professional development is both an affective and cognitive process.

12. Because inservice education, to be useful, must be related to the work situation, it is by its very nature a political as well as an educational process. Policies to guide the continuing education of teachers must start from this basic premise or they will be ineffective in dealing with the conflict that is produced when adult learners seek to use the knowledge and skills they have been taught in inservice education as instruments to reform the system itself.

13. Teachers are not the only school personnel in need of growth. Teacher educators, principals, custodians, secretaries, parents, aides, and others must be included in inservice plans. It should be a "we," not a "they," process; and the "partners" from the university who work on-site should be part of the "we."

14. In the past decade, we have been treated to a variety of parades: the right-to-read *show*, the differentiated *team*, the behavior objective *troop*, the teacher center *big top*, and the career education *shuffle*. If the commitment to inservice education for mainstreaming is to be realized, the teachers will have to be convinced that mainstreaming is not just another bandwagon coming out of Washington.

15. Although private purposes and individual self-interest are powerful motivators, significant amplification occurs when those interests are linked to active engagement with larger human and social concerns (e.g., P.L. 94-142). Experiences that occur when one works to understand and deal with a significant social problem have great developmental power and foster many kinds of learning. We need to build those experiences more frequently into inservice programs by helping prospective teachers to look outward as well as inward for purposes.

16. Teaching centers possess great potential as continuing education centers as well as collaborative governance mechanisms. They can be designed to deliver college and community resources, bring professionals together, and form a network of available educational services. Neither the public schools nor the colleges can live in splendid isolation. All partners in the education process can

cooperate in the operation of a teacher center: (a) teacher educators; (b) the schools; (c) teacher organizations; (d) the university; (e) the school board and community; and (f) the state or intermediate agencies. Anything less than a high level of interchange of experience and expertise among these partners will widen an already considerable gap between what is and what could be.

Conclusion

The most vivid truth that emerges from any analysis of the views expressed at the conference on the present state of the educational system, the goals and concepts included in P.L. 94-142, and teacher education is that we will not succeed if special education is kept in a conceptual framework apart from regular education at any level of the educational spectrum. Until we get rid of this dualism in our teacher education institutions, our public schools will continue to be a mirror image of the conditions present in teacher education. Therefore, we must prepare *all* teachers to implement the concepts in P.L. 94-142. We must reform *all* aspects of teacher education, not just special education departments.

The professional status of teaching and teacher education will be recognized when the corpus of validated knowledge and skills to which teachers and teacher educators subscribe is clearly identified and the public recognizes that the teaching profession possesses the skills and knowledge to perform a service that is a matter of life and death to this society and its people. Implementing the concepts of P.L. 94-142 would constitute such a demonstration.

The problem is not that we cannot prepare teachers to accomplish this essential public service but that we do not. Future teachers are not only getting a second-rate undergraduate education, they are getting a third-rate professional education. We have been unwilling to provide the time and money that are necessary for true professional preparation. We have taken a short-sighted cheap approach to teacher education and we are getting what we are paying for.

We are not faced with an insoluble problem. Nor, however, are we dealing with a problem which can be corrected by minor tinkering. As the authors stated in the AACTE Bicentennial Commission Report,

> What the teaching profession needs is a totally new set of concepts regarding the nature of the emerging human services society, its educational demands, the kinds of delivery systems necessary to provide public access to continuing educational opportunity, and the types of professional personnel and training required to reform public education. (Howsam, et al., 1976, p. 138)

Resources, both financial and personal, must be directed toward strategies that link schools that are seeking to change with teacher education institutions that are seeking to break out of established patterns. Shuffling courses about is not the answer. A major shake-up is needed in the form and substance of teacher education from the introduction to teaching through the teaching career of the teacher.

Throughout the conference, I kept thinking that this particular group of scholars would be a good group to turn loose on the task of changing the status of teacher education on their campuses. Because of their reputations and locations in different academic departments, they probably would have the power to make more of an impact, at least in some quarters, than their colleagues in colleges of education. However, it would take great courage; being an advocate for teacher education has not been the most popular role for scholars in the disciplines. The most popular role has been that of critic. As a result of this conference, however, this particular group of academicians would seem to have a special reason for taking on the task. All of the great ideas in this report can be acted on only if the importance of professional education in producing teachers who can provide free *appropriate* public education for all children is recognized.

The key to making the concepts in P.L. 94-142 come alive in the schools of this country is a new commitment to the pre-service and inservice education of America's teachers. Reform must move in both directions — to *universities* as well as to schools.

References

Chickering, A. W., Chickering, J. N., & Durchholz, P. Problems in the postsecondary education of adults. Paper prepared for the Latin American meeting on New Forms of Postsecondary Education. Caracas, Venezuela, September 1976. (mimeo)

Gruber, S. E. List of possible instructional modules for mainstreaming. Department of Exceptional Education, University of Wisconsin, Milwaukee. (no date)

Howsam, R. B., Corrigan, D. C., Denmark, G. W., & Nash, R. J. *Educating a profession*. Washington, D. C.: The Bicentennial Commission for the Profession of Teaching of the American Association of Colleges for Teacher Education, 1976

Olson, P. (Ed.). *Teacher education in America*. Lincoln, Neb.: Study Commission on Undergraduate Education and the Education of Teachers, University of Nebraska, 1975.

Ryan, K., Kleine, P., & Krasno, R. *Realities and revolution in teacher education*. Report #6, Commission on Public School Personnel policy in Ohio. Cleveland, Ohio: Greater Cleveland Associated Foundation, 1972.

Teacher Education Conference Board. Action!! On Task Force Report, *Newsletter*, 1977, **1**(4). (80 Wolf Road, Albany, N. Y. 12205)

Discussants

Who (What) is the Handicapped Child? Conceptions and Misconceptions

S. Phyllis Stearner[1]

Argonne Laboratory

It has been said that "Society achieves the kind of excellence it values." Historically, the records indicate that little indeed has been expected from persons who have some handicapping condition. This attitude has served to justify society's failure to provide essential opportunities to those persons who are different in one way or another, and so has created situations that serve only to perpetuate the handicapping conditions. Many aspects of the problems facing handicapped children and handicapped adults have their counterparts in the problems of racial and ethnic minorities and women in our society.

The conference addressed the problems associated with providing the "least restrictive" educational opportunities for handicapped children, as mandated in P.L. 94-142. Although little attention was given to the term "attitudinal barrier" in the many penetrating discusssions, much of what was said focused on problems associated with the general reluctance to accept the person who is perceived to be different in some way.

A few of the participants, however, seemed to have some difficulty in understanding that "different" is not necessarily the same as "inferior." The problems associated with attitudinal barriers should not be understated, for they are of fundamental importance. Society does not fully understand the kinds of limitations that are imposed by the various handicapping conditions. Out of this lack of understanding there have grown misconceptions, prejudices, and stereotyped ideas of abilities and disabilities. In large part, the segregation to which the handicapped have been subjected has served to fix and potentiate these mistaken ideas. It is appropriate, then, that one of the first approaches to this problem should be the

---

[1]Biologist, Division of Biological and Medical Research.

integration of handicapped and nonhandicapped pupils, that is, mainstreaming. If we can raise a generation that accepts those of us who are different — accepts us strictly on the basis of what we can do both mentally and physically — then we will have come a long way toward equality of opportunity. To put it in the simplest terms, integration is needed in order to fully educate the nonhandicapped as well as the handicapped.

Attitudinal barriers create problems for persons with various types of handicaps, mental as well as physical. In most other respects, however, these two types of handicaps involve different classes of problems. Implementation of mainstreaming, then, can be adequately approached only by understanding the differences. Most of what was said during the conference involved mental handicaps, in which there are different levels of learning capabilities or behavioral aberrations. My comments focus on the problems associated with the nonretarded but physically handicapped child. In this area, of course, I can speak with more authority, based on the experiences associated with my own life. As was emphasized during several of the discussions, handicapped persons who know the problems encountered in attempts to achieve equal opportunities within our social structure are on the side of experience. They want to move ahead in order to accomplish the task, to act to fulfill the need for equal opportunities. But resistance to change is a common trait of organizations. So the nonhandicapped leaders of organizations stress the need for reason and ask the question, "How are these needs going to be approached?"

From what we know about successful experiences in educating the handicapped child in a least restrictive environment, we need to deal with persons (people problems) rather than theoretical constructs. Thus we can get on to the immediate problem, the critical need to provide quality education to the handicapped child. "There is no limit to the resources of the human mind, but no resource is of value unless it is used. . . ." This statement was made recently in reference to problems of equal opportunities for women, but it also can be applied to the problems of the handicapped. In order for any human mind to be put to use at its fullest potential, it must have had opportunities for maximum development, and then it must be given a chance to express itself. These factors all too frequently are denied to the mentally alert but physically handicapped person. As a result, there is little chance for employment and a full and meaningful life as a productive member of society. As a child born with cerebral palsy, there were many road blocks along the way during my efforts to obtain an adequate education to become a biological scientist, and then in seeking employment.

I had little encouragement or guidance to direct me toward my goal as a research scientist. I was not mainstreamed; I had private tutors and attended special schools until I reached college. Most important was the support from my mother, who provided a wide variety of experiences during my early years. Then, later, it was she who gave constant encouragement in my academic efforts in college. I believe that a stubborn determination was the driving force in my life, but *lack* of counseling was probably also important. In my early years I never learned that handicapped children, especially those with a developmental disability such as cerebral palsy, do not grow up to be scientists. So I went on my stubborn and determined way and, eventually, succeeded.

The problems associated with the education of the nonretarded, physically handicapped child involve adjustments to the various physical limitations, but there are no special differences in learning. Thus, a variety of physical or manual adaptations may be needed that will require ingenuity and innovation on the part of teachers. This task need not be difficult when the primary focus is on what the child can rather than what he cannot do. Most important is the elimination of misconceptions, for there are few real differences between the physically handicapped and the nonhandicapped. The unit of concern is the education of the children. This education must necessarily include integration, not only based on sex and race but, also, handicaps. There can be no equality of life experiences based on separation, for only by experiential relationships can we truly come to know one another and so attain equal educational opportunities.

The fundamental problem in achieving successful mainstreaming is in developing a cadre of teachers who understand the nature of handicapping conditions, who are sensitive and innovative, and who have the initiative to adapt to a few special needs. Here the practice in operation in Vermont, of teacher training in the field by practicing teachers, can be effective. Of course, the use of classes that contain some physically handicapped children is required.

The concept is the basis for a program recently initiated by Martha R. Redden of the Office of Opportunities in Science, American Association for the Advancement of Science (AAAS). The program is aimed at providing quality science education to handicapped children on the same basis as that provided to their nonhandicapped peers. Dr. Redden's project involves the collection and sharing of experiences of individual teachers who have tried to teach science to handicapped children and succeeded. As part of this program, an inventory of the experiences will be prepared and reported so that other teachers will be encouraged to do the same thing; at the same time, they will be given guidance based on the experiences of their colleagues. In the process of inventorying these experiences, a nationwide resource list of people who are willing to share their experiences with other teachers will be prepared. Martha Redden and her group believe that this register will be important because teachers are more willing to try what they know their peers have done successfully. In this connection, effective use can be made of a resource group of handicapped persons who can serve as role models and aid teachers in adapting lesson plans. Since it appears that "teachers teach in the way they were taught," it will be necessary to emphasize the teaching of handicapped children during the preparation of regular teachers. With sufficiently trained, sensitive, and innovative regular classroom teachers, the need for special education classes will be vastly reduced.

Much of the discussion during the conference emphasized the special needs imposed by a handicapping condition. To one who is handicapped, on the other hand, a disability is only important in connection with one or a few of one's daily life activities. In all other activities the handicap is not a factor. As a result, the handicapped themselves usually emphasize their abilities and only rarely may consider that they are "handicapped." The difficulty with this kind of thinking, of course, is that society perceives them to be disabled and so creates the attitudinal barriers which have been discussed. Attitudinal barriers exclude many groups that are seen to be different in some respect or another. For racial or ethnic minorities, there may be outward differences, such as skin color; for the physically handicapped, there are structural or functional differences that limit a normal range of activities. These defects have been compared to faulty packaging. But is this sufficient reason to discard the contents? Yet society does indeed reject the contents if the package is faulty. It does so when it fails to provide basic needs for the physically handicapped, for example, accessible public buildings and transportation, as well as the right to equal educational opportunities and employment.

The question of why so little mention was made of physically handicapping conditions did not find a ready answer during the conference. Since then, I have come to wonder whether physical and mental handicaps are sufficiently distinguished by society so that they can be considered separately. Can it be that those who have a physical disability are perceived to be mentally handicapped also? This speculation does have some foundation in reality, for I, who am in a wheelchair, am frequently treated by flight attendants, shopkeepers, waitresses, and even some of my scientific colleagues as if I were incompetent to answer a simple question for myself. Common questions are directed to my companion who assists me. While I readily admit to an average level of paranoia, I find amusement in the look of surprise by a visitor to my office when I respond to his question of where he can find Dr. Stearner.

Clearly, society has misconceptions concerning the handicapped. Teachers are a part of our society and can be expected to be no better informed than society at large. The greatest need to insure the future success of education in the least restrictive environment, then, is to provide adequate experiential training to new teachers and meaningful inservice experience for those already in the profession.

Some New Ways of Thinking About Handicapped Children

Hadi Madjid[1]

Arthur D. Little, Inc.

The Prevailing Mode of Scientific Thought

In the main, I do not view myself as handicapped although I am blind. I find handicapped areas here and there in the course of my life, as an explorer might discover islands in the sea, but I do not feel that I am a blind explorer. I have learned to navigate the seas and am satisfied with my life. In my experience, the toughest and most treacherous reefs are the "practical," "scientific" modes of thought which were used by the people upon whose judgment I was dependent during many of my young years. When I lost my sight in an accident at the age of 15, the accepted place for an education was a school for the blind. I wanted the familiar surroundings of my previous school, however. I "mainstreamed," but it was tough getting in. I began with a dream and a deep commitment, but I had no clear, objective understanding of how I would manage the school work. The administrators, on the other hand, began with practical questions to which they needed answers, but there were no easy answers.

This narrowness is not confined to the field of special education; it pervades the whole of society. Science itself has become organized around one dominant epistemological model. It has been vastly oversimplified and turned into a dogma; thus organized, it has affected how we think, how we live, how we organize our institutions, and, perhaps most problematic of all, how we plan our research. This mode of science is effective for creating a ballistic rocket or placing a man in orbit; where the objective is clear, success can be clearly defined and all important uncertainties can be eliminated.

---

[1]Senior Economist

The mode of science that is effective for developing a ballistic rocket, however, is not effective for helping man to achieve meaning in life. Uncertainty and ambiguity are the very fabric of life, the very nature of being human. Eliminating them is a contradiction. The problem of meaning in life requires the incorporation of uncertainty and ambiguity into the scientific equation. Science that is directly helpful to human lives must be as limitless as the human imagination, as complex as man's experience, and as full of ambiguity as life. The mode of science that leads to the ballistic rocket requires rigid boundaries. The mode of science that nourishes man demands that there be no boundaries; it flourishes in the spaces beyond boundaries where man's imagination and spirit alone can make the judgments that guide thought and action.

Reading the papers for this conference, listening to the speeches, and taking part in the discussions gave me the impression that the work and research in the field of special education has been dominated by a narrow science that fails to reflect the real world because it does not allow ambiguity.

I believe that overemphasis of the narrow scientific approach is a great barrier; it complicates as much as it eases the task of learning for the teacher and the handicapped child. I do not wish to imply that science is the whole problem but that it is a terribly serious one. It becomes more serious each day because the prevailing mode of science is rarely questioned or systematically investigated.

What is a Handicap?

My impression at the conference was that by-and-large the assumption was implicit that "handicapped" describes a person as a whole. I found this apparent assumption striking because it does not match up with my perception of myself. It probably stems from the fact that much of the research in special education deals with mental retardation and emotional disturbance. However, the assumption is not true for the physically handicapped and it even may be only partially true for the mentally retarded.

At the conference, I used the term "hydraulic model" to describe the underpinnings of the assumption and contrasted it with the "gating model." The hydraulic model assumes that the handicapped child is fundamentally different in learning capacity and thus needs extra pressure to be put upon him by the teacher. The gating model assumes that a handicapped child is not significantly different from other children except in his handicap. The difference manifests itself only when the child confronts certain barriers or gates; for example, a stairway presents a gating problem to a person in a wheelchair. It is not what goes on during the learning process with the teacher that is a barrier but getting into the classroom in the first place. Similarly, the blind child must have printed material converted into a tactile or auditory form. Whether a handicapped child fits into the hydraulic or gating model is absolutely central to implementation of the new federal legislation or, for that matter, of any state action toward mainstreaming. Professional skills, organizational procedures, measures for classification and evaluation, costs, and so on, differ significantly in the hydraulic and the gating models.

I believe that the main reason for the dominance of the hydraulic model is the previously mentioned prevailing mode of scientific thought. This mode requires clear-cut objectives and, also, that things be classifiable — that a person be either handicapped or not handicapped, or legally blind, or paraplegic, or the like. The practice of "management by objectives" is unable to deal with the active person whose degree of handicap varies with different barriers. For example, I discussed with one of my colleagues his attitude toward me because I felt that he was avoiding working with me. The problem turned out to be that he was quite confused about how I was handicapped. He felt that I must be but he did not understand how; almost in desperation, he asked me to explain and to end his confusion.

The main purpose of clear objectives is to advance action, to put a man into orbit or to get handicapped children into school. The hydraulic model is well suited to the prevailing operations of institutions; in the field of education, it keeps the whole problem within the school system. Standard operating procedures in an institution set boundaries for the institution. Procedures first clarify what belongs inside and outside the boundaries of the institution and then they focus on managing what is inside. Thus, the hydraulic model of the handicapped child places the child entirely within the domain of the school system where he can be dealt with according to existing operating procedures, with only slight modifications for the individual case. The gating model, on the other hand, breaks open institutional boundaries and focuses attention on different institutions or providers of special services. The gating model looks at all the important aspects of a child's life that may influence his education and at how they relate to school. There are multiple barriers; eliminating one does not eliminate the others. The child must get from home to school in the first place; overcoming the barriers to this movement depends, in part, upon the availability of transportation and the physical barriers along the way. Then, the child who is hard of hearing can be helped by a special hearing aid, a blind child by recorded material, and so on. Overcoming barriers is a complex task and it cannot be accomplished by the school system alone. The family, community, government, and business are all interdependent. We can begin to understand the organizational difficulty in using the gating model of a handicap when we ask, whom shall we make responsible for the successful education of the child? Facing this question squarely places us in a terrible dilemma. If the child gets the right hearing aid, he will no longer be handicapped; if he does not, he will be. The responsibility thus becomes society's. We must choose whether a child is to remain handicapped. This choice turns the practical objective of mainstreaming handicapped children into an ethical and moral problem. When we view life in its entirety without boundaries, we are straight into a different epistemology, into a mode that cannot exclude ambiguity and uncertainty.

What is the Advice?

There are no easy answers. We cannot place all our faith in the narrow mode of science. We must learn to think more broadly, to carry out research that confronts reality more directly, and to so organize our institutions that they will be more rewarding to both the people who are served and the people who work in them. I believe one must begin at the very beginning by recognizing that ambiguity is an essential aspect of mainstreaming, no matter what we do. Ambiguity is all around us, if we only attend to it. Programs of special education have been developed for handicapped children. Yet those programs can be terribly misused, changing from a good to an evil, as in some of the central city schools when minority children who are not handicapped are classified as handicapped. From the narrow mode of science, this change is seen only as an error: The design of the rocket is wrong and we must build better rockets. A rocket built according to the same principles will perform in exactly the same way. But accepting ambiguity involves the design of a different vehicle. The automatic, set-trajectory ballistic rocket is inappropriate; what is needed is a vehicle that can be steered by a pilot.

In the gating model of the handicapped child, the objectives are multiple, as in any ambiguous situation. Furthermore, each objective contains its own opposite, where the same gate can be either a barrier or a solution. Where multiple barriers must be overcome, one generally cannot handle all of them at once. It takes time to deal with them, focusing on one, then another, accepting the third to be dealt with after, and checking all the time whether a barrier that has been overcome has returned as a problem. No preplanned program can handle this kind of situation. An educational plan based upon the narrow mode of science is likely either to exclude some handicapped children as too handicapped to be dealt with or to include them, but by providing them mainly with seats and no education. The important thing is to provide an appropriate map, someone to steer, and something to steer with.

I was struck that none of the papers discussed at the conference dealt with what happens to a child after he finishes school. No papers deal with jobs, family, or society. This omission is almost inevitable when the hydraulic model is used and the epistemology assumes that the task of science is to eliminate ambiguity. Where ambiguity is accepted, it is natural and almost inevitable to lay out the issues in a holistic manner. At the conference, I recalled my own days at school as a handicapped child and I could not help but think of my family's contributions, both positive and negative, and of how I wondered what I would do after I finished school. I was a much better student after I lost my sight than before, because I felt that if I did not get good grades in school and go onto college and graduate school I would not be able to deal effectively and freely with my handicap and earn a decent living. Ambiguity means that there are difficult choices to be made, that things do not go automatically. The family affects school and school affects the family; public law and regulations help and hinder; and the effects are continuously shifting. This interdependence is the substance of the map I have that helps me to make my choices. I never put boundaries around my awareness; I make my choices, fully accepting the ambiguity.

The handicapped child is often overprotected; his or her horizons may be severely restricted and opportunities for experience limited. Tragically, it is the very richness of experience that allows the handicapped person to be most independent and most responsible for his own fate. The hydraulic model works with a vengeance to negate the very independence we try to achieve. When the terrain is ambiguous, it is absolutely essential for the individual, no matter how young, to learn to take responsibility for his own destiny. The teacher or parent cannot be the pilot alone.

Any plan for mainstreaming should address the central question of how the vehicle is steered and by whom. From my own experience, I cannot help but believe that it must be the handicapped child himself. I have had to deal with a number of gates, many of which I have overcome satisfactorily, and always I have had to take a strong initiative or little would have happened. I have not heard of any curriculum which is designed to help a handicapped child recognize and assume his own responsibility for overcoming barriers.

If the handicapped child is the pilot, what then is the steering mechanism? Relationships between the handicapped child and other people seem to me to be the mechanism. It is in relationships with others where I am both most limited and most free. This is the one gate that affects all others. For everyone, life is relationships; the narrow mode of science does not see life in this way, however. The teacher is seen as someone who hands knowledge over to the pupil. I was intrigued by McDermott's presentation in which he argued that the relationship between a pupil and teacher is interactive. This paper relates to minority children, but I believe his argument is true for handicapped children as well. Learning to deal with ambiguous situations is relational. The boundary between the teacher and pupil disappears and the teacher, as well as the pupil, learns. For the handicapped child, relational learning does not apply to the classroom, only to the barrier. It is not always the teacher who plays the dominant role; it may be the parents or a friend who is skillful in using tools. For example, the canes available to blind people are badly designed: They bend easily and their reflective surface is quickly damaged in use. A friend who is skilled in using tools and I discussed the problem, a couple of years ago, and came up with an answer. He made me a prototype cane which has worked out very well. Educational planners need broad familiarity with the interests of many people in different lines of work; they need to identify people who can work with handicapped children to overcome their barriers and gain a sound education. An important aspect of planning for mainstreaming would be the development of a broad comunity base of such involved persons.

Finally, what is the vehicle being steered? A ballistic missile relies upon formulas, machinery, and repetition; a vehicle fit for traveling in ambiguous terrains must rely upon the human imagination, mind, will, and soul. A ballistic rocket places organization ahead of the individual. A vehicle for traveling in ambiguous spaces must place the individual first. The tendency of the narrow mode of science is to submerge the individual behind professional skills, organizations, routines, automatic machinery, and the like. This focused approach may be powerful and necessary in some activities but it is absolutely wrong to strive for it in all spheres as is done now. It seems to me that the teacher, school administrator, government official, parents, and, above all, the handicapped child himself must step forth and take responsibility for the journey as long as it remains essentially ambiguous. The national objective of mainstreaming children in schools is not just an objective target to be aimed for and achieved. If it is nothing more than that, it will take a long time in coming and will be fraught with difficulties. It should be seen as an ethical goal — a goal that gives all members of the society something to strive for. Mainstreaming should be a moral claim on the future by all of us.

Pursuing an objective goal in an ambiguous terrain inevitably leads to a sense of failure; going astray in the pursuit of a moral commitment leads to correction and redirection, while pursuit of the goal continues.

Reactions From a New Believer

John W. Melcher[1]

Department of Public Instruction, Wisconsin

The conference was a real "jet assist" to me as an on-the-line special educator. The over-100,000 special educators in this country have found their professional conscience and are no longer preoccupied with making special education into a sky-high monument. We now realize that in our eagerness to help the child with exceptional educational needs, we became preoccupied with our ability and with the quantitative growth of our movement; we lost sight of the child with handicaps as our prime concern and the sincere commitment to do the best for that child in a manner as close to the mode provided for other children in our "universal" school system. Historically, we chose special education delivery systems that provided service to children on the "separate but equal" logic that also afflicted the education of minority group children.

During the past decade, special educators have been encouraged to "intellectually cohabitate" with our colleagues in regular education. No longer do we see ourselves as the "experts" who are the sole qualified persons that can normalize or ameliorate the environments of children with exceptional educational needs.

This conference was a great opportunity for scholars in sociology, economics, history, psychology, and anthropology to share their candid attitudes with academic leaders in American special and regular education and representatives of local, state, and federal education agencies who are, ultimately, responsible for free public education of all children in our society. The especially astute and penetrating observations shared with the group by our handicapped friends — Dr. Phyllis Stearner and Dr. Hadi Madjid — dramatically illustrate how we have limited our source of professional knowledge by not seeking out the deep feelings, knowledge, and perceptions of the handicapped people we purport to serve. Their insights, profound wisdom, and ability to "acid test" the scholars'

---

[1]Director, Bureau for Handicapped Children

and practitioners' theories, practices, and prejudices were a highlight of the uninhibited meeting of the many frames of references reflected in the attendees' minds, attitudes, and long-term professional commitments. Greater consumer research is obviously a need we have just begun to explore; a business enterprise would not last a fortnight if it ignored what the people concerned think and feel. We need to converse much more with all levels of "consumer-children" enrolled in our schools' regular and special education programs, with adults who have been served by us in the past, and with the taxpaying society as it views our handicapped clients and friends and our attempts to assist in their educative process.

Throughout the conference, I observed the keen attention paid by the divergent individuals to the opinions of others in this select group. From this small sample of cross fertilization, I have come back to my pedestrian responsibilities with a *new* hope for amalgamated efforts of regular and general educators, handicapped persons, and scholars in the social sciences. The old isolationism of special education is passé, and the new sophisticated multifaceted attack on the complex problems now seems more probable to me. This type of wide-spectrum study of the education of the handicapped should be extended to college campuses, the total USOE, the total staffs of local and state education agencies, as well as to the handicapped groups and their associates.

Reactions

George P. Young[1]
St. Paul (Minnesota) Public Schools

I am much impressed, as I have been for several years, with the lobbying success of special education enthusiasts. With single-minded purpose they have obtained legislative action and court decisions which have built programs for special education from almost nothing, just a generation ago, to an unequalled array.

People denied any public education at all a generation ago now receive, and are recognized as having rights to, particular programs which have been designed for them specifically at public expense, an expense that exceeds by far the cost of educating the rest of the school-aged population.

This rapid and significant expansion has been welcomed and supported by those of us who implement the programs mandated by law and court orders. Our support for the programs continues, but the welcome is beginning to wear somewhat thin. I feel a backlash, and I believe that the university people and the parents of special education children, who have carried the main burden of the lobbying, must become sensitive to the growing danger facing special education.

At a time of general student decline in public schools, and the attendant financial stress, school administrators, boards of education, and parents of the general student population begin to question the increased use of local funds for special education, and special education is viewed, correctly, as harmful to the general population to the extent that local financial support for special education programs results in less program for the general population.

You must understand the financial implications of enrollment decline. Fewer students mean less financial aid from the state for the general student population because state formulas are based on numbers of students. Staff reduction accompanies enrollment decline, which changes the nature of the teacher group. Since staff reduction follows the seniority rule, the last in are the first out; the

---

[1]Superintendent of Schools

less expensive teachers are let go and the teachers left are at the higher salary levels. The nature of the student population also changes; an increasing number and percentage of the student population come from low-income families, and these students are often the ones who need the expensive special services.

At a time, therefore, when more services for the general student population are needed, expenses go up, services are decreased, and less money is available. Regular classroom teachers are released, student-teacher ratios go up, ancillary services are decreased, yet, at the same time, special education expands. We estimate, in St. Paul, that 30 per cent of the total cost of special education programs comes from our local budget, which exacerbates the financial problem for the rest of the district.

Adding mainstreaming adds significantly to the problem, and significantly to the view that something must be done to protect the welfare of the general population of students. In other words, backlash.

During the conference, a great deal was said about mainstreaming and the new mandates: testing procedures, identification procedures, and the segregation of special education students are attacked. To those of us who have carried out the mandates and court decisions on special education programs, the attacks, particularly when they seem to be directed at us, create confusion. Testing programs were constructed and used by special education advocates to make certain that children were "correctly" identified as eligible for special education programs, and to insure that the monies went to special education and were not drained off for ineligible children. Now it seems that the people who brought about the testing, who deliberately set up the labeling to provide evidence for the need for programs (money), blame the school administrators for the conditions special education people themselves established.

The administrator — myself for example — has long looked at and admired the strategies of special education people, both for fund raising and teaching-learning strategies. There is great value for the rest of us in the models of special education teaching-learning strategies. There is a large group of children whose ability levels lie below average but not low enough for eligibility for special education placement. Even with the models at hand, the strategies which seem to work are not incorporated into the rest of the system.

My support for mainstreaming, therefore, is as much based on the good that I believe can be accomplished for special education students as the good I see for the rest of the system. Mainstreaming may work to make the successful models available to the rest of us. It is, after all, not only the special education students who have been segregated from the rest of the school population, but the main school population has been segregated from the special education group.

The problems which I see are as follows:

1. Increasing financial stress on the public school program exacerbated by special education program mandates, which eat into the local budget.

2. The attendant backlash.

3. An apparent lack of concern by special education mainstreaming supporters for the significant reorganization problems faced by the rest of the system.

Someone at the conference mentioned that inservice programs, related to the need for assisting classroom teachers to cope with mainstreaming, is carrying culture to the primitives. Missionaries in the past went to some rather beautiful people, taught them to be ashamed of their beauty and, thus, they covered up and hid their beauty. Somewhere in that parable there is a lesson.

Closing Comments

Closing Comments

Nicholas Hobbs

For these closing comments, it seemed useful to me to try to identify the tensions that ran though the discussions: the conceptual tensions, the intellectual polarities, perhaps the theses and antitheses and their implications for the future of special education. I was able to identify nine pivotal themes.

1. The most pervasive tension in the deliberations was the relation between what we have known traditionally as special education and regular education, and the necessity at this time for some kind of reconciliation between the two. Renegotiation, a term contributed by Reynolds, is quite valuable because it implies the probability — the necessity — of mutual accommodation and growth precipitated by the "least restrictive environment" requirement. We are not on a one-way track where special education contributes something to regular education or regular education absorbs special education; rather, we are seeking a kind of mutual adjustment with the expectation of mutual benefit. The future is open-ended. It will be hard to predict how these negotiations between special and regular education will come out. We have what someone in the group called a brave new law (P.L. 94-142) but, as was pointed out several times in the discussions, we also must deal with systems that are resistant to change. We pointed out evidence of a strong backlash that certainly will have a dampening effect on the aspirations embodied in the laws. Several members of the group underscored the continued need for special placement, for special opportunities, for some kinds of handicapped children. Unless this need is recognized, we can develop an unwarranted sense of failure in mainstreaming. It seems likely that in the renegotiation process, the concept of the individualized educational program may well provide a matrix for development in regular education. It is a reasonable expectation that, in time, all education will be characterized by individually designed and negotiated child development programs.

2. Tension between stability and change was discusssed but, it still seems to me, we touched only the surface of this very difficult problem. We spoke of *others* who resist change. Who is it that re-

sists reasonable change? Not us. *They*. One might ask, who are "they"? But we know that they are we and we are they. There are simply many agendas that will have to be negotiated, to be worked out, in the public schools. The future of special education surely will be shaped by these many agendas, not by ours alone.

At least two models of change were suggested: (a) change resulting from external pressure, from coercion, and (b) change resulting from internal needs to grow. Someone pointed out the utility of resistance to change; you do not want organizations that are so labile that they have no continuing character. At that point, especially in the context of talking about change, we came up with a number of scapegoats, people or institutions that stand in the way of progress as we defined it. McDermott helped us to see how unproductive looking for scapegoats is likely to be.

3. Considerations of the sources of change brought references to (a) social trends and (b) policies. Social trends suggest influences over which there may or may not be much explicit control; policies, on the other hand, suggest influences that may be amenable to rational formulation and explication. But does policy precede or follow social change? One of the many admirable functions of the public schools in America over the years has been to provide an arena for resolving social issues. It is tough, it is distracting, it takes a lot of resources, but I do not think you will find the same circumstance elsewhere. Think about the school system in France. It just was not engaged in social change — not until 1958, anyway.

Since 1853, when the first compulsory school law was passed in Massachusetts, the American schools have been important instruments of social change. As I understand it, one of the reasons for this radical notion of compulsory education at state expense was the necessity of Americanizing large groups of people from quite diverse cultures. Schools were asked to take on that enormously difficult job. From my State of Tennessee, I am aware that a public school was the arena for fighting over issues of fundamentalist religions vs. an emerging emphasis on biology and science in general. In the past two decades, the civil rights movement found a forum in the schools. Picture Little Rock and the National Guard, and George Wallace "standing in the schoolhouse door." Civil rights were fought out in the schools. The concern for handicapped individuals which we are now seeking is part of this commitment to equity that has characterized our nation in quite glorious ways since World War II. The commitment is reflected in the civil rights movement, the women's liberation movement, and the enormous new investment in special education.

It seems to me that policy largely responds to change and very seldom shapes change. One needs limited expectations for what policy can accomplish. In the future, policies in the area of our concern are likely to be shaped by increasing awareness of finite resources, declining enrollments, and diminishing energy supplies. Educational policy will reflect these external realities. Every now and then, a particular policy statement gets out a bit ahead of its time, as I think occurred with P.L. 94-142; usually, there is a kind of harmony between technological change, ideological change, and social change, with policy following closely behind.

4. Individualization vs. categorical programing is another source of tension. We talked about the importance of basic constructs in its resolution. Although we often decry the categorization of handicapped children, we must recognize the social utility of our categorical classification system, untidy as it is. I suspect that we will end up in time with a mixture of individual and categorical programing. It will take a long time to effect a change in the direction that I would advocate, to a classification system based entirely on the service requirements of individual children. It was pointed out several times that in moving to a service-based classification system, there are tangible losses: identity, enthusiasm, support of partisan groups, and simplicity of thought, which help in the legislative process, and so on.

5. Education needs rational support systems. I found no opposite position for that argument; we agreed readily. Gallagher pointed out that the support system concept might be a major contribution of special education to the renegotiation process. The Bureau of Education for the Handicapped, in fact, recognized early the need for a support system and did something about it. Provisions were made for training, including the training of future leaders, for research, for the development and diffusion of teaching materials, for demonstration programs, and for information exchange. These provisions have been one of the major advances in our public school system in the last several decades.

6. The tension arising from local autonomy vs. centralized programing was examined. Timpane warned us to anticipate much centralized specification of requirements and much litigation as a consequence of this tension.

7. There was tension between concerns for the optimum individual development of children and social expectations that are in conflict with this goal. Several conferees pointed out that the schools will reflect the needs of the larger society. Schools will continue to sort people, for example, which may not be desirable. However, a major function of the educational system will continue to be providing people with credentials so that they can be identified for specific roles in a complex society. Individual efforts in the face of societal expectations can make some difference, in some circumstances; nevertheless, schools will do what society want them to do, for the most part.

8. The discussion of the proper focus for concern and attention as we renegotiate the relation of special education and general edu-

cation centered on the question, should we focus on the individual child or something else? Most of the talk was about the child, individual development, and child-teacher relationships. At times we focused on the classroom and, occasionally, on the school. When we talked about our social order in general, at least we intimated the need for fundamental changes in the structure of the larger society to solve some of the problems that create inequities in the schools.

There is a middle level of concern between these two extremes. It would seem to be an appropriate responsibility for the schools to focus on a circumscribed, ecological system that is defined by the being of an individual child, on the child in his natural habitat and in relation to significant others in his life. This emphasis is especially necessary when children — not just handicapped but any child — get into trouble because the normal system of supports has faltered or broken down. For example, a serious automobile accident or an illness in the family may disrupt the child's ecological system and seriously impair his ability to cope. A completely normal and capable child making his way effectively in the mainstream of regular education occasionally will run into events that require the school to deal with this larger system; for the handicapped child, the ecological system defined by the child's being is nearly always an imperative concern.

One of the implications of an ecological perspective is the necessity of increasing the involvement of parents in the educational programing of children. Parental involvement in devising individual education programs for children is required by P.L. 94-142. This is more than a formal requirement based on common sense. An enormous amount of research that is now available shows that programs work best when parents are involved. This finding is true for younger children, because that is with whom most of the research has been done. Parents should be involved in not only setting policy and planning individual educational programs but also, at times, in the actual operation of programs.

9. The issue that sparked the most interest and feeling was that of science and rationality in problem solving vs. experience, intuition, action, commitment, and existential engagement. The conflict, in my judgment, was overstated, but possibly on purpose because we all had manifested an overcommitment to science and rationality. So some adjustment was needed. It seemed to me that we will get into trouble if we try to follow either one route or the other, exclusively. There are simply many ways to construe the world, and many people who construe it with varying metaphor and often equal effectiveness: scientists, poets, philosophers, theologians, architects, musicians, mathematicians, and special educators. None is more veridical than the other. Various constructs will differ in utility in different situations. There may be some esthetic criterion by

which one might judge their relative merits, but I do not think that the criterion is likely to be "truth."

Schiefelbusch made the further point that we neglect engineering in our infatuation with science. He was not anti-science; he was pointing out the need for tough, hard, disciplined work close to where children, families, and communities live. In order to get the designs necessary for effective programs, we must have good engineering based on good science. It is difficult to get support for engineering work, but it is vitally necessary.

In conclusion, I would like to make a prediction that was not discussed. It is something that has occupied my thoughts recently. I think we may be moving through and possibly out of a period of great emphasis on equity, equality of opportunity, diversity, and pluralism. I am in favor of these obvious goals. But if they are carried beyond some point, there can be no community. I see signs in a number of places of re-examination of the extent to which these goods are being carried. There seems to be a revival of commitment to the common good. For example, an issue right now is immunization of children. It is a disgrace that 35% of American children are not completely immunized. We have epidemics of measles and we could have an epidemic of polio. This situation does not make sense; it need not exist. On the other hand, the problem is not easy because we must face the fact that if 10,000 children are immunized for measles, one will die, very likely. So how do we make the adjustment between a commitment to the individual and a realization of the common good? This question will be a tough one in much of the renegotiation between special education and regular education. If my prediction does come true, we can be sure that the fray will be set in the public schools.

Conference on Issues Relating to the Future of Special Education
Minneapolis, Minnesota
April 26-28, 1977

Participants

Moderator

Clyde A. Parker, Chairman
Department of Social, Psychological,
  and Philosophical Foundations of
  Education
University of Minnesota
Minneapolis, Minnesota 55455

Presenters

Arthur Chickering, Director
Center for Study of Higher
  Education
Memphis State University
Memphis, Tennessee 38152

Joanne Chickering, Counselor
Student Development Center
Memphis State University
Memphis, Tennessee 38152

James J. Gallagher, Director
Frank Porter Graham Child
  Development Center
University of North Carolina
Chapel Hill, North Carolina 27514

Reginald Jones, Chairman
Afro-American Studies
University of California
Berkeley, California 94720

Henry Levin, Professor
School of Education
Stanford University
Stanford, California 94305

Ray McDermott, Professor
Human Cognition
Rockefeller University
New York, New York 10021

Seymour Sarason, Professor
Department of Psychology
Yale University
New Haven, Connecticut 06520

Richard L. Schiefelbusch, Director
Bureau of Child Research
University of Kansas
Lawrence, Kansas 66044

Critics

Geraldine Joncich Clifford,
  Professor
School of Education
University of California
Berkeley, California 94720

Dean Corrigan, Dean
College of Education
University of Maryland
College Park, Maryland 20740

Nicholas Hobbs, Professor
Center for Study of Families and
  Children
Vanderbilt University
Nashville, Tennessee 37203

Dan C. Lortie, Professor
Department of Education
The University of Chicago
Chicago, Illinois 60637

Edwin Martin, Director
Bureau of Education for the
  Handicapped
U.S. Office of Education
Washington, D.C. 20202

Michael Timpane, Assistant Deputy
  Director
National Institute of Education
Washington, D.C. 20208

Discussants

Bruce Balow, Professor
Department of Psychoeducational
 Studies
University of Minnesota
Minneapolis, Minnesota 55455

Mary Corcoran, Professor
Department of Social, Psychological,
 and Philosophical Foundations of
 Education
University of Minnesota
Minneapolis, Minnesota 55455

Hadi Madjid
Arthur D. Little Company
32-11 Acorn Park
Cambridge, Massachusetts 02140

John Melcher, Director
Bureau for Handicapped Children
State Department of Public
 Instruction
Madison, Wisconsin 53702

Maynard C. Reynolds, Chairman
Department of Psychoeducational
 Studies
Director, National Support Systems
 Project
University of Minnesota
Minneapolis, Minnesota 55455

S. Phyllis Stearner
Division of Biological and Medical
 Research
Argonne National Laboratory
Argonne, Illinois 60439

George Young
Superintendent of Schools
St. Paul Public Schools
St. Paul, Minnesota 55102

Observers

Thomas Behrens
Division of Personnel Preparation
Bureau of Education for the
 Handicapped
Washington, D.C. 20202

Robert Herman, Associate Deputy
 Commissioner
Bureau of Education for the
 Handicapped
Washington, D. C. 20202

Sue Bye, Secretary
National Support Systems Project
University of Minnesota
Minneapolis, Minnesota 55455

Karen Lundholm, Assistant to the
 Director
National Support Systems Project
University of Minnesota
Minneapolis, Minnesota 55455

Reece Peterson
National Support Systems Project
University of Minnesota
Minneapolis, Minnesota 55455

Sylvia W. Rosen, Technical Editor
National Support Systems Project
University of Minnesota
Minneapolis, Minnesota 55455

Publications of the Leadership Training Institute/Special Education and National Support Systems Project University of Minnesota

*Distributors**

Audio Visual Library Services
University of Minnesota
3300 University Ave.
Minneapolis, MN 55414

Davis, J. (Ed.). *Our forgotten children: Hard-of-hearing pupils in the regular classroom.* (1977)

Reynolds, M. C. (Ed.). *Psychology in the schools: Proceedings of the conference on psychology and the process of schooling in the next decade.* (1971)

Reynolds, M. C., & Davis, M. C. (Eds.). *Exceptional children in regular classrooms.* (1971)

Spicker, H. H., Anastasiow, N. J., & Hodges, W. L. (Eds.). *Children with special needs: Early development and education.* (1976)

Council for Exceptional Children
Publication Sales
1920 Association Ave.
Reston, VA 22091

Birch, J. W. *Hearing impaired pupils in the mainstream.* (1976)

Birch, J. W. *Mainstreaming: Educable mentally retarded children in regular classes.* (1974)

Deno, E. N. (Ed.). *Instructional alternatives for exceptional children.* (1972)

Deno, S. L., & Mirkin, P. K. *Data-based program modification: A manual.* (1977)

Freeman, G. G. *Speech and language services and the classroom teacher.* (1977)

Hively, W., & Reynolds, M. C. (Eds.). *Domain-referenced testing in special education.* (1975)

Jones, R. A. (Ed.). *Mainstreaming: The minority child in regular classes.* (1976)

Martin, G. J., & Hoben, M. *Supporting visually impaired students in the mainstream.* (1977)

Parker, C. A. (Ed.). *Psychological consultation: Helping teachers meet special needs.* (1975)

Reynolds, M. C. (Ed.). *Mainstreaming: Origins and implications.* (1976)

Thiagarajan, S., Semmel, D. S., & Semmel, M. I. *Instructional development for training teachers of exceptional children: A sourcebook.* (1974)

Weinberg, R. A., & Wood, F. H. (Eds.). *Observation of pupils and teachers in mainstreaming and special education settings: Alternative strategies.* (1975)

---

*For information on single copy prices and quantity order discount rates, write to addresses given.

Leadership Training Institute/Special Education
253 Burton Hall
178 Pillsbury S. E.
University of Minnesota
Minneapolis, MN 55455

Reynolds, M. C. (Ed.). *National technical assistance systems in special education: Report of the conference in Washington, D. C.* (1976)

Reynolds, M. C. (Ed.). *Special education and school system decentralization.* (1975)

MISCELLANEOUS

Peterson, R. L., Bass, K. "Mainstreaming: A working bibliography." (mimeo) A periodically revised bibliography of books and articles relating to mainstreaming.

Peterson, R. L. "Mainstreaming training systems, materials, and resources: A working list." (mimeo) A periodically revised listing of training systems and other mainstreaming resources.

National Support Systems Project
253 Burton Hall
178 Pillsbury S. E.
University of Minnesota
Minneapolis, MN 55455

IN PREPARATION

Deno, E. N. *Mainstreaming: Learning disabled, emotionally disturbed, and socially maladjusted children in regular classes.* (Spring 1978)

Grosenick, J. K., & Reynolds, M. C. (Eds.). *Teacher education: Renegotiating roles for mainstreaming.* (Spring 1978)

Lundholm, K., & Prouty, R. W. *Change in the schools: A casebook.* (Spring 1978)